S0-BNW-143

THE CENTRAL AMERICAN IMPASSE

The Central American Impasse

Edited by Giuseppe Di Palma (Berkeley)
and Laurence Whitehead (Oxford)

ST. MARTIN'S PRESS
New York

 For information, write:
Scholarly & Reference Division.
St. Martin's Press, Inc., 175 Fifth Avenue, New York, NY 10010
First published in the United States of America in 1986
Printed in Great Britain

Library of Congress Cataloging-in-Publication Data

The central American impasse

Papers from a conference sponsored by Friedrich Naumann Foundation in San Jose, Costa Rica, in December 1984.

Bibliography: p.

1. Central America–politics and government–1979- .–congresses. 2. Authoritarianism–Central America–history–20th century–congresses. 3. Democracy–congresses. I. Di Palma, Giuseppe. II. Whitehead, Laurence. III. Friedrich-Naumann-Stiftung.

F1439.5.C458 1986B 972.8'053 86-6766
ISBN 0-312-12738-3

CONTENTS

PREFACE

This volume assembles a selection of the papers presented to an international conference on 'Transition to Democracy in Central America', which the Friedrich Naumann Foundation organised in co-operation with the Inter-American Institute of Human Rights at San José, Costa Rica, in December 1984.

The conference formed part of a programme of international dialogue designed to provide a platform for informal discussions between different parties on relevant international problems. Special emphasis is given to North-South issues.

The idea for this particular conference emerged during an international seminar sponsored by the Inter-American Institute of Human Rights in July 1983, which was devoted to the analysis of elections and democracy in Central America. There it became clear that elections are but one indicator of democracy and that it was consequently desirable to look at democratisation in a wider context: constitutional government, competitive parties, independent social organisations, respect for human rights and civil liberties needed careful investigation in the regional context.

Starting off with a paper submitted by Professor Giuseppe Di Palma, the question was raised whether there are any lessons to be learned for Central America from the experience of transformation from authoritarianism to democracy in other parts of the world, particularly in Southern Europe. In order to examine this question in more detail, the Friedrich Naumann Foundation decided to sponsor a conference on 'Transition to Democracy in Central America'.

Clearly this is a question of more than academic interest. It is directly related to possible political solutions to the Central American crisis.

To prepare the conference a steering committee was formed comprising eminent political scientists from Latin America, the USA and Europe. In the course of a preparatory workshop in December 1983, different democratic and non-democratic political scenarios were analysed in comparative perspective. Two main approaches to the problem emerged from this analysis:

a. the study of possibilities for social and political 'engineering' of

transition processes,
b. the examination of historical dimensions and future perspectives of the Central American crisis.

There are significant differences between European and Central American foms of authoritarianism. Thus it was necessary to clarify the distinction between totalitarian regimes, authoritarian regimes of Southern Europe before democratisation and bureaucratic authoritarian systems in the Southern Cone of Latin America. Moreover, it became obvious that no clear description and typology of the Central American variant existed. Consequently there was a need for an assessment of the internal and external factors which contribute to what can be called the Central American impasse.

In March 1984, the steering committee met in New York and designed the programme of the December 1984 conference. The following topics were chosen:

State and Society in Central America in Comparative Perspective
Comparative and Historical Experiences of Government Transformation (in Latin America and Europe)
The Dynamics of the Central American Crisis (Domestic, Regional and Geo-political Dimensions)
Actors' Perceptions and Motivations in Central American Government Transformation (Central American and External Actors).

It was obvious from the outset that these conferences could not solve one of the more vexing problems of our time. But in line with its objectives, the analytical papers brought together in this volume will contribute to a deeper understanding of the roots of the Central American impasse. Perhaps they can also contribute towards the resolution of conflicts by suggesting new answers to old problems by creating a climate favourable to the progress of liberty.

It remains for me to express the gratitude of our Foundation to the distinguished participants of the conference, to the Inter-American Institute of Human Rights, Costa Rica, and to the editors of this volume, Laurence Whitehead and Giuseppe Di Palma, who have put much effort not only into this book but also into the preparation of the conference itself.

Ralf Dahrendorf
Chairman of the Board of Directors
Friedrich Naumann Foundation

INTRODUCTION

Giuseppe Di Palma and
Laurence Whitehead

Problem-solving and theory-building seem two different modes of knowledge. The former is issue-oriented, policy-directed, value-laden, particularising. The latter appears the opposite of all the above. Yet in politics, the most Machiavellian of the social sciences, the two strands are called to meet. One purpose of political theory is knowledge in order to intervene as political actors. Thus, guided by theory, concrete problem-solving is less likely to be idiosyncratic, ephemeral and subject to reversals. Conversely, there is no political theory that cannot profit from being tested and extended against new issues. There are also areas of research and political concern in which, for a series of circumstances, some historical and some fortuitous, theory and problem-solving can profitably meet.

One such area is contemporary Central America. Here the past is in crisis, yet the future has not yet taken shape. For the truth of the matter is that the traditional social alliances upon which the old authoritarian regimes based themselves, while in crisis and subject to unprecedented challenges, have not yet and not everywhere been defeated. Conversely, new alliances, while in the realm of the possible, have not yet taken firm hold. This is exactly the type of conflictive predicament in which democracy may emerge as a 'satisficing' solution, an open compromise guaranteeing political survival – as several contributors to this volume argue – even to those who only embrace it as a second best. But what are indeed the concrete chances for such a solution in Central America?

Democratisation, and in fact any change of regime, turns out to be an exercise in problem-solving in which calculus, leadership, timing, coalition-mongering and conscious reflection, as well as chance, risk and surprise, intervene on the true or alleged necessities of history. Nowhere does the correctness of this theoretical perspective, but also the local constraints upon democratic problem-solving, appear to us to be clearer than in contemporary Central America. Geo-political location, physical size, competing international pressures, the cultural and political interdependence of the region, the presence of an active community of local (and South American) exiles and refugees, the poor institutionalisation and fungibility of otherwise repressive state apparatuses and *camarillas*, the lack of emerging socio-political formations with a hegemonic capacity, the endemic use of violence but also of manipulative solutions to regime crises, these are some of the factors pointing, for different and even contradictory reasons, in the same direction. In Central America democratisation demands a calculated and very difficult exercise in restructuring political choices among explicitly conflicting political projects, none of which is yet defeated or victorious.

As the chapters by Maira and Weeks make clear, the historical traditions of the region (Costa Rica excepted) provide a peculiarly unfavourable backdrop for any attempts at genuine democratisation. An agrarian structure lineally descended from the conquest; a post-independence record of patrimonialism of a peculiarly aggressive kind (partly a function of the relatively small size of each state which facilitated military control); a political convention that elections are held, and constitutional forms are nominally observed, only in order to regularise power outcomes determined by other means; and a socio-economic structure patently not geared to satisfying the needs of the majority of the population; all these constitute very serious obstacles to the brokering of peaceful political change. In fact, the most obvious lessons to be drawn from regional history are the very reverse of helpful: reformist experiments quickly degenerate; popular movements *can* be crushed by sufficiently ruthless deployments of force and coercion; there is always one law for the rich and powerful, and another for the rest.

These entrenched local traditions have been systematically reinforced by geo-political considerations. It is hardly necessary to belabour the point that the United States has long regarded this region as especially sensitive from the security standpoint. Even before the opening of the Panama Canal the Isthmus could be regarded as a vital line of US *internal* communications (coast-to-coast for heavy freight) that happened to pass through foreign territory. In the two world wars the control of these small, easily subvertible republics seemed an essential pre-requisite for defence of the canal route. To secure that route the US government needed the closest co-operation with the local military and police establishments, and needed the maintenance of order rather than the promotion of liberty or justice. From the other side of this relationship, the upper classes of the region also needed US protection, although the dangers they feared were slightly different. It is perhaps worth emphasising what the Mexican Revolution must have signified to the entrenched elites of Central America, or how much their reactions to that experience must have contributed to their resistance to anv genuine social or political reform. Their implacable resistance to the Cuban Revolution is more generally known, and has, of course, reinforced their alliance with Washington, but for them it was surely Mexico that provided the formative experience. Equally, of course, on the Central American left, once it had been clearly demonstrated (as in Guatemala in 1954) that neither the local elites nor the government in Washington would tolerate change on the Mexican scale, it seemed that only the more drastic alternative along Cuban lines remained available. These geo-political considerations reinforce the historical traditions already mentioned, and further limit the chances of a democratic transition.

Given the adverse characateristics of the region, both domestic and international, the reader may actually wonder whether exploring the chances of democratisation is at all worthy of scholarly attention, as we claim. There is a strong temptation, in contemplating the Central American quagmire, to move instead to higher, drier and safer grounds and fall back on some established and sobering scholarly wisdoms about democracies; namely, that they cannot prosper unless a number of objective social, historical, economic, cultural and institutional conditions are present, such as cultural homogeneity, group pluralism, a degree of prosperity, some level of education, a successful bourgeoisie, a more equitable social and economic system, modern land tenure and agrarian relations, non-dependent development, an established but moderate party system, an impersonal and non-political bureaucracy, a tradition of elite competitivenes, or some combination thereof.

Were we indeed simply to fall back on any of the theoretical approaches suggested bv this list of conditions, then Central America would be among the least likely candidates for democratisation, as well as the least likely to provide us with new analytical insights into the process. The case against democratisation would become so overwhelming that reflecting on it as an exercise in problem-solving and political leadership would mean reflecting on the nearly impossible or inexistent. Behind theories that emphasise rather demanding objective or structurally-determined root-conditions for democracy there is often the common view that democracy is a rare and delicate political arrangement. Democracy – so goes the view – is an incohesive system of government; it is a system of compromise, a set of rules for mediating plural and competing interests, which require specially favourable circumstances in order to exist and operate. Since these circumstances point to societal, political or behavioural features with an 'elective affinity' for democracy, it follows by this analysis that democracies that replace an authoritarian or totalitarian system do not fare well. For one thing, the very trauma of totalitarian or authoritarian demise builds resentment against democracy among those leaders and followers of the old regime who have lost benefits, power or more, as a consequence of its demise. For another, there are many who do not subscribe to democracy, irrespective of personal costs or benefits. These principled opponents are to be found not only among the loyalists of the old regime but also among those who fought it hoping to replace it with something other than democracy. Finally, to the extent that totalitarianism and authoritarianism are accompanied by societal conditions of 'backwardness' that survive the trauma of regime demise, such conditions are themselves detrimental to the new democracy.

The 'proof' that the sequence dictatorship-to-democracy is an inauspicious (and unlikely) one has been for a long time the fact that democracies have stably replaced dictatorships only in those exceptional cases at the end of the Second World War in which dictatorships were militarily defeated and democracies were installed under the supervision of the occupying powers. Accordingly, it is not coincidental that, despite or perhaps precisely because of the exceptional and exogenous circumstances leading to post-war democratic reconstruction, two of those democracies – France and Italy – have ostensibly given a poor account of themselves over the years. Further, even today, fears of a resurgent past and concerns with whether *any* of the post-war democracies has done enough to remove the legacies of dictatorship have been occasional themes in the analyses of political observers.

The implications of this line of analysis, and in particular of the latter points, for Central America are clear. Even if democracy were sponsored by a foreign power (i.e. the United States) determined and able firmly to remove the option of dictatorship from the region or from some of its countries – a mere hypothesis, since US attitudes towards Central America are far from the active commitment and even involvement in the process of democratic reconstruction which the US displayed in post-war Europe and Japan – there would be the further question of whether democracy could at all operate in the region in the absence of those 'elective affinities' which we mentioned before. Certainly the conclusion of a recent major comparative study (*Transitions from Authoritarian Rule*, edited by Guillermo O'Donnell, Philippe C. Schmitter and Laurence Whitehead (forthcoming, Johns Hopkins, 1986)) was that, short of outright invasion and conquest, international efforts to foster transitions to democracy could at best play only a supportive role; internal processes would be decisive. In that study, one of us argues that US policies in this area are likely to be relatively unsuccessful over the longer run. Washington is generally under pressure to create a 'showcase' that can redound to the credit of the particular administration that commissioned the funds. US policies to promote democracy are therefore mostly bilateral and tend to require high visibility and quick results. These characteristics are likely to run counter to the requirements for any genuine and lasting democratisation. One requirement in particular is of especial relevance to Central America. In order to establish a genuine transition to democracy, the major local forces must be given sufficient room to manoeuvre, to act on their own behalves and to establish their credentials as authentic groupings, not as 'puppets' manipulated by external powers. This requires a self-denying ordinance on the part of international backers, a form of restraint that may be particularly difficult to maintain when (as in the present case) genuine progress towards democracy would require a clearcut break with previous traditions of manipulation and violent imposition. Those on the right who stand to lose from such a transition will naturally use every method at their disposal to re-involve their traditional foreign backers, just as those on the revolutionary left will seek to prove that there can be no peaceful reformists, only 'puppets'.

In sum, established approaches to democratisation prevailing until recently (and a normal dose of instinctive common sense) suggest that the prospects for democratisation in Central America, no matter from what vantage point we contemplate them, are quite bleak. The contributors to this volume have not discounted those approaches; neither, however, have they sought total refuge behind them. It would be excessive to expect that a number of scholars called to assess what remains a highly volatile and difficult regional situation would agree where the structural constraints to democratisation end and where the task of political leadership begins – how overdetermined outcomes may be or how much space is left to or can be conquered by innovative problem-solving. In this sense, the volume's contribution to problem-solving and to the revision of established theoretical approaches is necessarily limited. We may confidently assert, however, that in reflecting on Central America most contributors – to paraphrase the words of one of them – have tried to balance the social scientist's inclination to order reality in terms of law-like patterns with the political actor's emphasis on human choice and leadership (a point stressed by Kaufman in his chapter). It is precisely the volatility and difficulty of the regional situation that, far from counselling a retreat behind the necessities of history, has urged a second and harder look.

One incentive to a more realistic approach, willing to come to terms with the Central American quagmire, has come from witnessing the new wave of democratisations that has taken place since the 1970s in other areas of the world. We have already pointed out how scholarly attention to the first big wave of democratisations – that which followed the fall of fascist and pseudo-fascist regimes at the end of the Second World War – was, if not scarce, at least of limited theoretical innovation. Since dictatorships seemed to have collapsed because of military defeat and democracy to have been reinstated under and because of Allied supervision, there seemed to be little to explain. Also, when called to account for the causes and nature of interwar dictatorships, most scholars, caught by the somehow unfathomable perversity of those dictatorships, felt it necessary to appeal to distant and objective root-causes (running the gamut from the socio-structural to the deviant and psychoanalytical) and could not therefore make theoretical room for the contingent and actor-oriented. Nor could they address the question of how regime support and regime loyalties could change, even abruptly. When it finally came to pinpointing the conditions for successful post-war democratisation, the emphasis fell on economic progress, the international solidarity of the advanced West and in general the need to replicate a special and particularly fortunate Anglo-Saxon model of society and development.

Our point is not that those early theoretical emphases are necessarily and totally incorrect, as that they are not always susceptible of extension to other contexts. This has become apparent with the democratisation of Southern Europe beginning in the mid-1970s. The reaction of the scholarly community to these processes has been different in emphasis when compared to the reaction to the post-war events, more alert and theoretically innovative. The examples, not only of Spain but also of Greece and Portugal, pointed to processes of democratisation that instinctively struck the analyst as being more self-reflective and problematic, and thus theoretically richer, than those which followed the Second World War. Above all, what the examples of Southern Europe suggested is that democratisation does not involve a neat confrontation between friends and foes of democracy, each defined by immutable and conflicting *Weltanschauungen*, but a more complex realignment and coalitional game, in which loyalties are not predetermined and frozen and in which the process almost always is set in motion by, or at least hinges on, decisive secessions within the operational core of the dictatorship.

Occurring at the same time as the events of Southern Europe, the unexpected crisis of bureaucratic authoritarianism in South America, the different forms and democratisation potentials that it has shown in countries like Argentina and Brazil, the dissynchronic (with respect to the rest of the continent) regime developments in Chile, are all phenomena which can add to the theoretical rethinking about democratisation, by comparing, combining or contrasting the South American and Mediterranean experiences of transition. The recent South American experiences demonstrate rather clearly that no single rigid or preordained model can account for the way authoritarian regimes rise, decline or collapse. To the contrary, social groupings that were once regarded as essential pillars of authoritarian rule have sometimes proved capable of surprising reassessments of their interests and purposes, so that apparently very solid regimes have been unexpectedly disarticulated. Equally, on the opposition side a process of learning and re-evaluation has in some cases made possible a far smoother and more collaborative transition than seemed imaginable a few years ago. But there has been nothing inevitable about the shape of their processes – they are typically hesitant, exploratory and unpredictable. In some cases, once a 'favourable dynamic' has been set in motion, all the participants may be swept along by forces they seem unable to control, or even fully to anticipate. In other cases, misjudgement or distrust has produced a vicious circle of missed opportunities and rising tension. No doubt there are always structural constraints on the outcomes that are politically possible, but the most striking lesson from these experiences is their degree of openness.

What can we learn from these recent European and South American developments that can help our assessment of the Central American impasse? One lesson, which in fact was already contained in the post-war democratisations, is that transitions to democracy are only rarely smooth and gradual evolutions over time. More often, they are discrete and conflicting events which scholars may tend to reconstruct after the facts as necessary, but in which human choice in the context of contingent and changing scenarios play in effect an unmeasurable and yet not discountable role. In this light, post-war democratisations themselves can no longer be considered exceptional in their unfolding. In particular, rethinking post-war democratisations with the contingent role of actors in mind brings out a point of special importance for Central America. This is the fact that the role played by international forces is far from being either unilinear or unmediated. The interaction with domestic realities requires careful and theoretically-informed attention to the context. What conflicting interests actually *mean* by the term 'democracy' (and – sometimes a very different thing – what they are eventually prepared to settle for under that label) is far more complex and elusive than standard political analysis would indicate. It would also be worth reanalysing, for example, to what extent – over and above military defeat and occupation – domestic actors involved in the post-war democratisations may in some cases have managed to appropriate a more crucial role for themselves, in the crisis of dictatorships or in democratic inaugurations, than has been conventionally recognised. The point of this observation, and its relevance for Central America, is certainly not to discount international forces but to stress the complexity and varieties of international-domestic interactions. There are, in sum, no privileged or most likely paths to democracy, making other paths exceptional, unanticipated, unpromising and somehow theoretically unproductive.

On the contrary, another and related lesson is that early analyses of democratisation, pointing to structural and objective explanations, have been based on the limiting example of countries that achieved democracy early on in their history, under apparently favourable circumstances, before the appearance of modern mass dictatorships, and/or without experiencing reversals and regressions. There has been a natural and theoretically justifiable tendency among scholars comparing these early democracies with late democracies, or with democracies that have experienced dictatorial reversals to emphasise the presence in the former of the kind of structural features listed at the beginning of this introduction – features which sustain the smooth functioning of an existing democracy. There has also been an equally natural but less than justifiable tendency to translate these functional features into genetic features of structural conduciveness, as well as to see early democracies as the product of a smooth, gradual and consensual process (see Danwart Rustow's classic article in *Comparative Politics*, April 1970, pp. 339-41). In effect, it is an open empirical question whether functional features also pre-existed the advent of democracies, even in those special and fortunate early cases. Features such as prosperity, equality, welfare, civic participation, mutual trust, tolerance, consensus and others we instinctively associate with democracy are themselves the product of (largely Western) democracies. It is equally an empirical question whether early democracies emerged from smooth, gradual, consensual, and indeed teleological processes. After all, there existed no record of established democratic practices at the time to which prospective democratic leaders could refer, and democracy was not even a word of common currency. A close analysis of the historical record would reveal a good amount of double-talk, group egotism, self-serving attitudes and hardened calculation on the part of many actors involved in democratic transformation. It is fair to say that early democracies have often been brought about by oligarchies whose style of political rule did not have much to do with democracy.

At any rate, whatever the early paths to democracy may have been, the lesson is that they are not the only ones, and they are no longer available. In Central America and elsewhere in the Third World scholars and political actors must assume the genetic difficulty and work from there. The features and conditions which in more advantaged countries may have at least in part pre-existed democracy – or may have constrained dictatorial interludes, if any, and eased the return to democracy – in Central America must be created in the very process of democratic inauguration and consolidation. In a region where dictatorship and violence as a political currency are endemic, and where the occasional use of pseudo-democratic practices for manipulative purposes has not helped popular trust in the promises of democracy, the task is frankly overwhelming. Plainly speaking, it is very difficult, given this background, to envision the circumstances under which democracy, or even some process of liberalisation, will effectually sustain itself as a second best and a way out of the present impasse. Political actors engaged, or somehow involved, in a democratic experiment are asked in effect to act without a safety net, and thus to work with infinite care – a quality in very short supply in the region. Not only groups that traditionally hold anti-democratic sentiments and interests must somehow be reconciled to democracy, since often their elimination in a democratic context is out of the question factually or normatively; also, popular scepticism about the true democratic intentions of the experiment must be confronted. Nevertheless, the very purposefulness that must guide any attempt at democratisation in the region – the very fact that democracy cannot be the fruit of natural and unplanned genesis – adds at least one element of sturdiness to the democratic prospect.

The ambition of the contributors to this volume, and to the conference that preceded it, has been to make a first tentative theoretical inroad into the Central American *problematique* by placing its analysis within the frame of the broader experiences and insights developed from the study of regime changes in other historical contexts. Accordingly, some of the contributors bring their specific expertise on Central America; others, without claiming such expertise, seek to apply to the region their special knowledge of regime transitions in other areas, as well as their knowledge of related intellectual issues – theories of totalitarianism and authoritarianism, democratic theory, militarism, the international dimensions of development and change. Contrariwise, it has also been our intention to test and refine old and new approaches to democratisation by confronting them with the realities of Central America, themselves under-studied and under-conceptualised.

While seeking a common intellectual ground for scholarly exchange, each of the contributors has brought personal perspectives reflecting the historical and regime experiences of his or her own region, as well as professional perspectives linked to scholarly specialisations. This is one reason why the volume cannot offer anything even remotely approaching a commonly-agreed blueprint for democratisation, and never planned to offer one. Another and more compelling reason has already been stated in these pages. On one side, conceiving of democratisation as a process in which there is space for human choice shows democratisation as an attainable goal – by volition and action. But by the same token the process also requires a special degree of political calculation, great sacrifices, a great capacity for compromise when necessary, great forbearance. In a region where so many interests clash at so many levels – from the international to the parochial – and in which revolution seems to many the only way out of frustration, it is difficult for scholars to agree upon and prescribe paths to political change that would transform those clashes into democracy's agreement to disagree.

Even assuming that the task is as simple as the neutral task of recommending or embracing paths to democratisation on the basis of their probability and feasibility, the fact is that the detection of the winning options, if any, before they are in, is extremely aleatory. If nothing else, given the central role of the human factor, pinning down what the present intentions of the various actors are and how they may change, as well as their significance and weight, is still a quite subjective affair.

Three of the contributors to this volume have supplied their personal interpretations of the current balance of forces, and distribution of perceptions, in the three republics most torn by violent conflict. These contributions are subjective in the good sense that they reflect close contact with some of the political actors most directly engaged in the tasks of democratic problem-solving, while at the same time observing immediate events with a degree of detachment derived from academic study of other comparable processes in other places or at other times. Mario Solórzano Martínez has a particularly close involvement with his subject-matter, given his other role as a leader of the Guatemalan

Social Democratic Party – a position requiring very great personal commitment – but he demonstrates that suitably-controlled subjectivity can be turned to advantage when examining the scope for democratisation. Rodolfo Cerdas is also directly engaged in the political life of the region, as a former member of the Costa Rican legislature, and a prominent television journalist in San José. His interpretation of the Sandinista regime in Nicaragua is undoubtedly personal and controversial, but again this is subjectivity of a helpful kind, closely involved, deeply concerned and drawing on an extensive historical and comparative knowledge. Similarly Terry Karl's assessment of the situation in El Salvador derives from first-hand experience and extensive interviews with key participants, and from her experiences as an adviser to US policy-makers. It also draws on her academic research concerning the Venezuelan Christian Democrats (COPEI). In the same way, Margaret Crahan's chapter on the Central American church is both a product of close and sympathetic study of local realities, and an extension of her long-standing enquiries into social and political trends in the Latin American church.

The organisers of the San José conference attached great importance to the comparative aspect of the question – i.e. what 'lessons from elsewhere' could be of most relevance. In addition to the West European and South American experiences mentioned above, two more specific chapters were also commissioned, covering situations that seemed of particular relevance to contemporary Central America – the current Colombian experiment with amnesty and pacification, assessed by Malcolm Deas; and Rosario Espinal's account of the long and complex process by which the Dominican Republic has evolved from the extreme repression of the Trujillo era and subsequent US intervention into an open and democratic (but still socially troubled) political regime.

Each of these authors provides his or her own distinctive view of what lessons should (and should not) be drawn. There are, however, some generalisations from this set of chapters that we as editors would like to propose:

1. Some encouragement should be derived from the fact that many apparently desperate and intractable situations (post-civil war Spain, Trujillo's tyranny, the Argentine military dictatorship) have proved surmountable, and have eventually been followed by periods of social peace and redemocratisation.
2. Neither socio-structural nor geo-political pessimism should be

allowed to obscure the scope for political leadership and for political initiatives to bring about peaceful reconciliation. When such reconciliation seems unattainable the question should at least be asked whether the explanation is some form of historical necessity, or whether the misguided strategies and misperceptions of leading actors may not be to blame.

3. It should not be taken for granted that private enterprise is at all times and places a force promoting authoritarian rule and intensified social conflict. In much of Latin, and especially Central, America this has often been the case, but both theoretical reflection and our lessons from elsewhere indicate reasons why this sector may be detachable from the 'reactionary despotic' coalition, and turned into a force for reform.
4. The apparent strength and momentum of the authoritarian right can be quite misleading, since this sector frequently commits such gross errors that it jeopardises its own position, and leaves the way open for its democratic critics. Concerning the armed forces in particular, it could be a serious mistake to assume that if they have acted as enemies of democracy and social peace for many years, or even for generations, therefore the only (or the best) strategy must be to defeat them in open conflict. Democratic politicians will be at a disadvantage in such a situation, and may be better placed if they seek to divide, domesticate, constitutionalise, browbeat or even bribe the military into a withdrawal to the barracks.
5. Even in countries with very little democratic tradition and where socio-economic injustice is very severe, the popular classes may quickly develop remarkably well-led and effective organisations that are capable of displaying the political skilfulness and long-term reasoning required for gradual democratisation and pacification.
6. It may not be practicable to tackle all the problems posed by a democratic transition at the same time. If a reformist dynamic can be established, even on a narrow front, it can set in motion a sequence of developments that may gradually extend and consolidate the process of democratisation.
7. It may not be practicable to pacify an entire country with a single pact, dialogue or amnesty. Some insurgents may always prefer to continue with the armed struggle, and so violence may even intensify for a time in the wake of a negotiated settlement. Similarly it may be impossible completely to purge the state apparatus of those who would prefer to provoke the restoration of a climate of tension and fear. Many years or even generations may be required before the

legacy of past civil strife can be completely eradicated. Nevertheless partial settlements (realistically negotiated and vigorously implemented) can radically shift the social climate and the pattern of incentives away from one that encourages political violence.

Not all authors in this volume would necessarily agree with all these formulations, but they do provide an indication of what was discussed at the San José conference. Notwithstanding the relatively reassuring tenor of these suggested 'lessons from elsewhere', the fact remains that for the present, and in this particular case, the prospects for a peaceful or democratic outcome to the Central American impasse seem quite distant. (In the final chapter Whitehead offers his personal interpretation of why this is so.) Our authors have not seen it as their task here to chronicle, or once more to denounce, the suffering and tragic waste that this involves. However, all their contributions are informed by an awareness that we are dealing with questions that are far from being exclusively theoretical.

Berkeley/Oxford

1 AUTHORITARIANISM IN CENTRAL AMERICA: A COMPARATIVE PERSPECTIVE

Luis Maira

The Authoritarian Regimes of Latin America

In the past decade Latin American social thinkers have turned their attention to one of the political phenomena with most direct impact on the region's history and future: namely the widespread existence of political dictatorships. Numerous authors have dedicated their efforts to tracing the origins and logic of the most recent authoritarian experiences in the region.

These writings have considerably advanced our knowledge of the subject and have enabled the development of a Latin American viewpoint on a topic which in previous decades was evaluated on the basis of theoretical schemas produced in other parts of the world, mainly Western Europe, where authoritarianism occurred in a very different economic and social setting. As a result, the appearance of new types of repressive government in Latin America no longer produces as before the knee-jerk reflex of applying labels derived from the experience of developed capitalist countries, debates, for example, over whether the state is 'bonapartist' or 'fascist' or a 'dictatorship of notables'. Although we must acknowledge that all authoritarian regimes share certain common characteristics, it must also be recognised that for a genuine understanding of an authoritarian political system the most important thing is to identify the specific rationality operating in a given case. This requires paying careful attention to the historical conditions giving rise to oppressive government and to the social conflicts in question. It also requires attention to the connection between the level of economic development, the character of the productive structure and the specific requirements of political domination that generate a resort to coercion.

Surveying the phenomenon of authoritarianism in Latin America we can identify two basic types of regime that currently exist in the region. Simplifying, we can refer to 'traditional military dictatorships' and 'new military dictatorships' (i.e. those based on the doctrine of national security and on counter-insurgency theories). It is fairly apparent that the two models generally occur in a historical sequence and that they correspond to societies at different levels of modernisation and with different social structures.

Traditional military dictatorships flourished in the earliest stages of consolidation of the Latin American nation states. Of course, this consolidation was often a complex and long-drawn-out process, particularly in some of the more important countries of the region. In most countries there was a nominal adherence to democratic objectives and the early adoption of constitutional charters which were quite often of a high technical standard. But in practice political reality continued displaying strongly authoritarian characteristics, and it was rare to find genuine applications of the principles of ideological pluralism, open electoral competition and alternation in power. A contributory factor was that the North American political model which provided a source of inspiration to Latin American constitutionalists (that is to say, the liberal democratic system with presidential leadership) proved hardly suitable for export and, in contrast with the English parliamentary model which spread easily through Europe and other parts of the world, North American practices did not adapt well in the Latin American countries where the greatest efforts were made to transplant them. Consequently, what happened – with very few exceptions (Uruguay, Chile, Costa Rica) – was an alternation between fragile democratic experiments and traditional military dictatorships. Thus, one of the principal figures in Latin American history from the second half of the nineteenth century through to the first half of the twentieth century was the military chief who became a dictator as a result of unresolved conflicts between the civilian oligarchic factions.

Within a social order governed by the values and practices of a traditional agrarian society, the owners of great estates controlled both economic and political power and manipulated fragile parties which, although called Conservative and Liberal, hardly constituted more than gatherings of landowners. In such a social order, authoritarian practices were likely to flourish whenever the delicate balance of forces within these ruling circles was disturbed, or whenever a military or civilian leader appeared who was capable of redistributing or concentrating within his own hands the elements of political power existing within the society. These traditional military dictatorships therefore shared certain common characteristics that appear with great regularity in a variety of countries. The legitimacy of these regimes was transitory. They were not in power 'for ever', but rather in response to moments of crisis which 'obliged' them to take power in order to re-establish lost equilibrium, whilst promising, after a prudent interval, to restore the political freedoms that had been interrupted, notwithstanding the fact that on many occasions these promises were broken. These regimes lacked a national project with any precise ideological basis, and this caused them to neglect their own institutionalisation or to adopt model constitutions which they then proceeded routinely to violate. They established few links with foreign forces and external factors, being characterised by their parochialism. They were not so much totalitarian as arbitrary. They lacked the capacity even to imagine the all-encompassing apparatuses of repression which have made their appearance in more recent years. Under these regimes, brutality was intermittent, primitive and discretionary. Lastly, we could say that they were reactionary or conservative in an intuitive way: they could not conceive of any alternative social order and that was why they worked within the established order and maintained the hierarchy that served the oligarchy which they themselves aspired to join.

In general terms, this first type of political dictatorship prevailed without competition until the Great Depression of 1929. That moment marked the end of Latin America's mechanical insertion into the established international order, and it represented a point of departure for regional efforts to increase national autonomy, to establish an independent industrial basis and to improve the terms of trade of the region's strategic raw materials and of the agricultural products which until then had been sent to the central economies without any real concern on the part of state officials to regulate these transactions. From 1930 onwards, the countries of Latin America began, in varying degrees, to experience a rapid process of modernisation, urbanisation, industrialisation and social change. These developments gradually rendered the traditional authoritarian model obsolete. The main reasons for this included the progressive incorporation into political life of the popular classes and in particular of the working class and the lower classes in the major cities; the expansion of the middle classes as a result of the increase of commercial and professional activity; the development of universities as centres of critical thought in various countries, whose students organised rebellions to bring dictatorships to an end; and more generally the enlargement of social organisations and the strengthening of channels of political representation, particularly political parties.

Thus it was in the decades following the Great Depression that a change became apparent in the mode of operation of the dictatorial regimes. Curiously, these did not become less numerous, as we can certainly observe by reflecting on the record in Central America during this period. However, there was a progressive evolution in their *modus operandi* and in the practices of the traditional dictatorships. Little by little, they abandoned their earlier empiricism and Caesarism, and developed institutionalised forms of political control. But even so, it was apparent that they were in retreat and would in due course have to be replaced by a different kind of model.

From the end of the 1929 crisis until the end of the Second World War, *de facto* governments predominated in Latin America. In the middle of the 1940s democratic political systems briefly reappeared, but these soon gave way to a new wave of arbitrary governments at the end of the decade. Finally, towards the end of the 1950s, the dictatorships suffered a greater setback in the face of a second wave of democratic experiments. This was the setting in which the Cuban Revolution began, a revolution that would constitute a watershed in the history of the continent. The concrete threat of 'Communist expansion in the region' was sufficient to unite both the United States and the conservative classes in the countries of Latin America in the search for a type of political regime capable of blocking the spread of socialism in the continent, and above all of resisting the methods of guerrilla warfare that the new left was adopting in the hope of destroying the old order.

The Brazilian model was the culmination of this process. After various experiments, such as the Alliance for Progress combination of social reforms and counter-insurgency policies, US policy-makers working in close co-operation with the major power holders in the Latin American region decided that a definitive solution of the problem would require state control and a highly organised political system. State apparatuses capable of winning an 'internal war' against all 'subversive' challenges were established. The national security state was in due course extended from Brazil to various other countries in South America. It rested on a very different logic from that of the traditional military dictatorships. Whereas social conflicts in the latter were considered temporary in character, in the national security state they would be viewed as permanent features requiring a systematic subordination of political logic to military logic as the only way to defeat the 'internal enemy'. The new model contains an all-encompassing view of the role of the military. National security doctrine can be seen as a comprehensive alternative to revolutionary theory which would supply the ideological guidelines for a comprehensive reorganisation of the state apparatus, of the political process, of international alignments and even of the productive structure. In accordance with this thinking, national security doctrines are as ambitious in scope as the Marxism that they seek to eradicate.

In order to administer this new state, the armed forces would be obliged to close the internal divisions which had characterised the military *caudillismo* of the traditional dictatorships. Authority would have to be exercised institutionally by the highest bodies in the military structure. Consequently, the decision to undertake a *coup* and the choice of policies thereafter would be decided by the high command as a whole, or by the top security councils of the Latin American military establishments. Liberal democracy would have to be postponed *sine die* until the forces defending Western civilisation had achieved a definitive victory.

From the outset, this new model of dictatorship was committed to a capitalist system of economic organisation and stressed the central role that businessmen and private enterprises would have to play in the promotion of economic expansion and national development. With some variations from country to country, all the new authoritarian regimes could rely upon direct support from the major employers' organisations. In consultation or collaboration with the leadership of these organisations, economic policies were drawn up and ambitious development strategies were adopted with the aims of strengthening the nation state and achieving self-sustaining growth. In recent years, the shortcomings of these experiments have been revealed. Indeed, they entered into crisis, so that in Argentina, Bolivia, Brazil and Uruguay it has been necessary to re-establish democratic forms. However, this eclipse should not be regarded as irreversible, since in all the countries of Latin America the forces and interests which traditionally revert to dictatorial solutions are still in place.

The Nature of Central American Authoritarianism

Turning now to Central America, let us see how the concrete historical experiences of that region compare with the two types of Latin American authoritarianism just discussed. First and foremost, we must recognise that the literature on the new authoritarianism does not apply directly to the cases found in Central America. These dictatorships are not based on national security doctrines of the kind found in Argentina, Brazil and Chile. But it would also be misleading to regard Central American dictatorships as nothing more than regimes of the traditional pre-1929 type. A key hypothesis is that the authoritarian regimes of Nicaragua, El Salvador and Guatemala, which have entered into a crisis over the past decade, represent (together with the patriarchal regime of General Stroessner in Paraguay) the last relics of those *transitional* authoritarian regimes which appeared throughout Latin America in the 1930s but which became less and less functional as social conditions changed and the modernisation of the region progressed. This explains the problems of internal reconstruction faced by these governments and helps to account for the scale of the crisis which has arisen in these countries.

In nineteenth-century Central America, one consideration of great importance helped to shape the development of authoritarian tendencies on the Isthmus. This was the structure of the productive sector, and in particular the patterns of rural land ownership. One essential clue to the economic history of the sub-region is the fact that Costa Rica began exporting coffee to world markets much earlier than the other Central American republics. Costa Rican democracy is, of course, the exception to generalisations about the political traditions of the Isthmus, and the early development of its coffee exports implied a displacement of the traditional landowning elites and the subdivision of the great estates to produce a class of medium-sized farmers in the central *meseta* of the country where the main cities are located. This soon gave rise to active political involvement by social groups more extensive than the old oligarchy.

In the second half of the nineteenth century there was a decline in the political hegemony of the region's conservatives and a process of liberal reforms got under way, notably in the early 1870s. This first took place in Guatemala, where the principal figure was President Justo Rufino Barrios. It soon spread to El Salvador, Honduras and Nicaragua, generating expectations of the spread of democracy and an opening of the political system. But this attempt soon failed and one of the keys to political evolution in Central America is the subsequent reversion to conditions of fierce authoritarianism. Never since the 1870s have there existed in these countries such favourable conditions for the establishment of liberal democracy following the US model. (At this time, the government in Washington already exerted great influence in the area, an influence which in those years was associated with far greater prestige and legitimacy than can be found today.) In practice, the failure of the liberal reform period signified that in countries like Nicaragua and El Salvador the power of the great landowners would be consolidated. In the second of these, the production of coffee commenced after the Land Tenure Laws of the early 1880s which had reinforced the *latifundio* system and which gave rise to the almost mythical image of the power of the so-called 'fourteen families' to regulate the destiny of the country.

It was after the failure of the plan to create liberal republics that the model of traditional military dictatorships achieved its fullest expression in the sub-region. In the last decade of the nineteenth century and the early years of the twentieth century, *de facto* governments became the norm, often lasting for very long periods. By contrast, governments based on the popular will were infrequent and short-lived. Their existence was always highly precarious.

Following the war with Spain in 1898, the USA became a determinant factor shaping the prospects for democracy in Central America. In particular the Roosevelt Corollary in 1904 explicitly asserted the USA's right to regulate the nature of the political regimes established in Latin America in accordance with American national interest, and a policy of interventionism was developed throughout the entire Caribbean basin. The protectorate which the Marines established in Nicaragua in the second and third decades of the century provides a high point of this policy. Under this model the country was occupied by the Marines, the activities of the Nicaraguan government were overseen by the North American authorities, and direct control was exercised over such public agencies as the Customs House, the internal tax system, the Treasury and so forth. There were also programmes of modernisation and reorganisation of the public administration together with attempts to professionalise the armed forces, linking them closely to the training and military doctrines of the US military. A National Guard was established under the protectorates, heavily influenced by the precedent of reconstruction in the southern states of the USA after the Civil War.

In practice, the US occupation of countries such as the Dominican Republic and Nicaragua gave rise to a new military structure which powerfully reinforced tendencies towards authoritarianism. It fostered some of the most long-lived dictatorships that have been known in the continent, namely those of Rafael Leonidas Trujillo and Anastasio Somoza, who both came to power after rising to the leadership of the National Guards established in their respective countries. The most important phase of authoritarianism in the sub-region orginated from the interaction of these political factors with the changes affecting the productive base of these societies derived from the 1929 economic crisis. All the countries of the Isthmus other than Costa Rica were subjected to a uniform system of political control, and these dictatorships were now better structured, more long-lived and capable of producing more lasting effects than their predecessors. The repression of dissidents became more scientific and systematic than before and certain apparently democratic political forms were adopted, the consequences of which we shall consider in the next section.

The governments of Rafael Ubico in Guatemala, Maximiliano Hernández Martínez in El Salvador, Tuburcio Carías in Honduras and Anastasio Somoza in Nicaragua are specific manifestations of this stage. All except Somoza exercised power for approximately fifteen years and their regimes came to an end as a consequence of the pro-democratic surge produced by the defeat of fascism at the end of the Second World War. It is important to note that these dictatorships originated close to the time when President Roosevelt came to power and the good neighbour policy was launched. A fundamental element of this policy was support and encouragement for the creation in Latin America of democracies on the North American model, together with a cessation of direct US military intervention in the region.

In practice, however, Washington lent its support to the dictatorships of Central America while US investment in the region expanded. The fundamental characteristic of these regimes is the capacity and the versatility of the oligarchic groupings that control them. Originating in the rural sector, these groups have extended their interests into new urban activities and undertaken a two-edged policy of alliances: on the one hand, they have linked up with the private US interests based in their country, thereby obtaining support from the US government; and on the other, they have also established strong links with domestic military elites. The authoritarian regimes of Central America therefore rest on two basic props, and if those begin to change the whole system becomes destabilised, creating the type of political crisis we now witness: the first prop is the maintenance of an equilibrium between the interests of the rural and urban productive sectors: the second is the maintenance of a degree of subordination (or controlled competition) between oligarchic groups and the military high command.

The first element is fundamental because the viability of this type of authoritarian government depends upon keeping the popular sectors of society disorganised. This is quite possible in a social system dominated by the great estate, even the type of large landholding now referred to as an agri-business, but it becomes far more difficult when urban economic activities become more extended and diversified and generate new networks of solidarity and organisation among the inhabitants of the major cities. Thus it was inevitable that the authoritarian governments of Central America would start to weaken as modernisation and urbanisation progressed.

The second equilibrating factor also proved fundamental for the survival of these dictatorships. This was the maintenance of a division of labour between the civilian and military elites. The former were to preserve effective control over the various branches of productive activity, while the latter were to maintain ascendancy over the state apparatus, fulfilling their administrative defence and security functions. Stability would be undermined if the military decided to encroach upon the prerogatives of the oligarchy in the area of business and enter enterprise management, seeking to establish themselves as the hegemonic nucleus of an alternative bourgeoisie by taking advantage of the opportunities provided by their control of the state apparatus to engage in what may be called 'primitive accumulation'.

This, however, is exactly what took place, from the mid-1960s, in Nicaragua, Guatemala and El Salvador. The Somoza family, in alliance with the senior levels of the National Guard, took increasing control over all types of economic activity and stepped up their demands for 'participation' in business, turning themselves into the most successful entrepreneurs in the country, and in the process generating intense conflicts which contributed to the eventual destruction of the Somoza dynasty. Especially following the 1972 earthquake, the Nicaraguan private sector began to view the protégés of the dictatorship initially as a source of unfair competition and subsequently as an outright threat to the development of the free enterprise system.

The same occurred in Guatemala and El Salvador. In Guatemala in particular, the military from the mid-1970s began organising their own enterprises which have grown at a rapid rate thanks to the advantages of direct control over political power. In El Salvador as well, the military, although playing a less prominent part in the leadership of the larger enterprises, have also played an increasing role, which has produced considerable conflict, with the traditional oligarchic sectors seeking greater political autonomy.

The political history of the past decades in those countries now facing the greatest upheavals has therefore been a story of progressive weakening of the hegemonic capacity of the oligarchic and military cliques that were in control of the state, due to cumulative divisions within the dominant power bloc, together with the appearance of new social forces capable of making effective demands for democratisation and motivated by interests that are increasingly irreconcilable with those of the established power-holders.

The frustration of all attempts at democratisation in the region has coincided with a process of economic growth which has complicated matters still more. During the 1960s and the first half of the 1970s the Central American sub-region grew by some 5 to 6 per cent a year at a fairly steady rate. And as the literature on authoritarian regimes will confirm, periods of economic growth and dynamism hardly favour the establishment of political openings, since prosperity tends to increase the legitimacy of those in power and to stimulate individualism in the society at large. In Central America this generalisation requires some qualification because of the character of the economic growth that took place. It was an essentially inegalitarian pattern of development which widened the existing differences between the richest and the poorest groups in each country, and which strengthened the transnational connections of the domestic business class, making the situation of the excluded sectors ever more intolerable. Thus, when the recession of 1974-5 precipitated the region into crisis (the fourfold increase of oil prices had a dramatic effect on a region which has no domestic sources of energy) the conditions were set for a revolutionary confrontation on a large scale. To sum up the period from 1945 to the economic crisis of the late 1970s, the following conclusion emerges rather clearly: significant changes on the economic front produced a perverse effect on the social structure; in the political realm, reliance was placed on the continued survival by repressive means of authoritarian regimes that had outlived their conditions of vitality. Various proposals for gradualistic reform were set aside by those in power, who preferred to gamble on a prolongation of the old system of domination regardless of the cost.

This is why the scope for reconstituting the authoritarian system in Central America in the 1980s is extremely restricted. When a balance sheet of the political history of the region is eventually drawn up, the most important conclusion will probably be that it is impossible simply by an act of political will to extend the life of authoritarian regimes which have completed their missions and become exhausted.

The Search for a Democratic Solution and the Weight of History

The outbreak of civil war in Nicaragua in 1977 attracted a great deal of international attention to Central America. As conflict spread to the majority of countries in the region following the victory of the Sandinistas and the overthrow of General Carlos Humberto Romero in El Salvador in 1979, this gave rise to a very pronounced internationalisation of the various political processes underway on the Central American Isthmus. The major international actors suddenly became interested in these countries whose history and political evolution had not hitherto concerned them very much. After a short lapse, the USA resolved to view the crisis from a strategic perspective, linking it directly to the East-West conflict, while political sources in Western Europe and the countries of the Contadora group paid more attention to internal factors.

Whereas the first approach – dominated by a military logic – envisaged the outcome of the crisis in terms of a complete victory of 'democratic' forces over those of 'communism', the second thought more in terms of a resolution of the issues in conflict based on negotiations and the achievement of a political consensus between the major local forces. These differences in international viewpoint undoubtedly constitute one more obstacle to the production of a solution to the problems of the region, but the root of these problems lies elsewhere. It is the exhaustion of an authoritarian political formula which has been implanted in Central America for so long that is the key issue.

The main interest of viewing the regional dictatorships in a comparative perspective is that it may help us to identify some 'shadows of the past' which obstruct the emergence of a political solution. In the rest of this chapter we shall briefly discuss three main obstacles.

1. *The Central American dictatorships have abused and discredited democratic forms.* In traditional military dictatorships problems of legitimacy were generally neglected and indeed the appearance of things disregarded. The old dictators confined themselves to exercising power as if they were the owners of landed estates so large that they embraced the territory of an entire country. For the most part, they had little interest in procedures which could in formal terms validate their control over the government. With the passage of time, however, such issues became more important. One element which contributed to this was the consolidation of the Inter-American System, whose founding documents expressed adhesion to the principles and forms of representative democracy. Another important factor was the pressure which began to emanate from Washington, in response to enquiries from the more liberal members of Congress who were seeking to distance the USA from the dictatorships of Latin America.

However this may be, it is clear that after the great wave of dictatorships of 1930, the *de facto* regimes of Guatemala, Nicaragua and El

Salvador began increasingly to adopt a 'democratic liturgy', even to the extent of misleading some observers. Elections were held with greater regularity to provide spurious mandates for the dictators, limited terms were established for the exercise of power (although these were subsequently extended according to the convenience of the moment), some opposition political parties were allowed to function and there was even a certain tolerance for the public activities of some opposition leaders. They even established legislative assemblies composed of a limited range of parties and municipal government was also institutionalised.

Behind this facade, however, the dictatorial will to monopolise power has remained unshaken. Consequently, the public front of democratic formalities indicates nothing of any substance. Thus, whenever an opposition political party manages to assemble a certain degree of support it will be dissolved and repressed; whenever a newspaper oversteps narrow bounds in its criticisms it will be closed, and its editor and his associates will be jailed; whenever a political leader begins to threaten the prerogatives of the government he will either be eliminated by the security forces or sent into unlimited exile. And when all these mechanisms fail, there still remains one last crucial resource: electoral fraud. This has become such a well-established practice in Central America that it is a normal and recognised thing for 'someone to win the election and someone else to win the count'.

The resort to fraudulent practices and the consequent discredit of democratic forms increased as the dictatorships entered into crisis. The Somoza family was always able to manipulate elections in order to hang on to power. But this was not the case in El Salvador and Guatemala. In El Salvador, the convergence of centre and left-wing parties gave rise to the creation of the Unión Nacional Opositora (UNO), a coalition of social democratic and communist organisations. The UNO clearly won the presidential elections of 1972, but its candidates for the presidency and the vice-presidency, José Napoleón Duarte and Guillermo Ungo, were deprived of their triumph, repressed and forced into exile. In 1977, the story was repeated. Once again, the winning opposition candidate, Colonel Ernesto Claramunt, was thwarted by the official candidate of the National Conciliation Party, General Oscar Humberto Romero. Moreover, dozens of demonstrators were massacred on 28 February in El Salvador, when they turned out to demand respect for the verdict of the polls.

Something similar occurred in Guatemala where the tradition of electoral fraud is very long established. In 1974, for example, the government candidate Kjell Laugerude was defeated by the opposition candidate of the Christian Democratic Party, General Efraín Ríos Montt. However, the government handed the presidency to its own candidate. The situation was repeated in an even clumsier manner in 1982. On 7 March of that year the official candidate, General Aníbal Guevara, Defence Minister in the outgoing government, lost the elections by a large margin but he was in any case declared the victor. This gave rise two weeks later to the military *coup* of 23 March, which this time permitted General Ríos Montt to take office – although not by electoral means.

This long history of fraud and aggression against the political opposition within a context of apparently democratic procedures is one of the causes of political polarisation in Central America, and it explains some of the present difficulties obstructing a solution to the crisis by means of a simple convocation to elections. In other authoritarian regimes, this type of proposal would be taken up by the opposition itself, but in Central America it is seen as the forerunner of some new conspiracy against the popular will. Because of that, the only way the electoral process could make some contribution to the generation of a political solution to the crisis would be if it was part of a clear and negotiated process of democratisation which included effective guarantees for all political actors and was part of a generalised political opening in which all the contending political forces would obtain their freedom of expression.

2. *There has been a precautionary destruction of the political centre.* The will to hold on to power at any price leads authoritarian governments to view with great anxiety the appearance of centrist political forces, particularly those grouped around Christian Democratic and Social Democratic ideologies. Since the 1950s this type of party has begun to organise itself in Guatemala and El Salvador, and also somewhat later in Nicaragua and Honduras. At the same time, there has been an evolution of some of the traditional Conservative and Liberal parties towards the centre, and they have begun to mount more active political opposition to the *de facto* regimes, establishing points of contact with the new centrist parties. Governments have reacted to this growth of the opposition by favouring, or at any rate tolerating without objection, the establishment of extreme right paramilitary groups who denounce the most moderate proposals for social reform as communist programmes. The Social Democratic and Christian Democratic parties were also subjected to policies of harassment and reprisal. In many cases, then, one of the principal objects of the Central

American authoritarian regimes has been to disorganise and destroy moderate political parties which were seen as the most immediate threat to the *status quo*. From harassment they have moved on to the physical elimination of reformist leaders. Such was the case with the Christian Democratic Deputy, Adolfo Mijangos in Guatemala in 1972; with former Foreign Minister, Alberto Fuentes Mohr, and with the former mayor of Guatemala City, Manuel Colom Argueta, both leaders of the Social Democratic movement, in 1978 and 1979. In El Salvador, the civil-military junta that replaced General Romero coincided with a great offensive by the far right organisation ORDEN against the more progressive wing of the Christian Democratic Party. Mario Zamora, the Minister of Justice and one of the leading figures of the Christian Democratic left, was assassinated at the beginning of 1980. And the assassination of Nicaraguan Conservative leader Pedro Joaquín Chamorro, owner and editor of the newspaper *La Prensa*, in January 1978, is widely remembered as the trigger event precipitating the final political crisis which brought down the Somoza regime.

In this way, the protracted death throes of these authoritarian regimes has also witnessed a destruction of the political centre and of the options associated with it. The leadership of these centrist parties has been weakened by the murder of their most influential figures and by the closure of opportunities for political expression. Their followers have therefore been subjected to a process of polarisation. Some of the them have bowed down before the established powers in return for very little, while others have chosen to join border fronts which, given the very nature of the conflict, have fallen under the leadership of left-wing forces with a military as well as a political capability. This accounts for a second difficulty in the way of attempts to democratise Central America and it explains the frequent presence among the opposition forces of Salvador and Guatemala of leaders who had formerly headed centrist organisations. The same occurred previously to opponents of Somoza in Nicaragua. Thus, in a climate of political polarisation and civil war, the centrist political groupings tend to be destroyed and will have to be practically 'reinvented' if they are to play an important role in future stages of democratic transition.

3. *The social movements of the sub-region have become highly radicalised.* Another consequence of the attitude of the dictators has been that the platforms adopted by social organisations in Central America have become very radical. This has affected even those organisations that were in their origins very moderate in outlook. In a context of

extreme authoritarianism and primitive reaction towards any challenge to the monolithic control of society, any collective demand, however basic, is seen as a subversive act and as a threat to the power structure. This has been very clear above all in relation to the labour movement: the most basic working-class demands gave rise to an enormous governmental repression. This caused the labour confederations to progress rapidly towards a critical position of the entire economic and political system, and the approval of anti-capitalist programmes of objectives.

The same process occurred in relation to the student movement and the peasant movement. The university federations have been for several decades key protagonists in almost all the mobilisations against the Central American dictatorships. Their manifestos and political programmes also express rejection of the capitalist system and propose solutions of the socialist type. More recently, a similar process could be observed among peasant organisations, which originated in the 1960s under the sponsorship of the Catholic Church. Consequently, all these groupings were initially very influenced by Social Christian thinking as can be seen from a review of their history in countries such as El Salvador and Honduras. However, demands for changes in the conditions of employment in the countryside and subsequent proposals for agrarian reform soon provoked fierce repression. This gave rise to a sharp shift leftwards among peasant leaders and rural organisations. In El Salvador, for example, a variety of peasant organisations, many of which had initially been very moderate in outlook, could be found by 1980 supporting the various fronts for the politically aligned with the radical left (such as the Bloque Revolucionario, the FAPU or the Ligas Populares 28th of February).

The radicalism of Central America's social movements has been crucial in creating the space and opportunities for the guerrilla organisations and for the armed struggle. But, taking a longer view, it also constitutes a strong pressure for far-reaching reforms as an integral part of any solution to the existing crisis. Thus, it is not possible to envisage a deal fixed up exclusively by the top political circles of a given country. If such an approach was attempted it would be rapidly undermined from below by a process of mobilisation involving workers, students, peasants and other sectors. Any political agreement must therefore include more exacting requirements than those that apparently permitted democratisation in southern Europe, for example, where the demand for democracy was a much more central platform of the opposition groups, given that there was far less injustice and inequality in those societies than we find today in Guatemala and El Salvador.

All these considerations, together with the distinctive international setting in which the Central American crisis is unfolding, set the limits within which a political solution must be found. The characteristic form of authoritarianism on the Isthmus that we have attempted to sketch in this chapter gives rise to a series of conditions that must be taken into account in any settlement aspiring to stability and effectiveness.

The restoration of an authoritarian political system is always difficult to achieve, all the more so when the crisis has reached such a point that political and economic objectives become irreconcilable. It becomes virtually impossible when the dictatorship in question is essentially anachronistic – that is to say, when it is out of line with the level of development of the society as a whole and when it has undergone a long period of erosion and disintegration.

The most difficult problem in Central America is that many solutions based on a simple democratic transition, and relying on formulas such as the holding of general elections or the summoning of a constituent assembly, will lack credibility and effectiveness because of the way these devices have been abused by past dictatorships. 'Political engineering' requires a more complex type of negotiation which takes into account the legitimacy requirements of any transitional government and which elaborates precise rules of the game guaranteeing the political freedom required by all contending forces who are to engage in negotiated settlement and subsequent open competition for power. At the same time, questions will arise as to how the various social organisations can be integrated into the emerging political system and how they can be won over to democratic processes. This is a complicated matter, given that in these countries one must both reinforce the density of civil society and at the same time ensure an effective bargain between social actors engaged in democratisation. Just as difficult will be the task of reorganising the armed forces and ensuring their subordination to civilian power and their commitment to their specific professional task. This is another prerequisite for the success of any democratic political solution. An equally delicate problem in the same area will be the 'reabsorption' into democratic political life of those elements currently aligned with the guerrilla movement, and the elimination of the paramilitary forces and the private guards of the extreme right who have been the major instrument of crime and repression in all these countries.

2 THE EUROPEAN AND THE CENTRAL AMERICAN EXPERIENCE

Giuseppe Di Palma

Transitions to democracy do not require exceptionally favourable circumstances. Dankwart Rustow gave us some of the reasons in a classical article published in 1970:[1]

1. Democracy does not demand any special prerequisites – any level of economic development, economic or social conditions, or any special cultural make-up.
2. Democracy is not born from consensus, it is born from conflict. It is born as a compromise to terminate or forestall an inconclusive struggle for regime supremacy.
3. Because it reflects a compromise, democracy is a second best for most concerned interests. Thus, the rules of the democratic game are initially adopted out of nothing more than a calculus of instrumental and, if you wish, self-serving compliance. Operational consent takes precedence over more demanding value consensus.
4. Because it reflects a compromise, democracy is not something that countries inadvertently back into either. On the contrary, transitions to democracy involve conscious choice, calculus, leadership. And they are events in which elite and organized behaviour play an extraordinary role.

To Rustow's analysis I have added[2] two analytical considerations, both bolstering the optimistic/game-theoretical view of democratic transitions:

1. Regime changes are not a smooth and natural response to slow and continuous change or even less to so-called functional imperatives of society.They are abrupt and time-bound occurrences in response to discrete events – usually internal to the regime and/or international.
2. Regime outcomes rest in turn on factors/events that are largely internal to the transition itself, and linked to each other by a Markov-type chain of causality. Thus the probability of later transitional events pushing towards a democratic outcome rests on earlier transitional choices and events that set the stage for a democratic

scenario – scenario that becomes progressively more difficult to deflect or reverse as it plays itself out.

I have used these analytical insights to account optimistically for European 'redemocratisations', such as those that occurred after the Second World War in Germany, Italy, Spain, Portugal, Greece.

On the other hand, if I reflect on Central America in light of the European experience, my optimism is considerably tempered. True, Central America is undergoing a period of potential regime changes in response to the type of discrete political and international occurrences just mentioned. But can those changes be veered towards democracy?

The following pages set the Central American case against that of Europe. If democracy does not require exceptionally favourable circumstances, as the case of Europe suggests, Central America appears to be afflicted by exceptionally unfavourable circumstances. Are there ways out of the predicament nevertheless?

The General Case for Democratisation – Europe

Central to my assessment of the European experience is a simple observation, but one that can take us a long way if properly dissected in its implications. The observation is that allegiance to democracy need not be absolute in order for democracy to occur; allegiance can also be, *and often is*, a relative choice. People and interests may keep or switch allegiance not so much because democracy is attractive *per se*, but because there are no other feasible alternatives, or because (much more interesting) the other alternatives are less attractive or are losing their attractiveness. Put in these terms, the fact that allegiance to a new democracy is often a relative (and recent) choice has its positive side. Indeed, it implies that democracy is still possible even in the absence of a pre-existing and fully-fledged democratic political culture.

If the above is true, it is then just as true that allegiance to dictatorship is not forever – be it allegiance to a specific dictatorship, or to dictatorship as a general type of rule. If such allegiances were forever, there would be little hope indeed for a new democracy. It would mean that allegiances could not be transferred to democracy but would have to be uprooted. It would mean that democracy would have to wait either for a defeat of the dictatorship in an international war, or for a civil war or revolution of some sort. But these are unlikely and extreme events. Also, in the case of civil wars and revolutions, the dictatorship would have an overwhelming advantage in the exercise of violence.[3] Even assuming that the dictatorship is finally overthrown by its domestic enemies alone, it may well be replaced by another dictatorship rather than by democracy, such being the perverse logic of meeting violence with violence. And even assuming a democratic outcome, the new democracy would be likely to inherit a divided country.

Fortunately, however, dictatorships are more likely to come to an end through more complex and less heroic processes of internal exhaustion, than at the hand of their enemies alone. These processes prove on the one hand that dictatorships are not as cohesive as we make them out to be, and on the other they make the transfer of allegiance more feasible. Dictatorships may start to come apart because, by the nature of their closed and self-serving system, they become sluggish, ineffective, unable to adjust to changing times, irrelevant or convulsively and yet futilely repressive. Or because, by liberalising, they trigger expectations and pressures for even greater change. Or because they substantially alter the place that some of their organised constituencies (most dangerously, the army) occupy in the regime. Or because they prove typically unable to solve the crisis of confidence that almost invariably accompanies the death or incapacity of the first dictator. It is in response to any combination of these circumstances that forces in the coalitions supporting or running the dictatorship may finally come to consider it as expendable and disposable, and begin to secede.

But secede towards what? Secession will most likely go hand in hand with an unprecedented mobilisation of many traditional enemies of the dictatorship (some of them with democratic aspirations, some with other or unsettled aspirations). This means that all sorts of coalitions of dissent from the dictatorship may take shape during the period of secession. The point is to transform these essentially negative, shifting and even conflicting coalitions into one coalition of consent for democracy. Though the transformation is by no means assured, democracy has some trump cards to play.

The best trump card is actually what we often consider to be democracy's weakness. It is exactly because democracy is a system of compromise, it is exactly because of its openness and open-endedness, because its game is never final, because nobody loses once and for all and on all arenas, that under certain circumstances the democratic game may finally appear attractive, convenient or compelling even to its earlier detractors – be they loyalists of the old dictatorship or enemies who may have fought it having in mind a goal other than democracy. In other words, a coalition of consent for democracy can rely upon and draw strength from a moderate compromise: a compromise that attracts a wide spectrum of opponents as well as former loyalists of the dictatorship, leaving out if necessary only a few, weakened dissenters.

Naturally, however, this type of compromise must rest in turn – and can in fact rest by the nature of democracy – on material bases. There are basically three such bases, three also being the key constituencies whose consent to democracy must be secured:[4]

1. Since democracies operate in the context of capitalist economies, there must be collective consent to the reproduction of capital. Though the matter seems obvious, this requires less obviously avoiding policies of democratic reconstruction designed to hamper significantly capital's capacity to accumulate and invest or, worse, designed to punish capitalists *collectively* for their real or alleged class role in the advent and running of the dictatorship.
2. Similarly, most of the state institutions that served the authoritarian regime (army, bureaucracy) are meant to serve democracy as well. Therefore, in order to secure such service, their internal self-rule may have to be preserved. Expressed in another way, in the transition to democracy, policies should be avoided that can be construed as retroactive punishment of the institutions' personnel *as a class*, rather than as necessary removal of legal features added by the dictatorship or as well-meant reforms. And reforms should come to terms with the preservation of internal self-rule and the institutions' involvement in those reforms.
3. Crucial to this first part of the compromise is the consent of the left. But how to secure its consent, and possibly even its participation, in promoting the compromise? The answer is that the left in turn must be granted ample space for democratic action in the party, electoral, parliamentary and labour arenas. Sooner or later, in other words, it must feel in the legitimate position to weigh publicly and contractually in the stimulation, allocation and social uses of privately produced wealth. I should add that this strategy of co-optation of the left, if successfully executed, may attract to the democratic game even a left that is potentially extremist by label or advocacy, if not by deeds.

Within these parameters a material compromise and therefore the transfer of allegiance from dictatorship to democracy are possible, without vitiating democracy. But possible means only possible. Forces whose allegiance has gone to other types of regime may not understand the material advantages offered by the democratic compromise, or, if they understand them, may not particularly value them. On the other hand, the alternative of uprooting those forces instead of conquering their allegiance is, as I have already indicated, neither that feasible nor without serious political cost for the prospects of democracy. Central America seems a good case in point in all these regards.

Indeed, my analysis concerning the winning capacity of the democratic compromise carries a strong Western European and social democratic bias. It reflects the special and indeed so far unique experience of a number of new European democracies. What is special about their experience is that, in replacing fascist or pseudo-fascist dictatorships, they could count on reviving or recycling for democracy a series of political and state institutions with a long historical tradition of their own – longer in fact than the lifespan of any particular regime and predating dictatorship. Some of these institutions (political parties, unions, lay organizations of the church) may have gone underground under the dictatorship; yet they did not disappear. Others may have served the dictatorship (bureaucracies, armies, judiciaries, business associations); yet they never became coterminous with it, never defined or were defined by it, and were possibly shunted aside by new and specifically totalitarian institutions (single parties, corporatist syndicates, special tribunals, party militias, secret police). It is true that in some cases, for example the army in Spain, the state apparatus or parts of it installed and partially or temporarily ran the dictatorship. But what is important to remember is that, in such cases, the dictatorship emphasised depoliticisation and demobilisation, while the state apparatus still presented itself as the historical and impartial guarantor of domestic law and order. All of which confirms the fact that in Europe the state apparatus has always been concerned (not always successfully) with protecting its impersonal, non-political, legal-professional status. Exactly the type of status which democracy can also guarantee.

Though not sufficient, this institutional weight of the past (and a past that had been liberal and even democratic) was, in my opinion, of prime significance in making European returns to competitive politics successful. In the first place, it helped state institutions placed at the service of dictatorship to secede, as a first step towards reaffirming their legal-professional autonomy within the state. And whatever the prime movers in the crisis of a particular dictatorship were (war, succession, reshuffling of the authoritarian coalitions), secessions made the crisis swifter and more resolute.

In the second place, of all possible outcomes of the crisis, the institutional weight of the past favoured democracy *tout court*, over another dictatorship or some 'guided' democracy. One consistent aspect of the various crises of dictatorship in Europe has been the prompt re-emergence of political parties and party allegiances, even after decades of interrupted competitive politics. But this re-emergence has been possible exactly and only because each of the two key European social formations – the bourgeoisie and the working class – had party traditions to which they could return and with which they could vie within the crisis. In turn, once and because these traditions were revived, it made much less difference what the 'natural and instinctive' regime affinities of those social formations might have been. What became instead of paramount importance was the preservation and consolidation of the party-political space of each social formation, in a political arena that proved immediately to be highly competitive.

Thus, once the crisis of a European dictatorship was underway, the country's institutions and social formations, each with their coveted spheres of autonomy and social presence, were compelled towards co-existence. They were compelled by the very weight of their diversity and co-presence, and so as to avoid the prospect of a protracted and inconclusive fight. That is why they accepted the three-pronged moderate institutional compromise which is at the heart of democracy. Much of this development also made for a clear and recognisable demarcation line between the authoritarian and post-authoritarian period in each European country. How clear the demarcation was, is shown by the uses of elections during each democratic inauguration.

Elections were never used as a tool to bring about democracy. Similarly, they were never used to arrest liberalisation at the threshold of democracy, by artfully constraining electoral participation and procedures. Nor were they ever successfully used to go beyond democracy, towards some kind of radicalising utopia. As a tool for democracy, they were not needed; as a tool against it, they were late and insufficient. Instead, elections were knowingly used to legitimise after the fact, and even with some delay, a democratic choice that had already been made by and through the revival of civil society and of state/institutional autonomy. Above all, they were used to decide the balance among the forces willing to play the competitive game. Thus, though elections were largely open to all political forces, including fringes whose loyalty to democracy was originally in question, the presence of such fringes never seriously endangered the firmness and irreversibility of the original choice.

The nostalgic right, abandoned by the bourgeoisie and the state apparatus, was never able to count on elections to reverse, delay or constrain competitive politics. The left, including by and large the communist left, came to recognise and employ elections, despite much rhetoric to the contrary, for what they truly are – an ineffective tool for radical social transformation, to be sure, but an effective one for the competitive representation of diverse interests. In fact, it is interesting to notice that in those exceptional cases in which the extreme left, realising that elections could not usher in the socialist society, denied their revolutionary legitimacy and tried to circumvent them, the left ended up by losing. The recent case in point is Portugal in 1975. Thus in post-authoritarian Europe, elections came to sanction a coalition of consent between right, left and centre. And elections were democratic not because they were *about* democracy, but because they were *within* democracy. In short, the issue no longer was, if it ever was, one of 'bullets or ballots'.

Central America: *Pars Destruens*

I have used the European experience as a model of successful transition to democracy. How does it fit contemporary Central America? What instinctively strikes me about recent dictatorial crises in the region is the inverse use of elections during such crises: elections seem to be *about* democracy rather than *within* democracy. They are seen in other words as *one* strategic tool employed during periods of protracted and uncertain transition – when a country is neither firmly authoritarian any more nor yet clearly on the way to democracy – in settling the contest between still dissenting political forces. While some forces may wish to use elections for genuine democratic aims, others may shun them as either destabilising or counter-revolutionary, and still others may consent to their use with mental reservations and for aims other than the achievement of democracy *tout court*. Nor is the use of elections alternative to that of armed force – even on the part of democratic actors. Since elections are a very delicate mechanism, electioneering under such a mixture of bullets and ballots may be ineffective, or produce unanticipated and undesirable effects.

Another way of putting this would be to say that elections in Central America suffer from the fact of being used despite the absence or weakness of the institutional conditions for a democratic compromise between the key state and social formations. But perhaps the most accurate statement is not that elections are used despite weak institutional conditions; the most accurate is that they are used, in a sort of *fuite en avant*, because of such weakness. To illustrate weakness and its effects on the uses of elections, let me consider the three potential partners to the democratic compromise.

Let me consider first the state apparatus and specifically the army, since the armed forces are so essential to the running of Central American politics. I have indicated that one component of the democratic compromise is the preservation of the institutional autonomy and the legal-professional status of the state apparatus and the army. It follows that an army that wishes to preserve or recapture its autonomy and legal-professional status may be induced for this purpose to transfer its allegiance from authoritarianism to democracy, even in cases like the recent Spanish one in which the army installed the authoritarian regime. But let us suppose that there is no such institutional status to preserve, and no aspiration to such status. Central America, where the very status of the army as an impersonal bureaucracy staffed and run according to legal-professional criteria is in question, is a case in point. The category that more closely describes Central American authoritarianism in that region is sultanism or neo-sultanism – to revive a Weberian term recently employed by Juan Linz and others.[5] Under such a regime the state is both object and agent of patrimonial appropriation, and the distinction between office and occupant is a weak one. In a very concrete and personalised sense, men of arms (even more than an army) are the regime. It is therefore difficult to see how armed forces that function to place their men at the core of sultanism might be interested in a legal-rational regime like democracy, that would alter radically their status and *raison d'être*.[6] Single military leaders still might – but they could not rally a veritable institution behind themselves. It is equally difficult to see how forces opposed to the dictatorship could place much trust in the democratic conversion of such state apparatus.

Certainly not the Marxist left, since it is likely to be locked by the military in the logic of violence, and since the price and the limit of a still unlikely military conversion to democracy seem to be the banning of the left. Besides, the left itself does not place undivided priority on the democratic compromise. The reason does not stop at dogma and ideology, which themselves need explanation. If the left cannot respond to the military logic of violence with any other winning logic, if its brand of Marxism is revolutionary and subversive, the reason is also and fundamentally that in Central America the left has not been in the position to build a party-political hegemony over its 'natural' social formations. Far from being a factor of subversion, such hegemony would be, in my opinion, a factor of calculated moderation. The left would not risk its historical assets by engaging in armed violence. Nor would it have compelling reasons to engage in risk-prone behaviour, since the almost spontaneous revival of its party-political traditions as the crisis of the dictatorhsip unfolds should act as a powerful disincentive for the military adventurism of *coups* and civil wars. In fact, the military itself might have less cause, out of fear, to meet violence with violence. Thus, on all these counts, there would be a premium on resolving the crisis of dictatorship by democratic compromise. But since these are not, as I said, the conditions of the Central American left, political crises in the region assume instead a violent and often non-resolutive character. Within their scenario, any faction of the left which tries to act reasonably, when party leadership and hegemony are not consolidated, runs the very real risk of being continuously overtaken and displaced on its left.

A moderate democratic centre may be more inclined to try the strategy of compromise, at least because there may be no other peaceful alternative to it. But by so doing the centre runs the risk of falling into all kinds of opportunistic traps and non-reciprocal concessions – especially since it appears unable to bargain from a position of institutional strength and solidity. We may consider in this regard the position of the bourgeoisie – the one social formation that should constitute the backbone of the political centre. To be sure, there is no reason to believe that the bourgeoisie as a whole should remain wedded to the authoritarian regime. When state and society are patrimonialised by politico-military cliques it is in fact not unlikely that sectors of the bourgeoisie will themselves be the object of political plunder by such cliques, and will in response set in motion the very crisis of the dictatorship by removing their original support. The point about the bourgeoisie is a different one, and is similar to that about the social formations of the left. The point is its extreme social *and* political fragmentation. Of the broad bourgeois sectors I can think of – agrarian, state-dependent, *comprador*, domestic – I would guess that only the latter may conceive of a democratic project. But neither it nor the other sectors can revive traditional networks of bourgeois party identifications and organisations which in fact never existed. Thus sectors of the bourgeoisie may be capable of seceding from the dictatorship, but not as capable of forging and imposing by their weight a coalition of democratic consent – either on the armed forces or, for that matter, on the left.

What, then, of free elections in this atomised context? I have already suggested how, in the conflictive uncertainty about the outcomes of the authoritarian crisis, elections in general are viewed as just one strategy in the arsenal of strategies used by various factions in the transition. Thus elections may be subject to all sorts of manipulations to influence results, and may even be used openly to confirm some new form of dictatorship.

But let us assume that an effort is made to run elections in a genuinely free, competitive, democratic fashion. Since conflicting strategies confront each other in the transition, a democratic coalition able to impose free elections could claim a major strategic achievement. Elections might finally test the ability of the forces for democracy to hold sway over society. No more may then be needed – no conquest of people's hearts and minds – to establish democracy's right to rule. Nor should we overlook the fact that in societies without party traditions to resurrect, calling for popular elections seems the most compelling way in which democratic forces in the transition can prove their strength, improve their standing *vis-à-vis* other competing forces and arrest violence.

And yet we cannot ignore the risks of free elections. Resorting to elections in order to build democratic partisan identities, exactly because these identities do not pre-exist, may amount to a premature or wasted move. Since free elections are likely to be held in a climate of actual or threatened violence, *contragolpismo* or civil war, their conduct and their results may fall short, or be denounced as falling short, of democratic intents.

As to the conduct of free elections, two conditions seem indispensable: that they be conducted in an orderly fashion and that they be open to all forces willing to take their verdict seriously. But in a climate of actual or threatened violence, these conditions are most difficult to guarantee. To secure orderly elections, the democratic forces may need the assistance of the old state apparatus, such as it is. Rightly or wrongly, they will then be accused of colluding with the old order, resorting to coercion and betraying their electoral promises. This is another reason why forces which have chosen the path of armed rebellion against the old order may not be willing to participate in free elections, even when so solicited. But by far the most important reason is that free elections constitute only one in a number of competing strategies. If the strategy wins, it would compel rebels to choose between compliance with the democratic game and political marginality. But since its winning capacity is yet to be proven (that is why elections are called) why agree to undergo the test? Instead, if elections are held under reasonable guarantees, and yet the turn-out is less than substantial, it is easy to discount their results. And if the turn-out were to be substantial, what 'better proof' that voters were coerced to the polls and elections were not, after all, free?

As to the results of such elections, only one result would do. Only a fully and unambiguously democratic vote can put an end to all the uncertainties and make democracy the winning option. But there is little guarantee that the results will be and will remain democratic. This is for the reason I have pointed out several times: the lack of traditions in the way of a national party system. In countries where a national party system has never taken root, where popular elections have been sporadic and shunned, where voting has been tied to parochial and personalistic concerns, where civil society appears fragmented socially and politically, and where therefore neither dictatorship nor armed rebellion are yet clearly ruled out as an option – in these countries it is not at all unlikely that reasonably free and orderly elections will not after all result in a national mandate for democracy.[7]

Central America: *Pars Construens*

The pages above have painted me into an intellectual corner. After accounting optimistically for the European experience of democratisation, I have raised very basic reservations as to the possibility of replicating that experience in Central America. When one looks closely at those reservations, they in effect say that some minimal conditions absent in Central America come close to being necessary in order to sustain a democratic scenario. Roughly speaking, they are a fairly professionalised state and socially hegemonic political parties. It is their coexistence that, once a country or region embarks on a period of regime changes, creates a stalemate among political forces, discourages risky winner-take-all action, and offers instead an incentive to unblock the inconclusive stalemate by means of a democratic compromise. Expressed in another way, the absence of these two conditions signifies that means other than democratic ones may still be available to pursue political power, and that political actors may favour them in the period of regime transition. In simple words, violence may still pay off. And this seems to be the Central American predicament.

I nevertheless raise the question I raised in my opening paragraphs:

are efficient ways out of the predicament still conceivable? That is, are there ways out of violence despite the inauspicious institutional conditions indicated above? By the logic of my argument about the lingering rewards of violence, such ways out would seem virtually unattainable, except in one fundamental sense – unless, that is, violence fails to deliver *in its own terms*, as a means to remove the adversary and subjugate uncommitted populations. Thus, the initial event is not dissimilar from that which Rustow's analysis emphasises:[8] an inconclusive struggle, the protracted ineffectiveness of violence, war-weariness and disillusion possibly leading (as Laurence Whitehead puts it in his contribution to this volume) to abrupt shifts in the strategy and even objectives of political actors.

The important cautionary note, however, is that war-weariness is only the initial step. It remains true that forces that do not have mass/organizational or corporate/institutional interests to protect or revive have 'little to lose', and may therefore put up with a very protracted struggle before giving in to war-weariness, or may be tempted by the prospect of a final assault aimed at total victory. Everything else failing, they may provisionally respond by going underground or by exiting – as hired mercenaries, political refugees and conspirators, exiled jet-setters or itinerant revolutionaries. Thus, in a region where repression and rebellion, violence in response to violence, are endemic political currency, violence may as easily flare up as it subsides and war-weariness may as easily dissipate. The distinctive characteristics of Central American (but not European) dictators, the volatility and in-fighting of military juntas, the inexhaustible supply of rebel leaders and liberation fronts, speak to the point. Thus the predicament of violence is also a vicious circle. Breaking it requires timing in the effective exploitation of temporary weariness.

Because weariness is not only temporary but also relative (one is tired of an ineffective strategy and readier to renounce it if a new one is made available), it seems to me that introducing the lure of a viable political settlement at the moment of weariness is possibly the best or even the only way to interrupt the vicious circle. It bears repeating that, because the structural incentives that were present in Europe are absent in Central America, the task of advancing a political settlement as an alternative to violence is an exceedingly difficult one, even when violence is a debased currency. It is nevertheless a necessary one. I am not at all sure that necessity is the mother of invention and that virtue is born of necessity. I only know that overwhelming virtue and invention must be committed in devising a political settlement when the moment of opportunity presents itself.

As to the content and form of the settlement, two factors directly affect them. First, the settlement stems, as stipulated, from a protracted stalemate with no victors *or losers either*. It therefore will most probably have to rely on overtly negotiated pacts – rather than unspoken concessions, temporary withdrawals, implicit accommodations, ambiguous muddling through or any other move that, by leaving in doubt the nature of the new game and the right of the adversary to play in it, fails to make it attractive. In this regard it is interesting to note that, of all European cases of democratic settlements since the war, the only one that approaches the explicit form of a *democracia pactada* is that of Spain in the 1970s: the only case in which the authoritarian regime was not overthrown by domestic dissidents or foreign enemies. Thus, barring explicit accommodations, the Spanish scenario at the death of Franco, even more than any other European scenario of authoritarian crisis, appeared in prospect that of a protracted stalemate without winners or losers – except at unbearable institutional costs. The fact of a protracted stalemate also requires that the settlement overtly allows the preservation and exercise of corporate interests by the main antagonists. To be sure, those interests and their exercise will have to be redefined and possibly curbed so as to fit a reasonably competitive political game. But there is no way in which they can be ignored or suppressed if the settlement intends to derive lasting advantage from the stalemate. The case of Spain is again instructive in this regard. But the case of Central America is both more in need of a corporate settlement and by the same token more challenged by its requirements.

Indeed, if the Spanish transition to democracy made use of a strategy of *democracia pactada*, it was only because the corporate interests that operated the old regime were undefeated. In Central America, on the other hand, the need for and yet the difficulty of a negotiated corporate settlement stem also from the more fundamental fact that local interests do not even have a corporate structure. And this is the second factor dictating the terms of a settlement in the region: part and parcel of a *salida pactada* (negotiated solution) to prevent a return to violence as normal political currency must therefore be the adoption of measures and reforms that would pursue what European polities had achieved *before* their authoritarian interludes: the consolidation and institutionalisation of coexisting and stabilising corporate interests. In this sense, it is not surprising that unilateral appeals to democracy as a proper and fair order for the region, pressures for the prompt resumption of democratic practices, and even the holding of reasonably competitive and open elections while the struggle goes on, appear hollow, self-serving and deceptive moves. Taken alone, promises of a fair game do not constitute a political settlement guaranteeing who is to play.

Let me briefly exemplify the enormous difficulties but also the possibilities of a political settlement by looking at the place that the armed forces and the political parties would have to occupy in it. A political settement resulting from a protracted stalemate with no winners or losers must by necessity come to terms with the armed forces, the backbone of Central American (but not of European) dictatorships. I have abundantly stated why the task is enormously demanding: praetorian armies have little reason to reform, nor can their record of personalised violence be easily absolved for the sake of reconciliation. Indeed, the task is so demanding that according to Guillermo O'Donnell and Philippe Schmitter the only way out of military dictatorships of the type we are discussing seems armed insurrection.[9] Be that as it may (my reservations are clear from the text), one advantage of a protracted stalemate is that few situations work better in dividing a praetorian army with limited professionalisation: its capacity to deliver as a predatory instrument is in question. In fact, there is no such thing in reality as a perfect praetorian army: at least in Central America today there exist sectors of the military attracted by the idea of a professional army or by ideologies of national security. True, professional armies and ideologies of national security have been behind South American dictatorships. It is also true, as I remarked earlier, that military cliques attracted by the prospects of professionalisation do not yet have a professional institution to back them up. Yet a professional army is rooted, more than a praetorian army, in corporate guarantees. Thus the conclusion must be that a successful political settlement minimally demands (though it is not secured by) efforts to reform the armed forces in a corporate/professional direction. At least some sectors of the army may support a settlement, not necessarily because they share its democratic implications but because it is good for the army as an institution as well as personally rewarding.

As to the democratic implications of the political settlement, they are most closely associated with the political parties. The parties, however, are not the counterpart and opponents of the army. Rather, they are likely to cover a spectrum of interests from predatory oligarchies buttressed by the military to armed parties of the revolution. The fragmentation of civilian interests and their intermingling with military and armed interests can make reconciliation among parties and between armies, guerrillas and parties quite difficult. As the events of post-authoritarian Portugal suggest, when military/civilian coalitions are directly and centrally involved in steering a *salida*, the temptation to steer it by force is considerable. I have indicated why calling for elections, even under a protracted stalemate, is not a sufficiently attractive alternative to violence: elections can be used with some risks to jockey for position in preparation for the next move – which may very well be a political settlement – and even to nudge the adversary towards such settlement, but they are not a settlement. The fact is that, even if they are conducted fairly, unilaterally organised elections have a way of turning to the advantage of the organisers and to the disadvantage of many opponents who not surprisingly fail to be attracted by their fairness.

On the other hand, though a political settlement is necessary, its terms can not be excessively elaborate, if they are to be agreeable to a wide spectrum of political parties and their armed components. Timing is essential in seizing advantage of war-weariness and militates against complex inter-party pacts that could easily be bogged down in the effort to anticipate all conflicting issues and demands. In fact, the more specific a pact is, the more it risks raising new reasons for dissatisfaction and the more difficult it is to renegotiate it under changing circumstances. All of this in fact speaks for *a series* of pacts.[10] The function of the first such pact should simply be to offer a wide spectrum of parties a fair and concrete chance to stay and to count in the competitive game. In other words, the first negotiations concerning the political parties resemble the negotiations for attracting the armed forces to a final settlement: in both instances the objective is to enable those organizations concretely to carry out their vital professional role in a democracy. And since in the case of the political parties that ability minimally translates – to put it squarely – in the ability of the parties to secure enough electoral support to stay in the game, this requires that the first inter-party pact be no less (but possibly also no more) than a collective pact about elections and their conduct.

Striking such a pact is not easy – as we know. It may, for instance, require that, *having finally agreed to compete electorally*, political actors only recently engaged in armed conflict now agree temporarily, in order to build and protect their electoral following and organisational basis, to share positions of power and control of direct relevance for the elections. Nor is the pact, even if carefully executed, sufficient to institutionalise that system of socially hegemonic parties which, as I stated, is crucial not only for the stability of democracy but also for its very inauguration. Let me, however, point out some of the advantages of making enemies enter into the spirit of an electoral pact. In the first place, attention will be shifted from fighting and conflict to rule-making and practical matters of co-operation, signalling that elections are potentially changing from an exclusionary weapon in the convenient arsenal of one or another contestant into an inclusive process to legitimise divergent interests – from elections *about* (or against) democracy into elections *within* democracy. In the second place, since the elections will finally be seen as the founding, instating or legitimising elections of a new competitive order, parties will assign them an inordinate and perhaps even unwarranted value in determining mass political alignments for years to come. In this sense, even though a socially hegemonic party system with properties of stabilisation is not yet implanted, elections conducted under a pact should appear as a first engineered step in that direction. What counts in this regard is the willingness of the parties to think in such terms and therefore to invest in their own survival as machineries for the organisation and representation of societal interests.

One last point about inter-party pacts bears emphasis. The pacts I am discussing, with no winners or losers, demand considerable realism, tough-mindedness and forbearance. They are necessitated by the fact that the divergent interests of the actors in the struggle can be satisfied jointly or not at all. They therefore must be at the same time democratic and accommodative of interests that are not only at loggerheads but also suspicious of democracy. Hazardous and unpalatable as it is, the task requires a strategy of attraction and inclusive measures that will keep democracy open to potentially anti-democratic forces. Proportionality,[11] the legal recognition of extreme parties, parliamentarism rather than presidentialism, as well as the carving of electoral districts so as to secure sufficient representation of both traditional and new interests, are measures that recommend themselves.

There is no question that the costs of such measures in the long run can be considerable. Typically, multi-party parliamentary democracies with a weak executive and a history of violence before their advent have experienced a rough life. To the extent that they had to preserve traditional interests, they fed disenchantment. To the extent that their governments lacked executive resolve, they spelled ineffectiveness. There is European evidence for this. But in Central America the life of such democracies would be much rougher. For reasons that are obvious by now, the type of *salida pactada* that I have been describing could well produce a spectrum of democracies which either alternately or at one and the same time are 'guaranteed' by a prominent army, possess a party system in which parties run the gamut from *personalismo* to clientelism populism and Third World radicalism, pay lip-service to and shelter myths of social revolution, embrace chauvinist and anti-imperialist creeds, and in the final analysis aspire to the status of modern and effective social democracies.

Yet I must assert in their defence that such democracies would be unquestionably and infinitely superior to what presently exists. Nor, for reasons I cannot spell out here, should we necessarily infer their imminent demise.[12] Even the notion that they are always impervious to later reforms needs careful consideration of circumstances. Finally, it seems to me that a *salida pactada* different from the one I have described – one that would aim at more immediate social reforms or at strengthening a narrower and more cohesive coalition of governing interests – would be at any rate less likely to prevail (and if it prevails, probably less promising in the long run). Not even a strictly negotiated and inclusive electoral pact can guarantee that the results of founding elections will satisfy all concerned. There are good subjective reasons why, whether or not their fears prove groundless, both the traditional right and the left may fear the verdict of elections which, exactly because they are founding, seem to invite the voters to try a fresh start. Thus – though there are limits to how far the will to accommodate should travel – an inclusive pact is practically a necessity. Why, otherwise, should forces who fear electoral losses enter into the new game?

Conclusions

The scenario for a political settlement presented in the last few pages should not be read, despite probable expository slippages, as a statement of likelihood about its occurrence but more as a statement of necessity and internal logic. I have tried to show what special form a successful *salida* would have to take in view of the fact that Central America lacks certain structural conditions which elsewhere have been decisive in making democratic transitions successful. As to the likelihood of the scenario under present circumstances, I should not commit myself without at least extensive analysis. I shall nevertheless conclude by venturing some preliminary and somewhat optimistic considerations. There are two ways we can construct a statement of probability. One way is to see the onset of a scenario for political settlement as a function of the number of actors that shall be involved in its unfolding. Since the settlement involves, by its very nature, a large number of actors who must converge on platforms which are not necessarily palatable, the prospect for a settlement would appear to be dim. As Laurence Whitehead notices in his contribution to this volume, a well-co-ordinated shift in perceptions and conduct by many actors is an exceedingly difficult feat.

There is, however, a second way of looking at how a scenario for political settlement is set in motion. True, the viability of a democratic settlement rests eventually on the involvement of many actors in the settlement. But it is usually the case that the action of only one actor or one set of actors will set the scenario in motion. The other actors will follow suit *seriatim* in response to a chain of events that makes involvement in the settlement progressively more attractive or compelling. This means that no joint change of heart is needed at the outset. It may instead be sufficient that one actor reacts to war-weariness by finally seeking options which he and the others had for a long time irretrievably discarded. The other actors, whether or not they are as sensitive to war-weariness, will be sensitive to the winning potentials of the new options and to the risks of being left out.

I cannot discuss here how actors calculate whether a new option has a winning potential, though one factor may simply be the realisation that more and more actors are attracted by it. Terry Karl's analysis in this volume of Duarte's electoral strategy in El Salvador seems to me a good illustration of how the actions of one actor may carry others along. Though El Salvador is not yet at the point of a political settlement, the successful pursuit of an electoral strategy by one party may reach a point beyond which it is too late to resist it and too costly not to join.

There exists the final question of whether, despite what I have just written, there exists any single actor who is both indispensable for a regional settlement and yet impervious to the settlement no matter what. The United States would seem to be the obvious candidate. Can a political settlement succeed irrespective of how the United States feels about it? Does a settlement require some geo-political guarantees for the United States? Does the very fact of an American political concern for the area encourage local oligarchical and military interests to weather war-weariness? In Western Europe's democratic transitions, the democratic stance of the United States was very clear but also, I would argue, unnecessary once the respective geo-political spheres of communism and the West were quickly defined. And even the weakest European democracies proved quite adept at defusing alone the danger of internal subversion. In Central America, however, geo-political spheres are perceived by the United States to be in question, and so is the capacity of prospective democracies and new regimes in general to domesticate extremism and keep foreign influences out.

As long as these perceptions remain, domestic political settlements do become more demanding. How much more demanding? To repeat, the answer depends on whether the United States is really indispensable. Since the United States is unable or unwilling to step forcefully into the local fray, its limited support for repressive forces is not such that these forces will always remain indifferent to the prospects of a political settlement triggered locally by their adversaries. Thus one point of investigation is whether even a great hemispheric power may not have to settle for local regimes which are second-best in its calculations.

Notes and References

1. Dankwart Rustow, 'Transitions to Democracy', *Comparative Politics*, vol. 2, no. 3 (April 1970), pp. 337-63.
2. Giuseppe Di Palma, 'Government Performance: An Issue and Three Cases in Search of Theory', *West European Politics*, vol. 7, no. 2 (April 1984), pp. 172-87.
3. If such advantage withers away, this is most likely to be preceded or accompanied by a crisis internal to the regime and its supporters. In such a case the scenario discussed in the following paragraph applies.
4. These points are explored in Adam Przeworski, 'Some Problems in the Study of the Transition to Democracy', in Guillermo O'Donnell, Philippe Schmitter and Laurence Whitehead (eds.), *Transitions from Authoritarian Rule in Latin America and Southern Europe* (Baltimore and London: Johns Hopkins University Press, 1986).
5. Juan Linz, 'Totalitarian and Authoritarian Regimes', in Fred Greenstein and Nelson Polsby (eds.), *Handbook of Political Science*, vol. 3 (Reading: Addison-Wesley, 1975) pp. 259-63.
6. Questions may be raised about whether the label 'sultanism' is obsolete and partial. Some authors stress a trajectory in the role of the military – from praetorian 'guardians of the dynasty', to masters in their own right, to more professional and modernising practitioners of counter-insurgency ideologies. My view is that *any* of those roles involves a self-image of the military as wielders of power which the military cannot easily dispense with and which is alternative to democracy.
7. Would the choice of electoral laws make a difference in this regard? Yes and no. It might be thought that a plurality system with single-member constituencies could stop party fragmentation and therefore help the structuring

and consolidation of a national party system. In point of fact, however, plurality can do nothing of the sort. It can, to be sure, reduce the number of *national* parties, but only if a structured system of national parties already exists. This is because a plurality system's only direct effect is to reduce the number of effectively competing candidates at the level of the local electoral constituency. That effect will not be felt at the national party level and will not thereby reduce the number of parties unless there already exists a consolidated network of national parties controlling local candidates. In fact, it could be said that in the absence of such a network, a party aspiring to become national would benefit from proportionality, while a plurality system would work wholly in favour of localistic parties and the rule of notables and bosses.

8. Rustow, 'Transitions to Democracy'.

9. Guillermo O'Donnell and Philippe Schmitter, *Political Life after Authoritarian Rule: Tentative Conclusions about Uncertain Transitions* (Baltimore and London: Johns Hopkins University Press, forthcoming).

10. See ibid. for many of the observations that follow on the role of pacts.

11. One valuable effect of proportionality, aside from giving every party a chance for representation, is that (as I stated previously) it is a better arrangement for the structuring and consolidation of a national party system.

12. Di Palma, 'Government Performance'.

3 LESSONS FROM THE SOUTHERN CONE

Robert R. Kaufman

Students of democratic change in South America's Southern Cone have few success stories to offer their Central American counterparts. The recent political openings in Argentina, Uruguay and Brazil, it is true, do provide some hope for the future in that part of the world. Still, the dominant motif of the last two decades has been immobilism and military repression, not mutual toleration and political compromise. If anything, South America might well be better off today if, over the course of the past twenty years, its leaders had sought to learn something from the experiences of Central America about the long-term costs of attempting to settle conflicts by military force. This is still a lesson of particular relevance to the civil-military elites that currently cling to power in Chile and Paraguay.

Compared to the nations of Central America, moreover, most of the Southern Cone countries have had some important advantages in attempting to avoid such costs. The South American countries are among the richest and most industrialised in Latin America, whereas El Salvador, Nicaragua, Honduras and Guatemala are among the poorest in per capita terms – with incomes substantially below even that of Paraguay, which is by far the least developed of the Southern Cone countries (see Table 3.1). With the exception of Paraguay, moreover, the Southern Cone countries have experienced prolonged periods of relatively peaceful populist politics; and prior to the military takeovers of 1973, Chile and Uruguay were usually placed among the world's most stable and institutionalised constitutional democracies. In Central America, only Costa Rica approximates this record. Finally, United States marines have never occupied or seriously threatened to occupy the countries of South America.

In view of the democratic breakdowns and military repressions that have occurred against this backdrop, much of the research on this region has focused on questions concerning how things could have gone so wrong. So far, there are few clear answers – and still fewer that might be exportable to other parts of the world. The unfolding Southern Cone experiences do, however, raise some broad issues about the mixtures of constraint and opportunity that surround political actors seeking to promote democracy and/or economic development.

Table 3.1: General Economic Data

	GDP per capita 1982*	GDP growth 1981-3**	GDP/CAP growth 1981-3**
Southern Cone			
Argentina	$1307	-9.0	-13.3
Brazil	1322	-5.8	-11.9
Chile	876	-9.9	-14.3
Paraguay	787	4.4	- 4.7
Uruguay	1651	-13.9	-15.6
Central America			
Costa Rica	1128	-13.4	-20.1
El Salvador	314	-15.4	-22.4
Guatemala	607	-4.9	-12.9
Honduras	393	-0.5	-10.3
Nicaragua	498	9.3	-0.9
Panama	1933	10.5	3.5

Sources* CEPAL, *La Crisis en America Latina: Su Evaluacion y Perspectivas* (E/CEPAL/CEGAN.8/L.2), p. 31 (1975 dollars).
** CEPAL, *Sintesis Preliminar de la Economia Latinoamericana Durante 1983* (E/CEPAL/G.1279), pp. 32-3.

And they raise some questions about the way these mixtures play themselves out in specific historical situations.

There are three basic points I wish to make along these lines in the following sections of this chapter:

1. Even apparently stable and institutionalised democracies (such as those of Chile and Uruguay) can collapse. But such collapses can be attributed at least in part to avoidable choices and miscalculations of the political class. Put somewhat differently, there is no convincing evidence that uncontrollable social or political determinants necessitated the turn towards authoritarianism during the 1960s and 1970s.

2. The military-authoritarian 'solutions' to the developmental impasses of the Southern Cone countries were failures: this was so in part because their leaders ignored the constraints imposed by the political realities of their respective societies.

3. Finally, the partial success of transitions to more liberalised political systems illustrates (to the extent that they have been successful) a point originally made by Dankwart Rustow: that democracy originates in the context of 'second best' choices made by groups that would rather have eliminated each other if they had had the power to do so.[1] In other words, such transitions depend in part upon leaders whose actions are structured by 'correct' perceptions of which parts

of the real world can be manipulated, and those which they must accept.

Though these observations will certainly appear obvious to many readers, they may none the less be worth stating explicitly, if only to offset natural tendencies to draw simplified 'lessons' from partially-remembered or imperfectly-understood developments outside one's area of immediate geographic concern. In any event, they are written in the spirit of Albert Hirschman's warning that the architects of multi-faceted socio-political transformations can never, given the complexity of their subjects, count on reliable blueprints. 'Not only is each house different from any other that was built before', he argues, 'but it also necessarily uses new construction materials, and even experiments with untested principles of stress and structure. Therefore, what can be most usefully conveyed by the builders of one house is an understanding of the experience that made it at all possible to build under these trying circumstances.'[2]

The Collapse of Democracy in Chile and Uruguay

First we need to pay some attention to the forces which ripped down the democratic houses in Chile and Uruguay in 1973. At a later point, we will broaden the discussion to include other Southern Cone societies. We start with Chile and Uruguay, however, both because their size makes them somewhat more comparable to the nations of South America than Argentina and Brazil, and because their problems seem particularly relevant to Costa Rica, where strong democratic institutions have recently encountered severe economic and political challenges. There is little dispute, of course, that the social-political crises faced by these systems were severe; the question is how overwhelming were the strains these crises placed on democratic institutions and what were the degrees of freedom available for coping with these strains? We can consider this issue under three general headings: (i) the 'manageability' of the underlying socio-economic conflicts confronted by these systems; (ii) the constraints and incentives implied by the structure of political institutions; and (iii) the choices and perceptions of the 'political class' itself.

The most salient socio-economic problems facing these systems, inflation and slow growth, undoubtedly did place serious strain on the long-term legitimation and accumulation capacities of each democratic state. Post-war growth rates were among the lowest in the region, and by the late 1960s and early 1970s, these issues had also become interlinked to a constellation of other problems – the zero-sum distributive conflicts among contending class organisations, urban terrorism and direct action fostered by the Tupamaros and by Chilean fringe groups, and growing attempts by the United States to stiffen the 'anti-subversive' will and capability of local military establishments. Such developments also raised a lively if still unresolved debate among academics and political actors about the extent to which they were rooted in long-term features of 'dependent development' and in the structural limits of import-substituting industrialisation.[3]

We shall take up the last of these issues – that of the 'root causes' of the socio-economic pressures on the system – in the last part of this section. For the time being, however, it is important to emphasise that such chronic, unresolved structural problems can contribute to democratic breakdowns only indirectly – through their escalation into acute forms of economic crisis and political conflict that can no longer be effectively managed or contained by democratic authorities.[4] Our principal focus here is whether and when such chronic problems had become unmanageable, and the extent to which this 'unmanageability' was a necessary outgrowth of the underlying structural problems themselves.

In the case of Uruguay, there are especially significant indications that, at least for the time being, the worst of the socio-economic crisis had passed by the time the military seized power in 1973. The stagflation of 1971-2, not quite as severe to begin with as that encountered in the mid-1960s, was already beginning to abate by 1973. The rate of inflation, though still very high, was down slightly from its 1972 peak, and for the first time in several years, the economy had begun to register positive rates of growth.[5] In the political realm, the Tupamaros, the ostensible target of the military incursion into politics, had already been defeated. And although the scene was marked by increasing labour union militancy, the principal electoral challenge to the traditional parties was a centre-left, reformist coalition (the Frente Democratico) which advocated rather modest changes in the socio-political system. In this context, military authorities may well have perceived a clear and present danger to the capitalist system, and members of the political class may well have lost faith in their capacity to govern. But there is very little clear evidence that in 1973 the democratic system itself was actually ungovernable.

The Chilean case is more complex, for by September 1973 there was little question that the economy had broken down and society seemed close to civil war. Still, as Arturo Valenzuela has argued forcefully,[6] there is no evidence that this acute crisis derived directly from the contradictions of Chile's dependent capitalist economy. If anything, as Valenzuela notes, growth rates, balance of payments and internal price stability actually improved significantly between the 1950s and the 1960s. And the standard measures of social mobilisation and mass political militancy reveal few major new shocks to the political system in the decade prior to the 1973 crisis. Although unionisation drives increased the number of organised workers, especially in agriculture, the growth of the union movement as a whole did not exceed that of the working-class population; and strike activity, as measured by average duration and man-hours lost, was actually lower in 1969-70 than at the beginning of the post-war period. Finally, although new voters did begin to flood into the system after the electoral reforms of the 1950s, their participation did not change the traditional balance between the parties of the centre, right and left. In fact, Allende's 1970 vote was actually a few percentage points lower than it had been in 1964 when he had been defeated by the combined strength of a centre-right alliance.

For the moment, these briefly sketched observations should be enough to suggest that both Uruguay and Chile conform with Juan Linz's more general suggestion that democracies rarely break down because of objectively unsolvable socio-economic problems. 'It is not the technical characteristics of the problem,' he says, 'but the political context in which they are placed, the constraining conditions on the regime, and the alternatives offered by the existence of one or more disloyal oppositions that ultimately trigger the process of breakdown.'[7]

But this raises a second general issue: the question of how the historical organisation of the political-constitutional system, and especially the party systems, structured the actions and choices of the political leadership. Even if the underlying socio-economic conflicts were not in themselves unmanageable, it is possible that the specific institutional organisation of political life encouraged conflicts and demands that eventually made them so. In Uruguay, the immobilism and patronage orientations of the traditional parties clearly presented a major 'structural' impediment to political leaders seeking to escape from the stagnation and the zero-sum conflicts of the past several decades and to make the system more representative of the socio-political forces struggling for power and resources.[8] In Chile, the centrifugal tendencies in the multiparty system created a different but no less severe set of dangers: before and after the 1970 elections, competition among different ideological sectors of the political elite inhibited accommodation on reform measures, while at the same time encouraged the mobilisation of mass demands that led to the crisis of 1973.

Did these systems, then, succumb to inescapable 'political-institutional' contradictions? We must, as in the case of socio-economic issues, distinguish between underlying weaknesses in the system and the escalation of these weaknesses into crisis proportion. Although as noted above, there were important institutional constraints on the problem-solving capabilities of each democratic system, it is difficult to argue that these were inherently 'fatal flaws'. In Uruguay, the party system which was overthrown in 1973 had after all already muddled through almost two decades of economic difficulty and social conflict; and by 1971, with the emergence of the Frente Democratico, there were even indications of possible reformist restructuring. In Chile, a long tradition of accommodation and compromise among competing ideological sectors of the political class had served very effectively in previous decades to contain the mobilisation of 'unmanageable' demands.

Finally, in the aftermath of systemic breakdowns, it is easy to exaggerate the defects of these organisations and to ignore their strengths. Like most institutionalised party systems, those in Chile and Uruguay did work to link political authorities to civil society and to channel competition for political office. Neither was closed to reformist tendencies – in Chile, on the contrary, the dynamics of the political system had done a good deal to facilitate social reform during the 1960s and early 1970s. And by organising the electoral process, each played a crucial role in legitimating the structures of a democratic state. Whatever the organisational liabilities of these party systems, their more positive attributes should not be overlooked.

This brings us to the role played within these economic and political-institutional parameters by the beliefs, choices and behaviour of members of the political class. The degree to which such factors matter, of course, can vary over time – and at the point of military takeovers themselves, there was little that democrats within either system could do to prevent such an outcome. On the other hand, as the complex process of democratic disintegration began to unfold in the late 1960s and early 1970s, it is reasonably clear that elite perceptions of crisis, loss of faith in the problem-solving capabilities of their systems, and a growing unwillingness to compromise political differences among competing sectors – all had important self-fulfilling components which contributed significantly to the probability that their systems would in fact break down. Without going into the details or dynamics of these processes, we can identify some of the major 'choice points' within each society where other kinds of elite actions and beliefs might arguably have turned the course of events in different directions.

In Chile, as already implied, a major choice point involved the nominating decisions made by party leadership groups in the presidential race of 1970. The right's decision to run an independent candidate, along with the inability of the left and centre to unite behind a single nominee, paved the way for Allende's victory by a narrow plurality and for the eventual polarisation of Chilean society. Even after 1970, however, moderate politicians within both the government and the Christian Democratic opposition missed a series of opportunities to avoid the political stalemates which eventually destroyed the system. In fact, there was substantial agreement on a number of issues, including an accelerated agrarian reform, nationalisation of foreign companies, and even the need for state control of key national industries. But in spite of this, talks aimed at constructing a working agreement between the government and the Christian Democratic opposition broke down in both 1971 and 1972, with the moderate leaders of both sectors each unwilling to risk the alienation of more extreme elements within their own coalitions. By the congressional elections of March 1973, the constitutional impasse between the president and the legislative opposition had made a *coup d'état* all but inevitable.[9]

In the case of Uruguay, Charles Gillespie has provided us with a number of avoidable milestones in the evolving crisis leading up to the military takeover.[10] These include attempts to rule by executive decree in June 1968, to repress strikes and curb media reporting in 1969, and agreement to the suspension of habeas corpus and the initiation of military trials in 1972. By the time the Tupamaros had been defeated at the end of 1972, the political class was too demoralised and divided to respond effectively as an 'incremental' coup gradually gained momentum during the course of that year. A key turning point came in Feburary 1973, several months prior to the closing of Congress and the dissolution of the unions, when the armed force openly confronted President Bordaberry with an ultimatum for greater military authority. When the President sought to affirm his control, no one answered his call for public support:[11]

> The Left was seduced by the illusory promise of a progressive . . . coup. The Wilsonistas had no confidence in Bordaberry as a democrat, and hoped for new elections to right what they saw as the

> unfair result of 1971. The Pachequistas might have been able to answer Bordaberry's call to fill Plaza Independencia to hear him denounce the army and air force insubordination from the balcony, but their leader had been appointed Ambassador to Madrid and they stayed home . . . By the time the politicians realised what a mistake they made, and tried to resist the *desafuero* [lifting of parliamentary unity] of Sen. Erro [a left-wing senator accused by the army of sheltering terrorists] in June, it was all too late.

It would be tempting to close this section at this point, with the conclusion that established democracies can be preserved by determined and enlightened democratic leaderships. Unfortunately, however, we must end on a rather more complex and uncertain note. For even if we grant the possibility that the political leadership could temporarily have averted the short-term crises, we do not know if it could also have taken the steps necessary to reconsolidate and strengthen its democratic systems. Here we must reconsider the question of structurally-determined 'root causes' mentioned at the outset. To what extent would failure to identify and resolve underlying developmental predicaments have continued to make each system vulnerable to destabilising crises? And to what extent were such problems resolvable at all within the framework of a competitive democracy? Such issues, left unanswered by the preceding analysis, are ultimately impossible to resolve without rewinding and redesigning the historical film. It is at the core of the academic debates over the causal weights to attach to such 'objective' factors as dependency, import-substitution and political-institutional structures in the analysis of broad patterns of social transformation.

But even if one believes, as I do, that the long-term opportunities for the consolidation of political democracy were weakened by the underlying political-economic configurations of Southern Cone development, there are several reasons for being cautious about overly pessimistic answers to the questions posed above.

First, of course, from the perspective of the beseiged democrats who might have preserved the system in the early 1970s, there was really no alternative to concentrating on the 'short-term' crisis management, since the constitutions had first to be preserved if they were also to be consolidated.

In the second place, in the world of political action, assumptions about the potential efficacy of human choice and leadership are a crucial counterweight to the social scientist's inclination to order reality in terms of law-like patterns. Such inclinations, as Hirschman has observed, may have an initial effect of converting 'the real into the rational or the contingent into the necessary'.[12] This does not mean, of course, that social scientists should stop looking for patterned constraints on democratic development. Nor do I intend to deny the fact that various intractable combinations of social, economic and political structures may substantially raise or lower the odds for the survival of a democratic system. Still, in view of the incredibly large margin of error involved in defining these odds, the clear and present danger of self-fulfilling prophecies appears overwhelming. In some instances, at least, the realisation may dawn 'that certain so-called attributes of backwardness are not necessarily obstacles, but can be lived with and sometimes can be turned into positive assets'.[13]

This is especially true, finally, when there is so little consensus among social scientists themselves about how to identify either the underlying social problems or their solutions. The very divisions within our intellectual community over these issues are at least one indication that democratic stability will depend not on the capacity of democratic leaders to find some particular set of solutions to some overriding set of developmental problems, but rather on their capacity to organise and mediate the debates on such issues in ways that reflect the underlying diversity of opinion while leaving room for incremental changes. I will take up this point again at the end of this chapter.

Ignoring Constraints: the Lessons of Bureaucratic-Authoritarianism

If social scientists frequently commit the sin of determinism, it is understandable that actors in the political arena often err in a very different direction: that of over-estimating their capacity to effect planned transformations and of under-estimating the intractable 'realities' that lie in their way. The Southern Cone experience of the past several decades provides a number of illustrations of how high the costs of this can be. One example is the adventurism of guerrilla and extreme left oppositions in the late 1960s and early 1970s. The incorrect and historically inaccurate lesson that such groups apparently drew from the Cuban experience was that 'revolutionary will' was sufficient to force through desired social transformations – even in the face of limited popular support and overwhelming opposition from powerful military and economic groups. Instead, of course, the maximalism of the extreme left merely fed the fears that contributed to the brutal authoritarian lurches to the right.

Here, however, we concentrate on another form of voluntarist hubris – that exhibited by the military authoritarian right, their technocratic allies and their supporters within US business and diplomatic circles. Beginning with the Brazilian takeover in 1964, to be sure, the leaders of these 'bureaucratic-authoritarian' coalitions argued that they were economic 'realists' not voluntarists – committed to imposing the harsh disciplines of the market in ways that would place their societies on sounder developmental trajectories. But although it was not entirely unreasonable to suppose that the Southern Cone economies needed to become more open to world market and investment forces, it was both unrealistic and costly to assume that political life could be suppressed through the use of military coercion while these transformations were being imposed. In the contemporary world, it is impossible to be an 'enlightened despot'.

The objective impossibility of such a project, by now made abundantly clear by the political and economic crises of the early 1980s, was nevertheless partially obscured for a time by the spectacular surge of Brazilian growth during the 1967-74 period. Even in the context of the current debt crisis and recession – and even after taking the growing disparities of income into account – this was an impressive developmental achievement. But the 'apolitical' and technocratic rhetoric of this period masks several important points that were ignored by admirers and would-be imitators of the 'Brazilian model'. First, the authoritarian regime benefited substantially from the cyclical dynamism of the Brazilian economy itself, as well as from a major period of international economic expansion. In this context, the role which authoritarianism actually played in promoting this 'miracle' remains an open question, particularly since similar spurts of industrial growth had occurred in the late 1950s under a constitutional regime.[14]

The second point, more important for our purposes, is that distinctive elements of political flexibility and economic heterodoxy were vital ingredients in the comparative success of the Brazilian model – a fact that was usually ignored by those who had attempted to transfer it into other settings. Concern for reducing the imposition of excessively delegitimating hardships was evident in some measure even in the course of the harsh anti-inflation measures adopted in the 1964-7 period. At a time when free market ideologies had acquired their greatest influence in Brazil, government spending programmes were still used to offset the shocks of credit and wage restrictions, while tariffs were lowered only gradually and selectively.[15] During the

1967-74 'miracle years', the experiments with indexing, the expansionary credit policies, increasing regulation of foreign capital and the growth of state enterprise – all deviated markedly from the dogmatic *laissez-faire* policies later applied in Chile and Argentina.

The Brazilians were also significantly more successful than their imitators in finding ways to combine the use of military coercion with other institutional mechanisms for channelling and reorganising political conflict. Even in the worst periods of police-state rule during the late 1960s and early 1970s, the regime also made ample use of the more subtle corporatist apparatus originally established duing the Vargas era.[16] Compared to regimes established later in the Southern Cone, torture, executions and political imprisonment were practised on a relatively small scale. Perhaps most important, the regime never abandoned its formal commitment to liberal democracy. By the middle 1970s, elections, parties and legislative assemblies, though established and circumscribed by military authorities, had become an important outlet for dissent and opposition. By the early 1980s, in the midst of a crushing economic recession, they had become important arenas for the relatively stable extrication of the military regime itself.

As of this writing, it is too soon to say whether this form of 'controlled liberalisation' will lead forward to a stable democratic system. It is certainly not my intention either to gloss over the past brutalities, costs and limitations of Brazilian authoritarianism or to suggest that the military has been 'won over' to eventual democracy. The 'lesson,' rather, is that both the economic and political 'successes' of the Brazilian model have been achieved in large part because of (rather than in spite of) the willingness of authorities to tolerate debates and to play the political game in ways that sometimes diverged sharply from their own anti-democratic mentalities.

The military governments imposed later, under more polarised conditions in Argentina, Chile and Uruguay tended to incorporate most of the harsher aspects of the Brazilian experience without its political subtleties. For long periods of time, drastic orthodox shock treatments replaced more moderate attempts to liberalise trade and investment policies and far more repressive forms of unmediated military authority attempted to abolish, rather than simply to reorient and control, party and electoral activity. During the late 1970s, the turn away from outmoded import-substitution models did contribute to brief spurts of economic expansion, led not only by exports, but also by increasing inflows of loans coming due in the 1980s. But particularly as the recessions of the 1980s began to set in, it became clear that these regimes had misread and oversimplified the complexities of the Brazilian experience, much as the extreme left had done with Cuba.

The political and economic consequences of these misperceptions varied from country to country. They seemed less destructive in Uruguay, for example, where the repression did not involve thousands of deaths and where orthodox economic policies were applied with greater moderation than in Argentina and Chile. The result in general, however, was that all three countries experienced the worst and most destructive features of bureaucratic-authoritarian rule. Much more than in the Brazilian case, military exclusion of previously activated parties and unions saddled each of these governments with 'delegitimating birth defects'[17] that made it difficult later to create workable 'constitutional mechanisms' of co-optation and participation. None of these regimes was able, for example, to establish a significant pro-government party or movement, or even to suppress the traditional party networks of the pre-authoritarian regimes. Economic authorities were also generally isolated from their own support groups by the absence of institutionalised mechanisms of feedback and consultation. This, of course, inhibited the possibility of finding genuine compromises over the role of state and multinational enterprises – an issue which plagued authoritarian and democratic governments alike. And in Chile and Argentina, the political isolation of economic decision-making authorities, even from the business community, contributed to the prolongation of increasingly costly policy miscalculations over interest and exchange rates. By 1980-1 these miscalculations had generated massive capital flight, the breakdown of local financial institutions and the run-up in Chile of huge levels of private-sector indebtedness.[18]

As the crises of the early 1980s have unfolded, the responses of political authorities have continued, in different ways, to reflect the increasingly high costs of their initial 'anti-political' course. Even in Brazil, the inability of the regime to institutionalise any clearly stable base of political support has left it vulnerable to internal stalemate and to a lack of clear policy direction – with no other option, from its own perspective, but to negotiate a partial retreat from power. With the recent defection by many pro-government politicos from the government's own presidential candidate, it now appears as if the military will have to accept a president from the civilian opposition for the first time in 20 years. The Uruguayan military, after having been shaken by the wide repudiation in the 1981 plebiscite, has followed a somewhat similar course of negotiated withdrawal. With the imminent resurgence of the Blancos and Colorados, there is little to show for their years in authority.

The highest costs seem to have been paid by Chile and Argentina, the societies that suffered the most 'anti-political' and repressive versions of military rule. Without any semblance of legitimacy to cushion the shocks of its economic miscalculations, the Argentine high command careered completely out of control in 1981-2. To deflect a resurgent union militancy looming on the horizon, the Argentine authorities at first launched the desperate Malvinas-Falkland adventure, then attempted to disguise the tragic blunders of this campaign with false reports of victory in the government-controlled press. By the time the bubble had burst, all of the political forces which the government had sought to repress had reappeared on the scene again, and a new elected regime was searching desperately for ways to reorganise and provide expression to these forces, while at the same time also finding a way out of a situation of national bankruptcy.

In Chile, the Pinochet government has clung tenaciously to power – despite the shocks suffered by its economy – sometimes by using limited forms of co-optation, but more often by a stern repression directed against elements of the centre-right as well as the democratic left. The government has not, however, been able to suppress the highly disruptive 'days of protest' by unions, churchmen, Christian Democrats and Marxists. And because it is now in the midst of its worst economic crisis since the 1930s depression, the regime has at last been forced to discard the *laissez-faire* ideologies that had once been its *raison d'être*. Indeed, the passage of time has made it increasingly clear that Pinochet attaches a far higher priority to preserving his personal power than he does to pursuing any particular project of socio-political transformation. In this sense, his government has come to look more and more like the personalist dictatorship of, say, a Stroessner or Somoza and much less like the 'modernising' military government of Brazil. And as in the case of the other traditionalistic dictatorships, the price of Pinochet's continuation in power will probably be a weakening of the centre and a strengthening of a revolutionary left.

A final irony can be found in the current economic failures of all four military regimes – the product of both internal mismanagement and of successive external shocks related to oil prices, debt and international recession. In important respects, these developments have brought each society nearly full circle to where they were when their military governments seized power. Between 1981 and 1983, the Uruguayan economy contracted more than any other Latin American country except El Salvador and Bolivia, with a decline of 13.9 per cent in its GDP, while inflation rates had climbed back to over 60 per cent by 1983. By 1984, Brazil was in its fourth consecutive year of zero or negative growth, with inflation almost twice as high as it had been at the time of the 1964 'revolution'. In Chile and Argentina, whose national income also declined at between 9 and 10 per cent, the manufacturing sector was hit especially hard by the combined impact of *laissez-faire* policies at home and recession abroad. As of 1982, per capita industrial production in Argentina was at 1965 levels, and in Chile, at a point equivalent to 1959.[19]

It would be misleading, of course, to ignore the fact that a great deal of this problem was attributable to external factors beyond the control of local authorities. Some democracies, such as Costa Rica's, have also suffered considerably during the 1980s – although it might be noted that others, such as Colombia's, have been more successful in blunting the worst edges of the crisis. But it is somewhat beside the point to argue that the authoritarian regimes of the Southern Cone have fared no worse than others. For even in terms of their own legitimating logic, only significantly better records could possibly have justified the kinds of political and economic sacrifices these regimes had previously imposed on their own populations.

On the Extrication from Authoritarianism

As has already been implied, political extrication from these authoritarian predicaments has proceeded at different paces and with different results. Only Argentina, after the abrupt and largely unplanned military retreat to the barracks in December 1983, has moved towards a full political democracy, and its future stability is very much in doubt. Brazil and Uruguay, as of this writing, are in the midst of more protracted and gradual transitions – more 'orderly' than Argentina's, but with far greater uncertainty about the degree to which anti-democratic forces will actually relinquish power. In Chile, notwithstanding some massive opposition challenges, efforts to dislodge Pinochet from power are temporarily stalled. Despite the diversity of these separate and still open-ended national processes, however, they do provide an opportunity to make some broad observations and to raise some unanswered questions.

From the perspective of the forces opposing authoritarian regimes, one of the most important set of issues is how to combine confrontation and negotiation in a way that will accelerate the process of political liberalisation. Some degree of opposition threat and pressure is usually a necessary part of this process, even in situations like Brazil's, where *abertura* has been an official government policy. An excellent example is the massive 'direct election' rallies and demonstrations held in virtually every major Brazilian city during 1983 – a process that was pivotal in inducing government party dissidents to support the opposition's presidential candidate. An opposition too timid or disorganised to seize such moments may well find them postponed for significant periods of time.

Yet some degree of negotiation and reassurance for moderate supporters of the old regime also appears to be an essential feature of liberalising transitions. Even in the case of the relatively abrupt Argentine transition, the Alfonsin government has been careful to set limits to the investigation and reorganisation of the still dangerous military establishment. And caution has been an even more important feature of oppositional behaviour in Brazil, where even former radicals like Leonel Brizola have been careful not to challenge the military authorities too openly. On the other hand, Pinochet may well continue to weather the storm of massive street confrontations, until moderate Christian Democrats and elements of the 'civilised right' are able to lure segments of the officer corps and the business class into neutrality or opposition. Pressure from below, like negotiation from within, is a necessary, but so far not sufficient condition, of moving a transition forward. While the first may increase the 'cost of repression' for anti-democratic authorities, the second will surely be essential for reducing the perceived costs of toleration.[20]

Striking an appropriate balance between confrontation and negotiation is probably the most important strategic dilemma facing any anti-authoritarian opposition, and it is one which is made significantly more difficult by the fact that 'appropriate balances' will change over time, depending on the spaces opened by the regime itself and on the resources available for mobilising a mass following. The massive direct election demonstrations that proved so important in Brazil, for example, would certainly have been counter-productive in the previous presidential succession period in 1979. On the other hand, the absence of a mobilised mass opposition behind Uruguay's traditional party elites may have weakened their hand in negotiating new liberalisation measures with the current military government.

Strategic decisions about negotiation and confrontation are made even more difficult by the fact that rival opposition factions must position themselves *vis-à-vis* each other as well as with respect to the authoritarian system. This has been part of the problem in the Chilean case. Strong antagonisms continue to colour the relations between the Christian Democrats and the parties of the left, and to frighten wavering supporters of Pinochet away from the ranks of opposition. Such fears are fed (but not caused) by a continuing maximalism, and a turn towards violence among some sectors of the left.

Of course, if we reflect even casually on the difficulties faced by oppositions in authoritarian situations, it should immediately become clear that finely-tuned forms of internal co-ordination or fully-orchestrated strategies of opposition are virtually inconceivable. The question, rather, is how much margin of error is available to opposition leaders – to what extent can they (or their allies) be 'too timid' or 'too confrontational' and yet still push the process of liberalisation forward? The experience of the Southern Cone countries suggests two important parameters:

On the one hand, a great deal depends on the political space provided (or vacated involuntarily) by the authoritarian regime itself. In Argentina, where by 1982-3 the entire military government had clearly lost the will and capacity to control the political situation, a wide and rather disorganised range of liberalising oppositions helped to accelerate the process, with little or no internal co-ordination. The latitude for tolerable error was still significant, but much more limited, in Brazil, where opportunities for opposition depended in part on the willingness of government reformers themselves to open institutional channels of protest and to protect these channels from the backlash of authoritarian hardliners within the regime. By the early 1980s, for example, it had become possible for union and left leaders to test the effectiveness of strikes and mass mobilisations without excessive risk that a military backlash might reverse the entire liberalisation process. On the other hand, unlike Argentina, it is still far too early and too risky for the opposition to touch the issue of accountability for past military security or economic operations. In Uruguay, and *a fortiori* in Chile, where the military authorities remain much more powerful and united, the margin for opposition error, and indeed the room for any kind of manoeuvre at all, remains very slim.

A second parameter of tolerable error, unlike the first, involves a factor that remains partially under the control of opposition leaders. This is the decision to use, or to condone the use of, violent challenges to the political authorities. In some instances, where there are really no institutional or political spaces for other types of opposition, guerrilla rebellion may be an unavoidable option, even for a democratic opposition. In one other instance, that of the Lanusse government in Argentina, the regime was already so demoralised by 1970-3 that guerrilla activities spurred negotiations leading to the transfer of authority – although it should be noted that the continuation of this urban and rural terrorism later proved also to be a major factor in undermining Lanusse's elected successors.

On the whole, however, the Southern Cone experience suggests that with regard to accelerating the distintegration of the powerful economic and military coalitions supporting bureaucratic-authoritarian regimes, guerrilla activities have been counter-productive. In Brazil in 1968 the attempt to organise anti-authoritarian insurgencies furnished an important pretext for a major repressive crackdown. And one of the striking uniformities of otherwise very different liberalisation experiences in contemporary Agentina, Brazil and Uruguay has so far been the absence of such insurgencies. Again, one must note the contrast here with the violent orientations among some segments of the Chilean left – although it is difficult to tell how much this is a cause and how much it is an effect of Pinochet's uncompromising rule.

At this point, we can take up the reference made in the introduction to Dankwart Rustow's classic essay on transitions to democracy. The origins of most European democracies, he suggests, derived not from any consensus about the value of democratic rule, but rather from deliberate, instrumental bargains among the leaders of contending social forces. Such bargains, in his view, almost always involved 'pragmatic compromise' and 'second-best choices' – a process in which 'non-democrats' were often 'forced, tricked, lured, or cajoled' into democratic behaviour.[21] Some of the aspects of the liberalisation experiences we have just discussed may usefully be understood in these terms as well. They are processes in which contenders with varying degrees of loyalty and opposition to the old regime begin to assess the limits of their power, against the backdrop of prolonged, costly and inconclusive struggles for authoritarian domination. Though tragic and avoidable, the authoritarian experiences of earlier decades have provided opportunities for moderates in both the regime and the opposition to learn and explore the advantages of mutual toleration. In an analytical sense, a successful end to this phase of the process, presumably, would be the point where growing opportunities for public contestation produce both a government and loyal oppositions through some kind of competitive elections.

What might happen after this, of course, is a matter almost purely for speculation in the Southern Cone context, since so far only Argentina has actually reached a stage of competitive elections. But despite the lack of facts, I would like to conclude this chapter with some comments and questions about the way the election of a democratic government might transpose old conflicts and raise new issues.

The main new challenge faced by democratic leaders in power, of course, is that of governance and consolidation. In my judgement, the priority in this situation is (or ought to be) on institutionalising and deepening commitments to the 'second-best choices' made in the course of the liberalisation process, a task which is different from, although not unrelated to, the search for solutions to the pressing economic problems left over from the authoritarian era. To an important degree, meeting this challenge can be understood as the continuation, in a new setting, of the same strategic issue faced earlier by democratic oppositions: how to find the appropriate combinations of threat and accommodation required to neutralise anti-democratic opponents and to build support for the democratic system among competing power contenders. In some ways, undoubtedly, democratic governments may find it harder to resolve this issue than anti-authoritarian oppositions. But even tenuous formal control of the political system also gives democratic leaders important new resources they did not possess before: symbolic, legal and material leverage for co-ordinating relations with democratic opponents, for organising mass support and for renegotiating old bargains with groups affiliated with the old regime.

In this connection the opportunities and constraints surrounding three specific sets of issues warrant at least brief comment.

The Military Ultra-right

For a very long time after any free election in the Southern Cone, the military establishment will pose the most clear and present danger to a democratic system. Still, most new democratic authorities will not find it possible to follow the relatively ambitious, if still prudent, reorganisational steps currently being adopted by the Alfonsin government in Argentina (i.e. reductions in the size and budget, the civilianisation of the 'military ministries' and the dismantling of some of the 'military-industrial' complex). There will also be very limited room for manoeuvre on the explosive issue of investigating and punishing past repression. This means leaving a long list of unresolved potential time-bombs in the future evolution of civil-military relations. Still, it would seem best to err on the side of caution and moderation.

With regard to a more limited range of issues, however, democratic governments may be able to exploit their formal powers to assert control in a number of areas which are crucial to the survival of the system. The past experience with democratic breakdowns, for example, suggests that it is crucial to insist on civilian supervision of police and judicial functions, as well as over economic issues and questions of constitutional organisation. In the aftermath of authoritarian failures, moreover, there may also be considerable latitude for encouraging a belief within the officer corps that their best professional and institutional interests lie in avoiding the divisiveness of governmental responsibilities and the risks of excessive political entanglements. Third, it is possible that civilian authorities will be able to retire or transfer their most visible hardline military enemies, although there are obviously profound risks involved in 'interfering' too directly in promotions and assignments. In the last analysis, finally, the most crucial steps in neutralising the military threat may depend on how democratic leaders handle questions of support and opposition in the broader political context. Here, there are a different set of problems, but also other points of leverage.

The Anti-democratic Left

Even small guerrilla movements can inject large doses of poison into a new democratic system. They can furnish the pretext for coups, or for incremental expansions of military authority, or they may force the government itself into anti-democratic emergency measures. There is no easy way to handle this, and there may be circumstances in which such emergency measures may be the best option for the government.

Still, the experiences of Uruguay, Argentina and Chile during the early 1970s suggest that there are steps available to both governmental authorities and opposition leaders that can reduce the scope of the dangers this poses to the constitutional order. On the government side, it is important, as noted above, for civilian officials to retain control of police and judicial functions and for emergency measures to be formally defined and limited in scope. Even more important, the government is in a position to provide a definition of the conflict situation by distinguishing clearly in its rhetoric and policy between illegal forms of violent opposition and legitimate if sometimes disruptive and noisy acts of protest, such as strikes, demonstrations, etc.

But political isolation, as well as governmental coercion, is crucial in containing the impact of insurrectional movements – and in this regard the leaders of democratic opposition forces have a role that may be just as crucial as that played by governmental authorities. To the extent that opposition leaders define their interest as one of collaborating in the construction of a democratic system, they also have a strong interest in closing ranks with the government in the condemnation of insurrectional activities. This is even (especially) true when there is an overlap between the alleged social and economic objectives of the insurrectional movements and those sought by the loyal opposition.

Defining Relations between Democratic Government and Opposition

Democratic systems will not be able to survive for very long without a considerable degree of co-operation between their main components, the government and opposition forces. In the Southern Cone, however, this will certainly be made more difficult by the contemporary economic crisis, which will deepen the underlying struggle over material resources. Thus, the 'economic questions' which have recurred throughout this chapter will not go away.

In assessing the democratic options available in these circumstances, it is impossible to ignore some extremely hard realities: (i) given current levels of debt, inflation and recession, new democratic governments will not in the medium term be able significantly to raise the living standards of popular forces who were economically excluded during much of the authoritarian era; (ii) for the time being, they will also be constrained to accommodate the international and local capitalist interests which have come to play such a pivotal role in the process of accumulation; (iii) any economic recovery strategy charted by a new democratic government will encounter strong criticism and opposition from some of the groups entitled to participate in the democratic process. Heated debate will surround both the 'short-term' question of how to distribute the costs of stabilisation, and the longer-term question of the kinds of structural adjustment required by the local economy.

None of this, to say the least, is very encouraging. For it implies that the list of unsolved socio-economic problems will remain at least as long, probably longer, than it was before the advent of the authoritarian era. Still, as noted in the discussion of democratic breakdowns, it is important to distinguish between the solution to economic problems, and the way conflict over these solutions is organised politically. Even if competing political elites cannot always do much about the first set of issues, they may be able to exert a great deal of influence over the second.

While opposition leaders will certainly be constrained by the expectations and demands of their mass followings (as will the government itself), they have an important influence over the way these demands are articulated – whether incrementally or categorically, whether in ways that help to validate the structure of the democratic system or that raise questions about its legitimacy. Government officials, with more control than in the past over implementing the political rules, can narrow or widen substantive differences over economic policy by the way they define the political resources available to power contenders – particularly through the assurances regarding present and future opportunities for contestation, organising unions and associations, strikes and demonstrations, etc. The key to this sort of behaviour is the government's understanding of the fact that the mobilisation of vigorous challenges to its policies and its incumbency may also be an important component of building popular support for the system as a whole. As in the case of the opposition, the government's use of symbols, its interpretation and affirmation of its commitment to democratic guarantees may be a critical part of this process. So also, of course, will be the effort to promote consultation and narrow differences over substantive policy issues.

These forms of collaboration between the government and opposition may be difficult to bring about, but they are hardly inconceivable. Whether or not they are currently in office, competing currents of the 'political class' do share an interest in political freedom – institutionalising the long-term opportunities for competing for power and influencing public policy. The more secure these long-term expectations are, the greater is the incentive to accept immediate losses in the struggle for political and economic resources, particularly when the alternative may be another round of military repression. And an essential feature of democracy, as Rustow has argued, is 'the habit of dissension and conciliation over ever-changing issues and amidst ever-changing alignments'.[22]

Notes and References

1. Dankwart A. Rustow, 'Transitions to Democracy, Toward a Dynamic Model', *Comparative Politics*, vol. 2, no. 3 (April 1970), pp. 337-65.
2. Albert O. Hirschman, 'The Search for Paradigms as a Hindrance to Understanding', *World Politics*, vol. XXII, no. 3 (April 1970), p. 343.
3. E.g. David Collier (ed.), *The New Authoritarianism in Latin America* (Princeton New Jersey: Princeton University Press, 1979).
4. I am following here the very important general analysis provided by Juan J. Linz, *The Breakdown of Democratic Regimes: Crisis, Breakdown, and Requilibration*, in the series edited by Juan J. Linz and Alfred Stepan (Baltimore and London: Johns Hopkins University Press, 1978), pp. 54ff.
5. See the graphic display on Uruguay, in Robert R. Kaufman, 'Industrial

Change and Authoritarian Rule in Latin America', in Collier (ed.), *The New Authoritarianism*, p. 195.

6. Arturo Valenzuela, *The Breakdown of Democratic Regimes, Chile*, edited by Linz and Stepan (Baltimore and London: Johns Hopkins University Press, 1978), pp. 23-33.

7. Linz, ibid., p. 55.

8. Cesar Alberto Aguiar, 'La Doble Escena: Clivajes Sociales y Subsistema Electoral', Presented at the conference on 'Democracy and Uruguay', Woodrow Wilson Center, Latin American Program, Washington, D.C., 12-14 September 1984.

9. See Valenzuela, *Breakdown*, esp. pp. 50-81.

10. Charlie G. Gillespie, 'Unravelling the Breakdown of Democracy in Uruguay', prepared for the conference on 'Democracy and Uruguay', Woodrow Wilson Center, Latin American Program, Washington, D.C., 12-14 September 1984.

11. Ibid., p. 12.

12. Albert Hirschman, 'The Search for Paradigms', p. 339.

13. Ibid., p. 339.

14. Kaufman,'Industrialization and Authoritarian Rule in Latin America'.

15. Alejandro Foxley, *Latin American Experiments in Neoconservative Economics* (Berkeley, Los Angeles, London: University of California Press, 1983).

16. Philippe C. Schmitter, *Interest Conflict and Political Change in Brazil* (Stanford: Stanford University Press, 1971).

17. Juan J. Linz, 'The Future of an Authoritarian Situation or the Institutionalization of an Authoritarian Regime: The Case of Brazil', in Alfred Stepan (ed.), *Authoritarian Brazil* (New Haven: Yale University Press, 1973).

18. See Foxley, *Latin American Experiments.*

19. Data are from CEPAL, *Sintesis Preliminar de la Economia Latinoamericana Durante 1983 (E/CEPAL/G.1279*, 20 de diciembre de 1983), p. 33, and CEPAL, *La Crisis en America Latina: Su Evaluacion y Perspectivas* (E/CEPAL/ CEGAN.8/L.2, 27 de diciembre de 1983), Cuadro 2.

20. Reference is to Robert A. Dahl, *Polyarchy: Participation and Opposition* (New Haven: Yale University Press, 1971).

21. Rustow, 'Transitions', pp. 344-5.

22. Ibid., p. 363.

4 AN INTERPRETATION OF THE DEMOCRATIC TRANSITION IN THE DOMINICAN REPUBLIC

Rosario Espinal

The multiplicity of factors that affect a process of political change has always constituted a challenge for social scientists in their efforts to decipher the variables that account for such a process. A look at various socio-political theories shows the variety of approaches that have been utilised to analyse politics and the tension that has prevailed between the reductionism of politics to a single factor, whether an economic or a socio-political one, and the complexity and lack of precision of the theories that try to integrate different elements into the explanation. This dilemma is evident in the study of democracy and democratic transition, as it has also been in the study of authoritarianism. In trying to account for the democratic transition in the Dominican Republic, the interpretation that we provide is not free from such difficulty, particularly since we try to emphasise the role played by some internal factors related to the class structure and class organisation of Dominican society. Therefore, we acknowledge that our interpretation is not a comprehensive, but a partial one. None the less, it is our view that by emphasising the role of such internal factors we can start pointing out the unique experience of the Dominican Republic in the context of those Caribbean and Central American countries which share a similar history of external economic and political dependency and authoritarian politics.

Because in Latin America authoritarianism has prevailed over democracy, the study of the latter has been of secondary importance in socio-political analysis. Moreover, as a result of the influence of modernisation theory in the 1960s, which suggested the historical correlation between economic growth, industrialisation and political democracy, an in-depth analysis of the democratic possibilities or the impossibility of democracy in Latin America was delayed. On the other side of the theoretical spectrum, the most popularised versions of dependency theory did not leave much room for democracy in the region. In the context of such a theoretical milieu, there is no doubt that the emergence of authoritarian regimes in the Southern Cone of Latin America in the 1960s and early 1970s helped to reformulate the theory of Latin American political development. With the formulation of the concept of bureaucratic-authoritarianism[1] the debate was opened not only concerning the new type of authoritarianism in the most industrialised countries of Latin America, but also, later on, concerning the democratic possibilities, at least in the larger countries of the Southern Cone. However, in the case of the smaller and less industrialised countries of Central America and the Caribbean, the main theme of political analysis continued to be, at least until very recently, the old type of authoritarianism rooted in military dictatorships that emerged from the US-trained National Guards in the earlier part of the century during American expansionism in the region. It has been precisely the drastic changes of the old economic and political structures in these societies that has brought the region to world attention in the last 25 years. However, the timing and form of that change has varied in important ways from country to country, which helps to account for the variety of political experiences that one encounters today in the region.

It is our purpose to offer some suggestions for the study of politics in Central American and Caribbean societies based on the concrete experience of the Dominican Republic. We look at the process of political transition from a polarised and repressive society to one of greater political diversity, participation and respect for basic human and political rights. This transition had its turning point in the 1978 elections when the Dominican Revolutionary Party (PRD) defeated Joaquín Balaguer of the Reformist Party (PR), who had been in power since 1966.

In order to understand the process of political transformation that led to the 1978 election and the transfer of power from Balaguer to the PRD, it is important to consider historical factors as well as the *coyuntura* of the mid-1970s, which facilitated a political transition through electoral means from a government that had relied systematically (although selectively) on coercion to one committed to the defence of civil and political rights. We begin with a working hypothesis that we analyse throughout in the context of different political *coyunturas*: the democratic transition in the Dominican Republic was based on the development of civil society, which resulted from the privatisation and diversification of the economy and politics. This process began to take place gradually during the Balaguer regime, but confronted substantial limitations due to the authoritarian traits of that regime. In order to examine this hypothesis we look at state policies and their impact on the class structure and class organisations, and the organised expressions of class action. We have chosen to concentrate on the working class and the bourgeoisie, with special reference to the industrial sector, since they constitute the main economic agents of the process of economic expansion that took place in the late 1960s and early 1970s with the implementation of import-substitution industrialisation. That is, they are the social basis of the process of modernisation. None the less, we recognise the importance of other social classes in Dominican politics, and the need to integrate them in a comprehensive analysis of the politics of the Dominican Republic. We will also refer later to the party system, especially the PRD, as a viable democratic alternative, and the role played by external powers such as the United States and the Socialist International in the 1978 elections.

The Reconstruction of Dominican Society after the Fall of Trujillo

Even though many Dominicans already nursed democratic aspirations before the fall of Trujillo, attempts to democratise the country in the aftermath of the fall of the dictatorship had all failed by 1965. The US military intervention of 1965 ended the civil confrontation (civil war) of April of that year, and with such intervention, the political mobilisation and instability that had prevailed during the early 1960s following the fall of Trujillo were replaced by de-mobilisation and 'political order'. Balaguer, a former collaborator of Trujillo, emerged as the winner in the 1966 elections, which were held under the shadow of US military intervention. Balaguer then put forward a plan to stabilise the country economically and politically. With substantial power concentrated at the top of the political structure, Balaguer achieved not only the political pacification of the country, but an important level of economic growth and expansion aimed at promoting private capital. That is, unlike Trujillo, who monopolised political and economic power, Balaguer favoured the expansion of a private bourgeoisie. Although government officials had benefited economically from state protection during the Trujillo dictatorship, the protection afforded to the business community went beyond the ruling political elite. A private entrepreneur class, which was not directly involved in the management of the state, benefited substantially from the government's protectionist measures. Thus, during the Balaguer regime, a 'private bourgeoisie' developed and was diversified, unlike the past, when economic and political power had been monopolised by a dictator. It is important to stress this course of events because the government could have pursued different policies. For instance, the state was the largest entrepreneur in the country after it had confiscated Trujillo's enterprises, but the government nevertheless did not promote a policy of economic expansion in the public sector, in the sense of controlling more enterprises either to benefit the high-ranking governing elite, as Trujillo had done, or to redistribute more equally the resources among the population. On the contrary, the objective was clearly to favour the development of private capital.

The protectionist measures to promote private capital meant a number of economic and institutional incentives such as wage regulations, financial facilities, tax exemptions and the availability of foreign exchange. The economic model promoted during the Balaguer regime was based on the expansion of the industrial sector (basic import-substitution of consumer goods). Along with it, the state directly promoted the expansion of the construction sector through investments in infrastructure such as roads, housing, hydroelectrics. That is, industry of easy import substitution, construction and the related expansion of the financial and service sectors constituted the basis of economic modernisation. During the early 1970s the rate of growth of the gross domestic product (GDP) was particularly high both in manufacturing and construction (Table 4.1). In relation to other Latin American countries, the growth of manufacturing for the period 1965-70 was higher in the Dominican Republic than in any other country, and for the period 1970-5 it was higher than in any other country except for Brazil and Ecuador.[2]

The Austerity Law (Law no. 1) of 1966 and the Law of Industrial Protection and Incentives (Law no. 299) of 1968 constituted the main legal framework of incentives for private capital. But the Austerity Law also allowed for public savings in current account. Such resources were used by the government to promote the expansion of the construction sector, create jobs and develop a clientelistic policy by means of which those who benefited from construction contracts were able to accumulate capital, and in return became a sector loyal to the government. The decline of current expenditures in relation to investments is presented in Table 4.2, and the concentration of resources by the president is illustrated by the percentage of the national budget directly administered by the presidency, in Table 4.3.

Law 299 provided industrial investors with tax exemptions on imports of capital goods, raw material and fuel, except for gasoline. It also provided tax exemptions on reinvestments. The extent of these incentives varied somewhat depending on whether production was for the internal market (import-substitution industries) or the external market (export industries). In either case, however, tax exemptions were high (Table 4.4). The provisions of Law 299 were not applied automatically to each and every enterprise. The procedure involved

Table 4.1: Rate of Growth of the GDP by Sectors of the Economy (Percentages)

Sectors	Years								
	1970	1971	1972	1973	1974	1975	1976	1977*	1978*
1. Primary Sector	5.5	5.3	15.2	16.7	1.9	0.3	10.4	1.0	–0.03
Agriculture	6.6	6.4	2.5	9.7	–0.1	–5.8	9.1	–0.2	5.4
Livestock	3.3	4.2	5.3	3.9	0.4	5.6	4.1	7.1	8.5
Mining	6.5	1.7	23.9	65.6	9.7	10.7	20.5	–1.2	–19.3
Fishing & Others	2.9	–1.9	8.7	25.3	–1.6	–5.7	1.7	–11.0	6.7
2. Secondary Sector	19.3	18.1	13.5	11.4	4.2	7.5	5.1	8.5	0.2
Manufacturing	19.3	13.2	10.3	11.2	4.7	7.3	6.7	5.7	0.6
Construction	20.5	34.3	22.4	12.0	2.5	8.2	0.4	16.8	2.3
3. Tertiary Sector	9.9	10.1	10.5	10.1	9.0	6.3	5.9	6.1	4.4
4. Total	10.6	10.6	12.4	12.1	6.0	5.2	6.7	5.5	2.3

*Preliminary data.

Source: *Memoria Anual del Banco Central*, Central Bank of the Dominican Republic.

Table 4.2: Central Government Budget (Millions of pesos)

Year	Government Revenues	Government Expenditures			Balance
		Current Exp.	Investments	Total	
1966	200.2	124.6 (64.1)*	21.5 (11.1)	194.3	5.9
1967	198.7	110.5 (54.8)	35.0 (17.4)	201.5	–2.8
1968	205.7	107.8 (51.7)	43.8 (21.0)	208.3	–2.6
1969	232.0	114.8 (61.7)	63.6 (26.9)	236.7	–4.7
1970	267.1	122.1 (46.4)	76.4 (29.1)	262.9	4.2
1971	303.6	129.2 (42.4)	107.2 (35.1)	304.9	–1.3
1972	335.8	138.5 (41.5)	126.3 (37.8)	333.8	2.0
1973	386.9	150.7 (38.9)	151.6 (39.1)	386.9	0.0
1974	520.5	178.4 (34.8)	203.1 (39.6)	512.6	7.9
1975	657.4	198.7 (30.4)	292.3 (44.7)	653.3	4.1
1976	583.9	216.9 (38.1)	229.4 (40.3)	569.3	14.6
1977	629.3	235.2 (38.0)	236.1 (38.2)	618.7	10.6
1978	628.2	282.5 (41.8)	210.2 (31.1)	675.5	–47.3

* Numbers in parentheses are percentages.
Source: *Memoria Anual del Banco Central*, Central Bank of the Dominican Republic.

Table 4.3: Portion of the National Budget Administered by the Presidency (Percentages)

Year	%	Year	%
1966	7.3	1973	45.0
1967	16.6	1974	50.2
1968	22.4	1975	48.1
1969	27.6	1976	45.9
1970	30.7	1977	47.2
1971	37.5	1978	43.5
1972	41.5		

Source: *Ejecución del Presupuesto*, Oficina Nacional del Presupuesto.

applying for classification to the Industrial Development Board (DDI), composed of representatives from the government and business organisations. Based on each application, the DDI would make a recommendation to the president, who would make the final decision. From 1968 to 1981, the government granted 866 classifications, of which 76.5 per cent benefited import-substitution industries. It is important to note that the incentives granted by Law 299 applied only to private enterprises. A special financial programme was also devised to promote private investment. The Investment Fund for Economic Development (FIDE) was created by the Central Bank in order to provide low-interest-rate loans to private investors. The industrial sector received 45 per cent of the total amount lent between 1966 and 1981.[3] Along with these tax and financial incentives, the government also guaranteed wage stability by freezing all salaries in 1966. The minimum wage was set at 60 pesos a month for both private- and public-sector workers and employees.

Table 4.4: Industrial Incentives Provided by Law 299

Incentives	Categories for Classification*		
	A %	B %	C %
1. Import-duty exemptions on capital goods	100	–	–
2. Import-duty exemptions on intermediate goods and raw materials	100	95	Up to 90
3. Import-duty exemptions on oil and related products (except for gasoline)	100	90	90
4. Tax exemptions on reinvestments	100**	Up to 50	Up to 50

* Category A refers to export industries. Category B refers to import-substitution industries introducing new products in the market. Category C refers to those industries substituting imports.
** 100% for foreign companies. Dominican companies enjoy 75% during the first year and 50% thereafter.
Source: *Incentivos Fiscales*, INCAT, the Ministry of Finances.

The incentives provided by the government also helped the expansion of foreign capital in the Dominican economy. Due to the limited information available on foreign investment in the Dominican Republic, it is difficult to assess the exact weight of such investments *vis-à-vis* the local bourgeoisie. What can be said, however, with the information available, is that foreign capital expanded throughout the Balaguer regime in most areas of the economy after a period of decline since the 1940s when Trujillo began to monopolise the economy. The flow of foreign investment was particularly high in the early 1970s, as illustrated by the case of food production. Comparing 23 Latin American countries, in 1970, the Dominican Republic was the third largest recipient of net direct foreign investment as expressed in percentages of the gross inflow of foreign capital; in 1975 and 1976 it was the fifth largest.[4]

Besides the economic growth and expansion of the late 1960s and early 1970s, there was also a process of social transformation of the bourgeoisie. Balaguer tried to incorporate the bourgeoisie into the decision-making process, although in a centralised manner. The political partnership between business and the government was made manifest in 1967 when the government declared that year as 'the Year of Development'. A committee of government and business representatives created by Balaguer to organise the activities for the occasion became, at the end of 1967, a permanent national planning board known as the National Council for Development (CND). The members of the council were selected by Balaguer, and the council became a mechanism of planning and consultation attached to the presidency. Originally, the CND had 49 members distributed as follows: 25 private citizens, 2 representatives of business organisations (these were the only ones selected by interest groups directly), and 22 government officials. Later, the number of representatives in the category of private citizens increased, as Balaguer promulgated 195 decrees between 1968 and 1978 appointing new members. During the first half of the regime, the CND played an important role, first, as a consulting mechanism for the president; second, as a mechanism of direct private-sector participation in the planning process; and third, as a mechanism of access for the business community to the top of the political structure (the presidency). For instance, the CND played an important role in backing Balaguer's first re-election in 1970 and formulating the plan to be implemented during his second term in power. However, as the bourgeoisie expanded and diversified during the economic boom in the early 1970s, it became more difficult to bring about consensus among different business factions in such a highly centralist and personalistic corporatist structure as the CND. The obstacles became greater in the mid-1970s, when the international economic crisis began to hit the Dominican economy.

Throughout the 1970s, the business class underwent an important process of internal organisation. Although some business organisations had been formed in the early 1960s, after the fall of Trujillo, the organisational trends had slowed down in the mid and late 1960s. In the context of the economic expansion of the early 1970s, new business organisations were formed (Table 4.5). The formation of these organisations is taken here as an important indicator of the growth and diversification of the Dominican bourgeoisie and the 'privatisation' of the economy. Although more information is needed in order to measure more accurately the economic expansion and social power of the Dominican bourgeoisie, our indicator compensates for the lack of other useful information.

Given the economic and organisational weakness of the bourgeoisie when Balaguer came to power in 1966, and the state of social and political fragmentation prevailing in the country after the fall of Trujillo, it was fairly easy for Balaguer to integrate the bourgeoisie in personalistic and vertical structures or by granting rights of representation to business

Table 4.5: Certified Business Associations in the Dominican Republic

Period	Industrialists' Associations %	Merchants' Associations %	Service Sector %	Mixed* %	Total %
1961-5	2 (7)	12 (15)	12 (28)	3 (60)	29 (18)
1966-77	20 (69)	41 (50)	25 (60)		86 (62)
1966-71	7 (40)	7 (17)	12 (48)		27 (28)
1972-7	13 (60)	34 (83)	13 (52)		59 (72)
1978-80	7 (24)	29 (35)	5 (12)	2 (40)	43 (20)
Total	29	82	42	5	158

* Including various categories of business.
Source: Calculations based on list of certifications, *Indice General de la Legislación Dominicana* (1961-80).

organisations controlled by a business elite, as in the case of the National Council of Businessmen (CNHE), or the Industrialists' Association of the Dominican Republic (AIRD). This system was efficient as long as the bourgeoisie had limited economic power and precarious organisations. However, once the bourgeoisie expanded and diversified, and while the government continued to maintain outmoded basic structures, a tension emerged between the aspirations of the various fractions of the bourgeoisie and the nature of the government. It is precisely this tension that helps to explain why a class that had benefited so much from the protectionist measures of the Balaguer regime withdrew its unconditional support for the government in the 1978 elections, when Balaguer was defeated by the PRD. By the time the international economic crisis began to affect the Dominican economy, which became more evident with the drop in the price of sugar after 1975, the CND was no longer an efficient consensus-building mechanism. There were also internal tensions within the bourgeoisie itself which led to internal transformations of the organisational system of the business class: the CNHE expanded its membership (from 1963 to 1974, the membership of the CNHE consisted of 4 business associations, while by 1982 it had incorporated 40 associations); in 1978 the CNHE relinquished its seat at the Industrial Development Board (DDI) in favour of the Association of Industrial Enterprises of Herrera (AEIH), a growing association of medium-size industries concentrated in Herrera, a suburb of Santo Domingo; and in 1980 the Association of Merchants and Industrialists of Santiago, the most important regional association in the country, joined the CNHE after a public and heated debate with other industrialists' associations over the negative effects of Law 299.

There were three main problems facing the bourgeoisie in the mid-1970s. First, the rising rate of inflation had forced the government to increase the minimum wage in 1974 and put pressures on business to control price increases. The latter had created serious conflicts between the commercial bourgeoisie in retail sales and the government. Secondly, the traditional landowning class withdrew from active co-operation with and support for the government. The most important expression of such withdrawal was the resignation in 1974 of Luis J. Pérez as president of the CND, in opposition to the implementation of the agrarian reform approved by the government in 1972. Thirdly, the industrial and financial sectors, who had benefited most from the incentives granted by the state, sought to improve their bargaining capacity from a position of organisational strength. A crucial problem for the industrial bourgeoisie was related to the increase in oil prices and the drop in the price of sugar, which meant limited availability of foreign exchange, vital to an industry highly dependent on imports. In the context of these fragmented interests, but with a bourgeoisie that was better organised than it had been in the past, national elections took place in May 1978. When the PRD defeated Balaguer and the high-ranking bureaucracy of the regime attempted a coup, the reaction of organised business was to favour the electoral results and the transfer of power. Such a reaction was a little unexpected from a class that had benefited substantially during the twelve-year Balaguer regime.

Besides the intra-bourgeois tensions that emerged in the mid-1970s, the economic difficulties and the organisational development of the bourgeoisie, all of which seem to have contributed to a democratic transition in a search for alternative solutions to the problems, it is our view that the support on the part of the business class of a democratic transition should also be explained in part by the fact that the Balaguer regime, despite its authoritarian traits, was represented by a civilian government. In addition, the bourgeois groups that developed during the years of economic growth were not always related to the old oligarchy linked to the traditional export economy. As we have already indicated, after the fall of Trujillo, all the properties of the Trujillo family were confiscated by the state. Thus, the basis of oligarchic power had already been weakened since the early 1960s, while the state directed a process of economic and social modernisation in favour of a fairly new bourgeoisie. In our view, because this business class emerged and was consolidated under a civilian regime, it was more prone to favour a democratic government, particularly when the popular classes did not constitute a challenge for the establishment. Here may lie a difference between the Dominican case and other countries in Central America, where the connection between traditional oligarchies and modern capital seems to be stronger.[5] The fall of Trujillo represented a breakdown of traditional oligarchical power, but, furthermore, the fact that Trujillo was not overthrown in the context of a revolution facilitated a faster reconstruction of capitalist development based on the protection and expansion of private capital.

Besides the impact that the incentives to private capital had on the bourgeoisie, it is important to note the expansion of the middle class with the spread of professionalisation and the growth of the service sector. This may be suggested as another factor in favour of democratisation. Due to the lack of voting data correlating electoral behaviour and class position, it is difficult to know precisely how the middle class behaved in the 1978 elections. None the less, two pieces of information help to show that the middle sectors were more inclined towards the PRD. First, at the time of the attempted coup on 17 May 1978, most middle-class associations came out publicly in support of the electoral procedure and the transfer of power. Second, it was in the areas of heavy working- and middle-class concentration that the PRD defeated Balaguer's Reformist Party with a larger margin; i.e. in Santo Domingo, La Romana and San Pedro de Macorís.[6]

As far as the working class is concerned, the Balaguer regime can be characterised as economically and politically repressive. The wage control policy was central to the project of capital accumulation throughout the life of the regime. Wage regulations helped to neutralise the bargaining capacity of labour on legal grounds. We have already indicated that the austerity law of 1966 froze all wages in the public and private sector, and the first increase in the minimum wage took place in 1974. However, such an increase had very little effect in terms of improving the standard of living of the working class, once inflation had been taken into account (Table 4.6). Earlier modifications of the austerity law in 1969 allowed for collective negotiation over salaries in the case of businesses that declared a profit, 'whenever the nature of the business allowed for a wage increase'.[7] Such negotiations had to be approved and regulated by the Labour Ministry. Thus, the viability of collective bargaining was decided by the employers and the state. In this respect, the wage control policies set restrictions not only concerning wage levels, but also on the possibilities of collective negotiation. The policies had economic and political implications. First of all, they guaranteed stable salaries to investors in order to promote profitable investments. The consequence of this for labour was the deterioration of the purchasing power of the working class. Secondly, they limited the possibilities of labour conflicts concerning wages and helped to minimise overt class conflict on legal grounds. The state sought to neutralise labour conflicts and, protected by the state, the business class was not faced with the need to develop mechanisms of bargaining and negotiation.

Table 4.6: Minimum Wages in the City of Santo Domingo (Monthly salaries in pesos)

Year	Nominal Wage	Price Index 1969=100	Real Wage
1966	60	98	61
1967	60	100	60
1968	60	102	59
1969	60	100	60
1970	60	105	57
1971	60	108	56
1972	60	117	51
1973	60	134	45
1974	60	152	39
1975	95	174	55
1976	95	189	51
1977	95	212	49
1978	95	219	43

Source: Calculations based on basic information from the nominal wage set by the austerity laws and the price-index from *República Dominicana en Cifras*, National Bureau of Statistics, 1980.

In addition to the wage control policies, the state sought to neutralise labour conflicts through other means: repression, the formation of rival unions and the replacement of union boards. The implementation of such anti-labour policies was facilitated by (i) the structure of the labour market, which was characterised by high rates of unemployment and under-employment (in 1970 they were calculated at 24 and 40 per cent respectively);[8] (ii) the legal provisions of the labour code which stated, as the main requirement for forming a union, that 20 workers at the same plant or sharing the same occupation should agree to do so; and (iii) the lack of job security for workers, including union activists, who were not protected from being fired by their employers.

These mechanisms of labour control and anti-labour policies allowed the government to limit the mobilisation and organisation of the working class that had taken place in the early 1960s. As indicated in Table 4.7, fewer unions were certified in the early years of the Balaguer regime than at any other period of the post-Trujillo era. Overall, at a time of

Table 4.7: Unions Certified by the Labour Ministry

Periods	Average Annual Certifications
1956-61	7
1962-5	45.4
1966-77	25.2
1966-71	11.8
1972-7	38.6
1978-81	87.5

Source: Calculations based on list of unions certified by the Labour Ministry.

economic growth and protection of private capital, the labour movement was repressed and weakened, and the working class saw its standard of living decline as salaries and services deteriorated. There was no consistent government policy of incorporation of the working class, either to facilitate the resolution of labour conflicts through negotiation and/or co-optation, or to gain political support from this class. The lack of institutionalised and established structures of labour integration can be demonstrated not only by indicating the anti-labour policies implemented, but also by the fact that towards the end of the Balaguer regime the trade unions, backed by the government, had been dismantled by their own leadership. This was the case for the National Confederation of Free Workers (CONATRAL) and the Trade Union Confederation of Organised Workers (COSTO). It should be mentioned, however, that the government developed mechanisms of legitimation among lower-income groups through clientelistic politics. Although it is not easy to provide empirical data on this issue, it seems that the construction programme carried out by the government, and tightly controlled by the presidency itself, played an important role in generating a base of support for the regime. Other clientelistic programmes were implemented by the Reformist Party, as is the case of the Cruzada del Amor, devised to deliver food, health care and other social services to the poor.

The rural population constituted an important force in support of Balaguer. This could be explained by the limited degree of mobilisation and politicisation of peasants after the fall of Trujillo in the early 1960s. The explanation for this phenomenon is not, however, quite clear. More research is needed on the political behaviour of Dominican peasants, but such a task is beyond the scope of this analysis. We would suggest only that the political passivity of the Dominican peasantry is rooted in the ideology of 'order' consolidated during the Trujillo dictatorship; it may also be related to the partial incorporation of some peasant groups into the agrarian reform programme carried out by Balaguer in the 1970s.

The Politics of the Democratic Transition

In order to understand the characteristics of the democratic transition in the Dominican Republic, it is important to take into consideration two traits of the Balaguer regime. The first is the civilian nature of the regime, despite the importance of military power within the government and the frequent use of coercion, particularly during the first years of the regime. The second is the selective use of coercion. That is, repression was not generalised in order to create a collective fear in society as a whole, as it had been during the Trujillo dictatorship. Coercive measures were used selectively, particularly against the Marxist left and the militant trade unions. Furthermore, as the regime was consolidated and the political instability of the 1960s was replaced by political 'order', the use of coercion decreased, which favoured the resurgence of a moderate opposition, as in the case of the PRD, and, later on, the partial integration of the left into mainstream politics, beginning with the legalisation of the Dominican Communist Party (PCD) in the mid-1970s.

In spite of the short civil war of 1965, which may have constituted the most serious threat to the status quo in the Dominican Republic, the limited degree of organisation of civil society at the time made it relatively easy for the Balaguer regime to restore political order within the context of a project of economic modernisation, without having to destroy all the political opposition as a long-term project. In our view, both the civilian nature of the Balaguer regime and the organisational weakness of the popular sectors (workers, peasants) were factors that facilitated a democratic transition through electoral means acceptable to the dominant class. This acceptability needs explaining in a society lacking a democratic history and with a largely impoverished populace.

Although the 1978 elections may be regarded as an unexpected event that took place by chance, due, perhaps, to external factors such as the human rights policy of the Carter administration, it is our view that there is more to it. The 1978 elections, the PRD victory and the transfer of power[9] reflected a previous process of transformation within the society, characterised by the consolidation of the bourgeoisie, the expansion of the middle sectors, the organisational weakness of workers and peasants and the consolidation of the political party system. With reference to the political opposition and the restructuring of the party system, the PRD is the main factor to consider in accounting for the democratic transition. The PRD represented what Przeworski has called the 'viable alternative' to authoritarianism,[10] or what O'Donnell has described as the 'moderate opposition' to bureaucratic-authoritarianism.[11]

The PRD had represented the democratic aspirations of Dominicans since the early 1960s, and it was able to channel such ideological power through a well-organised party in order to bring about the democratisation. Both the ideological power and the strong organisation were key factors for the electoral victory of 1978, after 15 years of failed attempts to take and maintain power. The PRD was formed by exiles during the struggle against Trujillo and was able to express the democratic aspirations of the Dominican electorate in 1962. It retained the monopoly of such representation after the coup of 1963; the participation of the party in the civil war of 1965 was a turning point in the party's history. After the 1965 defeat, due to US intervention and the emergence of the Balaguer regime, the party went through a period of redefinition of goals, strategies and tactics. The moderate and radical elements came into conflict, and in 1973, Juan Bosch, who up to then had been the main party leader, broke away from the party to form one of his own with a more radical project of social transformation (the Dominican Liberation Party, PLD). After the division, the PRD reaffirmed its moderate position under the leadership of José Francisco Peña Gómez. Paradoxically, however, Peña Gómez represented (and still represents) the more radical wing within the party. Not only had Peña Gómez participated actively in the civil war of 1965, but he is also a charismatic leader with strong support among low-income urban groups. In the 1974 national elections, the PRD, in alliance with other political organisations on the centre and left of the political spectrum, attempted to run a campaign and participate in the elections. Although the government imposed voting conditions that made a victory of the opposition unlikely, the capacity to mobilise people during the campaign was an important indicator of the potential of electoral politics should the government be compelled to implement fair electoral rules. Besides the capacity to mobilise the masses and the need to force the government to guarantee free elections, the PRD had to gain the confidence of a broad sector of the dominant class and consolidate its international ties. It should be borne in mind that the PRD had not been the party of preference of the United States.

In the case of the bourgeoisie, it should be pointed out that the PRD had, since its inception, enjoyed the support of certain sectors of this class who identified themselves with democratic politics. For instance, the president and vice-president of the two PRD governments, Antonio Guzmán and Jacobo Magluta (1978-82) and Salvador Jorge Blanco and Manuel Fernández Mármol (1982-6) have been linked to commercial, agrarian and professional groups. But the decisive support came from a better organised bourgeoisie, which developed under the civilian, but personalistic and authoritarian government of Balaguer. In our view, the economic difficulties of the mid-1970s increased the problem of centralised structures of decision-making for the bourgeoisie.

In the search for international support, the PRD developed close ties with the European social democratic movement and the social democratic forces of Latin America. The support of the Socialist International for the PRD during the 1978 elections was particularly evident, with the visit of Portugal's Social Democratic leader Mario Soares during the campaign. This international support was particularly helpful during the negotiations concerning the transfer of power after the attempted coup. Given the support shown by the Social Democrats in favour of the PRD, it would have been difficult for the Carter administration to back a coup at a time when preaching human rights was a central element in American foreign policy, particularly when large sectors of Dominican society, including sectors of the dominant class, were in favour of the elections and the transfer of power. It could be argued that due to the extreme economic and political dependency of the Dominican Republic on the United States, the decisive factor for the democratic transition was just such a human rights policy. It is our view, however, that such a policy helped to discourage the post-electoral attempted coup, but it does not account for the longer process of transformation within Dominican society that made the democratic transition possible. Had that been the central factor, a coup would have taken place after the Reagan administration came to power. It is also important to keep in mind the short duration of the human rights policy of the Carter administration.

Another issue that could be discussed in the Dominican context is the role of force and diplomacy with reference to US foreign policy. It could be argued that the use of force in 1965 (the US intervention) was necessary, in order to bring about a negotiated democracy later, as in 1978. On this point it is our view that the argument of force first and negotiation later cannot be justified when based on the Dominican experience. Regardless of the moral considerations involved in such an approach, which would lead us to reject it automatically, we argue that although coercion played an important role in weakening the popular classes, which in turn made democracy more acceptable to the dominant class, who did not therefore feel threatened by democratisation, there were a number of other factors which were extremely important. We have referred to them earlier, and it will therefore be sufficient simply to summarise them at this point: the breakdown of oligarchic power with the fall of Trujillo; the civilian nature of the Balaguer government, in spite of the authoritarian traits of the regime; the process of economic and social modernisation which led to the expansion – at least – of the bourgeoisie and the middle class; the fact that repression was selective and the government allowed for the reconstruction of the party system in the mid-1970s. Furthermore, although the organisational weakness of the working class can be partially explained by the use of force, the Dominican labour movement is also weak because of internal divisions between parties and ideologies. This has been a marked characteristic of the labour movement in the post-Trujillo period.

Concluding Remarks

The democratic transition in the Dominican Republic in the late 1970s is of extreme importance for a country whose history has been characterised by authoritarian rule. The respect for basic political rights has undoubtedly been enhanced since the PRD took power in 1978. Also, in the context of democratic rules, party politics has begun to acquire a life of its own. None the less, there are two main problems linked in different ways to this democratisation. First, it is a democracy that has been achieved in the context of – or perhaps one should say, based on – the weakness of the popular classes. That is, workers and peasants have relatively powerless organisations and, to a large extent, have been excluded from power. They constitute an important 'mass' useful in electoral politics, but excluded from the decision-making process on a permanent basis. Because of their exclusion and the weakness of their organisations, it is very difficult for them to struggle effectively for their economic and social rights. For instance, except for wage increases largely promoted by the government to compensate – at least partially – for the dramatic inflation of the early 1980s, the working class has not been able to make any important gains in seven years of PRD government. Second, the economic crisis has worsened in the 1980s and now affects most sectors of society, including the industrial bourgeoisie dependent on foreign imports. This economic crisis makes it more difficult for the PRD to pursue 'constituent policies'[12] that could help to link society to the government and the party in power. Two additional problems are linked to the future of democracy in the Dominican Republic. One, the lack of well-organised parties (with the exception of the PRD) which could help to channel political discontent through electoral means. The other, the historical memory of the Dominican people. Dominicans may associate 'economic progress' too closely with authoritarian politics: Trujillo during the post-war period, and Balaguer in the early 1970s. The effect that such association might have at a time of social crisis in favour of authoritarian alternatives is unknown, but it could be important.

To compare the Dominican experience with that of the Central American countries is not an easy task given the unique historical experience of each society and the variety of political events that have taken place in the last two decades. None the less, the fact that the countries of the Caribbean and Central America share historical traits such as dependency on a primary-export crop as the basis of economic growth, the timing of capitalist development and industrialisation, the economic, political and geographical vulnerability with respect to the United States, the enduring power of traditional oligarchies, and the authoritarian legacy, all encourage comparisons. It is not our purpose to pursue such comparisons here, but to suggest that a look at the internal structures of these societies would show that the ways in which the question of the distribution of power has been solved in various contexts has had an important effect on the subsequent development and the options opened to each society. Where and how the various national crises of power have been resolved establish different agendas for further political transformation. For instance, the assassination of Trujillo in 1961 without a popular insurrection generated different options for the Dominican Republic than was the case almost 20 years later for Nicaragua, when Somoza fell from power as a result of a popular revolution. In addition, the polarisation that characterises political life in El Salvador or Guatemala makes it more difficult to implement intermediate solutions or to propose compromises leading to a liberal democracy in the future. For instance, the extent of the Dominican civil war in 1965 was a minor struggle in comparison with the struggle in Central America. In our view, a social theory that seeks to account for the political transformation in the region has to consider these events, and when and how they took place. This should help, then, to account for the similarities and differences among the countries of the region. From the political point of view, it is an open choice how best to struggle for political compromises, democracy and the welfare of the large majority of the population of these countries. Achieving all of these objectives is a formidable challenge facing the entire region, including the Dominican Republic, where the more formal aspects of democracy have been to a large extent achieved, but where the large majority of the population lives in very precarious conditions and continues to be excluded from power.

Notes

1. See Guillermo O'Donnell, *Modernization and Bureaucratic-Authoritarianism: Studies on South American Politics* (California: University of California Press, 1973).

2. ECLA, *Statistical Yearbook for Latin America* (New York: United Nations, 1981), p. 70.

3. *FIDE*, Informe Trimestral, March 1981, Central Bank of the Dominican Republic.

4. *Statistical Yearbook*, p. 107.

5. Such a connection has been suggested in the case of Central American countries by Luis Maira, 'The U.S. Debate on the Central American Crisis' in Richard Fagen and Olga Pellicer, *The Future of Central America* (California: Stanford University Press, 1983), pp. 94-6.

6. *Informe Electoral*, Gaceta Oficial no. 9483, 7 October 1978.

7. Law no. 478 of 1969, the Labour Code, Santo Domingo, 1982.

8. This is based on estimations of the National Bureau of Statistics. See, *Hacia una Política de Empleo en la República Dominicana* (Santo Domingo: ONAPLAN, 1980), p. 24.

9. It should be noted that as a result of the conflicts that emerged with the attempted coup and the uncertainties about how a PRD government would behave, the Reformist Party of Balaguer retained the majority in the Senate through an electoral fraud.

10. Adam Przeworski, 'Some Problems in the Study of the Transition to Democracy', The Wilson Center, March, 1980.

11. Guillermo O'Donnell, 'Notas para el Estudio de Procesos de Democratización a partir del Estado Burocrático-Autoritario' (Working Document), CEDES, Argentina, p. 16.

12. See, for the use of this concept, Juan Linz, 'Transition to Democracy: A Comparative Perspective', San José, Costa Rica, 1983, p. 60.

5 THE COLOMBIAN PEACE PROCESS, 1982-5, AND ITS IMPLICATIONS FOR CENTRAL AMERICA

Malcolm Deas

At the beginning of September 1984 President Duarte criticised President Belisario Betancur's ceasefire agreement with Colombian guerrillas as a simple truce unlikely to last 24 hours, no sort of sincere and lasting peace. Yet a month or so later, his agreement to meet guerrilla leaders in La Palma, though it did not achieve a ceasefire, could not but strike an observer familiar with the Colombian negotiations as decidedly *Belisarista*: white flags, crowds, 'history' in a small municipio, the theatrical articulation of the popular desire for peace. The criticism and scepticism aroused were also familiar enough: where is the follow-up, where are the guarantees, what if anything has really changed? Who is being sincere about what?

To draw lessons from the Colombian experience for Central American peace-making is of course hazardous. Circumstances and history differ, the governments and the guerrillas differ. Nor is the Colombian process yet complete: it is a risky business and there are still ways in which it could go dangerously wrong. None the less there are also similarities, and a look at what has happened in Colombia certainly stimulates concrete and detailed thinking about what making peace with guerrillas implies. This chapter seeks to provide a reasoned outline of Colombian successes and failures that will enable students of Central American situations to begin to draw their own conclusions about their relevance. Of all the Contadora nations, it is Colombia that has the greatest recent experience of 'polarisation', guerrilla war, amnesties and *indultos* (pardons: not the same thing) and power-sharing, and by and large it has been Colombia that has made the running in Contadora diplomacy so far. The republic's own experiences are therefore certainly on the face of it pertinent to Central American affairs. Colombia is in certain senses 'closer' to Central America than the other two peripheral members of Contadora, Mexico and Venezuela, who have no such comparable recent history.

Before examining that more closely it is best to take a brief look at Colombia's political past and the elements that have shaped it. Colombia is a large country on the map – even when only the settled regions are considered it is still a large country – and it has not been dominated by any single one of its regions. Though the nineteenth century saw frequent civil wars and ended in the midst of one of the longest and bloodiest, what evolved was a system of civilian government by party and regional compromise. There was no alternative: civilian politicians were powerful enough to prevent the emergence of the army as a major political actor, but no single civilian group, either party or regional faction, ever exercised its dominance for long. Civilian politics retained, until recently, the power of generating widespread sectarian violence, particularly in rural areas where the country's civil wars and vigorous electoral past – there has been little interruption in elections over the entire span of republican history – have left a pattern of local antagonisms whose influence can still be seen in present guerrilla activity. Some elements in today's guerrillas can be traced back directly to the early *violencia*, the intense period of struggle between the two traditional party currents, the Liberals and Conservatives, a phase that may be dated 1946-53.

Historians frequently study how wars begin, much less often how wars end. As one side has never succeeded in crushing the other, civil wars and periods of near civil war have in Colombia been ended by more or less generous compromises. Some civil wars were ended by formal treaty. Overall there has been progress towards guaranteed representation of minorities. There is a long history of *indultos* and *amnistías*: one writer traced them back to 1784, and one jurist has counted 52 *indultos* and 15 *amnistías* in the 160 years after 1821. Old polemics show that the problems of providing guarantees of physical security and civil rights, of deciding what actions can legitimately be pardoned or forgotten, of finding a degree of openness in the political system, are nothing new. These recurrent tasks were perhaps easier at the end of the more formal nineteenth-century civil wars than they have been since 1946 with the *violencia* and its aftermath: formal civil wars better preserve a chain of command which can negotiate and enforce agreements.

Since 1946, when violence between Liberals and Conservatives began again in the Colombia countryside after the divided Liberals lost the presidency to the Conservative minority, the broad history of amnesty has been as follows:

1. After the 'Nueve de Abril', the 9 April 1948 Bogotá riots and scattered provincial insurrections that followed the assassination of Jorge Eliecer Gaitán, the government of 'national concentration' under the Conservative Mariano Ospina Pérez offered an amnesty as part of its efforts to contain the situation. This had little effect. Fighting

between Liberals and Conservatives intensified under the presidency of Laureano Gómez, until the *golpe de opinión* (change of military preferences) that produced the government of General Gustavo Rojas Pinilla, on 13 June 1953.

2. General Rojas was initially extraordinarily popular. He issued several amnesty decrees, the first covering soldiers involved in the abortive 1944 Pasto coup against the Liberal President Alfonso López Pumarejo and the second, the most significant, a year after his assumption of the presidency – Decree 1823 of 13 June 1954. His amnesty policy met with widespread success among the Liberal guerrillas of the eastern lowlands: these were the largest and most disciplined armed contingent of the party, and though there are some signs that they were evolving more radical ideas in the stress of conflict, they were still predominantly concerned with the overthrow of would-be-hegemonic conservatism, and not yet ready to reject the conventional leadership of the party. Several thousand guerrillas stopped fighting and a large quantity of arms were surrendered to the army. Decree 1823 merely set the seal on the process. Though the guerrilla leadership in the lowlands eventually submitted 24 formal conditions for accepting the amnesty, most of the guerrillas embraced it spontaneously.

3. There was less acceptance among guerrillas elsewhere in the country, though a number of these did also stop fighting. In Toloma and Caldas, the best-known cases, the guerrilla bands were more fragmented, the chain of command weaker and the situation complicated by previous struggles over land, both in indian areas and in areas of comparatively recent colonisation.

4. The years of military government, 1953-7, brought the leadership of the two parties together in opposition, and this produced the power-sharing Frente Nacional coalition which governed the country from 1958-74. Many of its arrangements, for example in the allocation of governorships and ministries, are still adhered to. The Frente was made easier by the relative absence of strong policy disagreements between Liberals and Conservatives. It was effective in reducing the incidence of political violence of the old sectarian type, which is now unlikely to recur. This should be seen as a major achievement. The government of Alberto Lleras Camargo in 1958 set up a Comisión Especial de Rehabilitación, and issued a further amnesty decree, Decree 0328 of 1958. The annual death toll diminished. A number of 'sectarian' guerrillas – Conservatives as well as Liberals – degenerated into banditry and were eliminated by the army. The army also over-ran the so-called *républicas independientes* established by guerrillas of Moscow-line CP orienta-

tion in Tolima and Huila, but these operations did not bring the guerrilla to an end. The FARC dates its formation from that year, 1964, and the mobile self-defence then begun is the 'long march' in the movement's legend of itself. Other guerrilla movements, ELN (Castroite) and EPL (Maoist) appeared. Electoral frustration after 1970 gave rise to the M-19, a more national movement less Marxist and less tied to a rural strategy. This movement was particularly active during the presidency of Julio César Turbay, 1978-82: it stole thousands of weapons from the army arsenal in Bogotá shortly after his election, and survived the subsequent capture of most of its members. It held numerous ambassadors to ransom in the embassy of the Dominican Republic. With some support from Cuba it mounted a small guerrilla invasion in the south of the country. President Turbay offered an amnesty (Law 37 of 1981), but its provisions were not considered ample enough and it was overshadowed by his Security Statute. The political conditions were not yet right: Jaime Bateman of the M-19 emphasised this: 'The problem of the amnesty was profoundly political, not juridical. He did not understand the political moment, . . . that an opening would have destroyed the guerrillas, because if they had not negotiated a peace, they would have been politically finished.'

Before considering the implications of Bateman's remarkable statement – it was made sometime in 1981, before Belisario Betancur's election – and how much political conditions have changed, it will be best to give a resumé of how matters stood towards the end of President Turbay's government.

Colombia had the oldest guerrilla problem in the Americas. The total number of guerrillas was not large – problems of definition make any statistic hazardous, but FARC combatants may number around 5,000 and the other organizations are much smaller – but nearly 40 years of varied exercise showed that though the guerrilla was far from victory, the army was equally incapable of eradicating the guerrilla. If the guerrillas attempted more spectacular operations, they took heavy losses and were forced to fall back. When the army's ambitions went beyond containment, it was tempted into expensive and often counterproductive campaigns. Guerrilla numbers appeared to be on the rise, though one should not be deceived by the FARC's ability to multiply 'fronts' on paper: some are much less serious than others. The stalemate has recently been analysed with great clarity, economy and authority by General (ret.) José Joaquín Matallana, one of the Colombian army's most successful anti-guerrilla commanders of the 1960s. The Colombian army is too small, its rank and file of recruits too unprofessional, Colombia is too large and too wild, the guerrillas too rooted for a continuation of operations on the current scale to achieve any solution.

The guerrillas were not doing any better. The FARC had numbers, though it is hard to regard 5,000 as such a great achievement – the population of Colombia is approaching 30,000,000 – especially given that many of the FARC's ranks are recruited using methods as blunt as those used by the regular army. A high proportion of Colombia's present guerrillas are adolescents, in contrast to the Liberal forces in the lowlands in the early 1950s. Judging by their penchant for photographs of young *guerrilleras*, their supporters think this has propaganda value, but it points rather to manipulation of the young, and reduces their military capacity. The FARC have also to some extent remained bound by their early concept of self-defence. They have probed widely, and have multiplied 'fronts', but they have refrained from causing spectacular disruption. They do not blow bridges, power lines or pipelines.

Much of the M-19's leadership has passed through the FARC and appears to have left through boredom and impatience. The M-19 has been capable of spectacular deeds – the Bogotá arms raid, the Dominican embassy, various seizures of towns – but has paid for these with heavy losses.

Internal dissensions can be seen from time to time in all these movements. They have been particularly lethal in the case of the ELN. Relations between them can be described as wary at best. There has been talk of the unification of Colombia's guerrillas for decades, but it did not look any closer as Turbay's term drew to a close.

Nor was a new 'cumulative revolutionary dynamic' apparent on the horizon. President Turbay's government has been held to be more than usually repressive, but it is important to grasp that this is a relative judgement. The arms robbery not surprisingly provoked the army into vigorous pursuit of the M-19, and some suspects were tortured. The state of siege and the Security Statute, however, look much stiffer on the page than they were on the streets – they did not stop the M-19 lobbing mortar-bombs at the palace. There was no censorship: criticism of the government was merciless, continuous and personal – 'They even criticise me for dancing in Cúcuta', as Turbay himself put it after getting a little carried away in a fiesta in that city. A less patient man might have allowed himself to be goaded into more drastic countermeasures; not Turbay. His critics not only under-rate this rather dim virtue but also his real political abilities as a negotiator, the solidity that comes from decades of tireless vote-gathering, and even his novelty and representativeness. Turbay was arguably the first 'non-oligarch' to gain the presidency because he was, through his own political weight, unstoppable. There are thousands of emulators of Turbay in the Colombian political system. It would be an unpardonable omission not to state that one of the difficulties facing Colombian guerrillas is that, though imperfect, the political system is democratic: elections occur regularly and it is not always certain who is going to win.

Social change in the last decades has not favoured the rural guerrilla. Urbanisation has swung the demographic balance in favour of the cities. The M-19 is the only group with a strong urban element, unless you count (as you well may) the Moscow-line CP as the urban branch of the FARC. Some rural changes produce tensions than can feed a guerrilla, but this is not everywhere the case. The cocaine business has been their best benefactor among rural developments of recent years. It brings them a lot of money, but there are obvious complications.

Even if this equilibrium could be considered stable, the cost to the country was enormous: subversion contributed substantially to Colombia's extraordinarily high rates of crime, particularly in kidnappings and extortion: in much of rural Colombia it has been impossible to run any substantial enterprise without paying for protection. The costs – in insurance, in guards, in loss of investment, in lost national production – are incalculably high.

It would be naive to think that internal peace would bring a rapid decrease in spending on the armed forces, but in the list of guerrilla costs one item has been placed by the armed forces themselves: the necessity of constant anti-guerrilla activity prevents them from attending to other tasks. In the wake of the Falklands War they are much more aware of the needs of national defence.

Colombia's international stance at the end of President Turbay's government was one of risky isolation. Colombia had problems with Nicaragua over San Andrés, Providencia and various lesser islands and keys, and was disappointed that despite the general diplomatic support she had given the United States over many years, that support was not immediately reciprocated in this matter, in itself one of no importance to the United States. Colombia had problems with Cuba: the Cubans considered that Colombia's competition for a seat in the Security Council of the UN was inspired by Washington; the Cubans trained the M-19 guerrillas for their incursion into the Putamayo, after giving them a heroes' welcome when they arrived from the Dominican embassy. Colombia had taken the most pro-British line of any Spanish American republic (with the possible exception of Chile) during the Falklands War, in marked contrast with Venezuela. Colombia had unsolved border differences with Venezuela. Much of Colombia's old diplomacy was laudably correct and much of it realistic, but in 1982 the country looked dangerously alone. Some of the danger was in Central America, and the Nicaraguan claim to islands and keys was the least of it. Colombia might become a target for subversion spreading from Central America. The guerrillas and the army watched Central American developments with interest. A guerrilla victory in El Salvador would undoubtedly have a powerful effect in Colombia: in that sense the republic was the largest though the least discussed 'domino' in the area.

In President Betancur's reorientation of policy, the domestic and the foreign elements cohere. Colombia's diplomacy has been given a facelift by entry into the non-aligned movement – a guesture that indicates that following the 'polar star' of the United States has been abandoned. Relations with Cuba, broken by President Turbay, have not been formally re-established, but they have been vastly improved. Colombia's position on the Falklands has become more Latin American. In a better financial and economic state than the other republic concerned, Colombia was able to take an energetic lead in the Contadora negotiations. This unprecedented burst of diplomatic activity was in itself initially highly popular – ordinary Colombians were noticeably gratified by it – and combined naturally with the announcement of a more generous amnesty and of a peace offensive within the country. The Colombian government was to support peace negotiations at home and abroad, while proclaiming that Colombia's problems were essentially Colombia's problems, and Central American problems Central American problems.

Thus the Centro-Americanisation of Colombia's guerrilla struggle, something that had looked a danger at the end of the Turbay administration, was to be avoided. Colombia would not present such an obvious target. But what chance did such legerdemain have of ending guerrilla and terrorist activity that was in sight of its fifth decade? (The Colombian example at least serves to remind Central Americans that there is no law of politics that says that states of conflict have a foreseeable end.)

First, the changes of policy were 'in the air'. President Alfonso López had good relations with Cuba, and with General Torrijos of Panama, and cannot be accused of excessive deference towards anyone – he would insist also on being non-aligned with the non-aligned. President López was also the Liberal Party's candidate to succeed Dr

Turbay, and made it clear that his policy would be to make a determined bid for internal peace: many left-wing intellectuals supported him precisely for that reason, including the country's most famous (though not most reliable) commentator, Gabriel García Marquez. No Colombian president of recent years has taken an intransigent repressive line about guerrillas, but in this election both candidates clearly thought the time ripe for some new sort of dialogue. In this, Dr López made the earlier and clearer pronouncements.

Secondly, once elected, President Betancur had some advantages over Dr López. He was the opposition, not the *continuista* candidate – one can overdraw the contrast, but it still exists. He had not been president before – Dr López would have had to explain why he had not made such moves more plainly in his first presidency. Betancur was a Conservative, free to seek a 'one nation' popular cause. Above all, he was enormously popular: no Colombian leader has enjoyed such popularity since the reluctant General Rojas Pinilla was persuaded temporarily to relieve the civilians in 1953. He was also an intuitive and calculating master of public relations. Colombian guerrilla groups are usually keenly interested in public relations – this is especially true of the leaders of the M-19, which calculated its actions precisely to that end and which sometimes measured its success in column inches and in television time. They had now met their match.

Betancur's popularity cannot be explained by an objective contrast between the new government and its predecessor nor by the material promises of the campaign. Dr Betancur campaigned strongly on two issues – housing for the poor without down-payments and the setting up of a radio and television-based university. These seem to me to have little more than symbolic significance. The psychological relief afforded by his victory, confirmed in his extraordinary high standing in the polls, was that he beat 'the old gang'. He confounded those who said that conventional politics could not produce anything new. He embodied some sort of *apertura*, an opening.

Now that euphoria has subsided and nerves have been set on edge by the hazards and imperfections of the peace process, Betancur's critics argue that the guerrillas are merely taking a tactical advantage of this opening. To evaluate this argument it is well worth taking a closer look at them and at how they were positioned politically in 1982.

The M-19 is the most obviously political group. Its origins are to be found in the electoral frustration of 1970, which may or may not have been won by the candidate of the Alianza Nacional Popular (ANAPO), the dissident-populist alliance of the discontented led by General Rojas

Pinilla. The electoral triumph of Dr Betancur served as a catharsis for the failure of 1970. Some leaders of the M-19 had extensive experience in more conventional politics. The late Jaime Bateman had successively passed through the opposition to Rojas's military government, the Young Communists, the Movimiento Revolucionario Liberal (MRL) of Dr Alfonso López, the movement of Camilo Torres, the FARC and the ANAPO, apparently in that order. The late Carlos Toledo Plata was long prominent in the Santander department ANAPO leadership before becoming a founder-member of the M-19; he had studied medicine in Argentina; ANAPO appealed to him because it reminded him of Peronism. He spent most of the 1970s in what might be called semi-clandestine activity: he had always wished to engage in 'ample political activity', and only took to subversion after the electoral 'robbery' of 19 April 1970. Iván Marino Ospina (still alive at the time of writing) organised the Federación Estudiantil Caldense in 1953 while in secondary school, representing conservative youth, passed to the young Communists, resisted Maoism and supported the MRL: 'I am still a *Lopista*', he could joke in 1981.

These leaders of the movement have wide political experience and many conventional political acquaintances, even friends. The interviews recorded in Patricia Lara's *Siembra Vientos y Recogeras Tempestades,* from which these quotations are taken, date from 1981, before Betancur's election. They show much evidence of a disposition that favours 'dialogue'.

They talk a great deal. They repeat their desires for amnesty, an end to the state of siege and negotiations – these are seen as part of the Colombian tradition. They emphasise the Colombian historical context and show many signs that they themselves are not immune to Colombia's pervasive legalism.

Though some spent time in the Soviet Union, there is little evidence of reverence for any Russian line:

> We all fell in love in the Soviet Union . . . Russian women are fascinated by Latins. Perhaps it's the dark skin . . . But I got bored in the Soviet Union and came back in 1962. Obviously I don't like to mention that I was there – one loses prestige. Seriously, don't laugh – *desprestigia berracamente*!

They say they are flexible: 'One must improvise at all times. Otherwise we would not be able to survive.' They do not speak ideologically:

> if revolutionaries go around talking about the contradictions between peaceful coexistence and armed struggle or the advantages of China over social imperialism or that sort of thing, nobody understands a damn! Such talk just weakens the revolution . . . We must nationalise the revolution, put it on a Colombian footing, *darle sabor de pachanga, hacerla con bambucos, vallenatos y cumbias*, make the revolution singing the national anthem. Making politics well is like cooking a stew: you have to put in a bit of this and a bit of that, let it simmer, watch it, see it doesn't burn . . .

Bateman made his particularly interesting criticism of President Turbay in the last year of his government:

> He did not understand that an opening would have destroyed the guerrillas . . . he would have destroyed us too probably because we did not have the resources to beat clientelism in an electoral struggle, and with an amnesty (of a more generous sort) the M-19 would have suffered an irreparable split. But the government united us. Obviously it could have destroyed us, but to do that it would have had to open its legs just a little while, just a little while . . .

These quotations from 1981 are given here at some length to give both the flavour of this particular 'stew' and to show that M-19's thinking before Belisario Betancur's election certainly contemplated a political solution.

The M-19 in terms of combatants is usually accounted much smaller than the FARC, but it has a broader penumbra of sympathisers, particularly among urban youth. It is also more belligerent than the FARC, and has been prepared to suffer heavy losses in its more spectacular operations. Some of these have used neither typical guerrilla nor typical terrorist tactics – they have been more open, more vulnerable, more public. More openness and more publicity are an obvious temptation to such a movement.

An analyst of the stance of the FARC at this same juncture might not find such picturesque language or such a sense of urgency – the FARC has a longer history, an older leadership and the stolid intellectual orientation of *los mamertos*, the Partido Comunista Colombiano – but all the same he would not find a hopeless case for dialogue. It sometimes seems that Manuel Marulanda Velez is the veteran of more conversations than combats. For all its multiplication of fronts and relative logistical solidity and discipline, FARC's aggression has always been limited, something that frustrated while in its ranks those future members of the M-19: 'In Colombia there are guerrillas in all the departments and nothing happens: the army has them completely under control . . . We should take the war where it hurts most.' This was not where the FARC was intermittently taking the war. The organisation's theory itself was timid: 'they required so many preconditions that there would have been no room in power for all those who were needed to get there.'

Though there is no source as seemingly direct as Patricia Lara's *Siembra Vientos*, a growing number of *reportages* provide some clues. (These works have also an importance of their own in the process, which may be positive: they are the first symptoms of the possible incorporation of their protagonists into the broader stream of national history.) There is a more symbiotic relationship with the Colombian army, not surprising after so many years of intermittent conflict. There is a strong emphasis always on the early resistance to Rojas's Villarica offensive, on the *republicas independientes* of Tolima and Huila and the long retreat year 1964-5, on peasant self-defence, as it was then called – the phrase is no longer fashionable but the concept lingers. The M-19 leaders are occasionally referred to as 'los muchachos'! Cultural echoes are sometimes decidedly antique, as one might expect, for example, from an ideologue as old as the FARC's Jacobo Arenas, born 1924: Victor Hugo, Homer, Shakespeare, Miguel de Cervantes, Bertha Singerman . . . He recalls the old Bogotá of trams like any nostalgic sexagenerian *cachaco*. There is a marked emphasis on history, on local Colombian history, among these veterans. They recognise that for the FARC some times have been much easier than others: 'A difficult time for the FARC was . . . the government of Carlos Lleras Restrepo, the masses had a certain trust in him. We don't only see things from a military point of view, politics also counts. Each epoch has its own difficulties, it's not all the colour of roses.' There is a certain modesty about claiming to be the vanguard, about the leadership –

'Do you consider yourself equal to Fidel Castro, Che Guevara, Augusto César Sandino, Farabundo Martí?

'Well, I simply consider myself Manuel Marulanda Velez.'

– and even about the degree of threat posed by the movement: 'The army high command argue that we are a real threat, but we don't think that we yet are. The military command is trying to justify repression and halt the revolutionary process. We know we are not a threat yet, we still have some way to go.'

The geographical origins and evolution of FARC have their local causes, but its national role has been for most of its history to maintain the revolutionary credentials of the PCC, a legal party of conservative habit.

It can thus be seen that both M-19 and FARC were unlikely to turn an entirely deaf ear to overtures from a fresh government. There is no evidence that they received instructions from abroad that it would be diplomatically convenient if they were to engage in a semblance of dialogue – in the case of M-19 it is not clear from whence abroad such suggestions would have been acceptable: it is a consciously nationalist movement. It is possible that Havana and Moscow should have sent such a message, and the Cubans particularly must be anxious to show no sign of subverting Belisario Betancur – they argue that the M-19 invaded the Putamayo not from Cuba but from Panama, and that bad relations were essentially caused by President Turbay's consent to serve US ends in the Security Council affair. There is, however, no evidence for outside influence, and there are sufficient national explanations for the course events have taken.

Both the guerrillas and the government were aware of Central American events.

The M-19:

> In Central America imperialism will show what it intends to do. The future of our struggle depends to a great degree on the future of the struggle in Central America. If imperialism gets involved in [*se mete en*] Central America, there will be a new stage in the Latin American anti-imperialist struggle. And conditions are not the same as they were.

Senator Germán Bula Hoyos, proposing the amnesty law:

> Very close in Central America a cruel war is being waged between brothers. I never believed that Colombia could easily get into the same situation, and now I am filled with content thinking that my compatriots are getting ready to reach a great national accord, which will mean that no such threat will ever hang over our territory.

The amnesty law, Law 35 of 1982, was promulgated on 20 November 1982. Though in some individual cases it had immediate effect, the government had to wait longer than it had hoped for a collective response from the main groups in the form of a ceasefire. The M-19 was thrown into some confusion by the death of Bateman in an air crash. Contacts with that movement were made abroad – a device for which there is plenty of precedent in Colombian politics, much used in the years of the formation of the Frente Nacional. The Colombian army, in the person of the Minister of War, General Fernando Landazábal Reyes, certainly still recognised that a solely military solution would not achieve peace, but its critics allege that it was reluctant to give President Betancur the necessary military and geographical 'space' needed to take his dialogue forward. Nor was President Betancur helped by the persistent belligerance of the M-19, which was deliberately to persist in bravura aggressions up to the eve of its signing the truce, and its arrogant demands for de-militarised zones. The Colombian army is debarred from uttering political opinions. The position of the Minister of Defence, in recent years always a soldier, is always delicate, and newspapers and politicians are alert for the slightest sign of exploitable comment. General Landazábal, the author of several books, overstepped the mark in January 1984 and was dismissed, together with several colleagues. General Gustavo Matamoros became Minister of War, despite having done some deliberating himself: he had given his opinion on the renewal of diplomatic relations with Cuba – 'a moral impossibility' – though that matter was clearly outside his province. This was a moment of palpable tension between the president and the high command. President Betancur asserted his authority, and it may have helped give his peace overtures more credibility among the guerrillas, but his relations with the armed forces were damaged. It might have been possible to silence the generals in a more politic fashion early on; there is no evidence that any sort of coup was being planned.

FARC upstaged the M-19 and the other groups by signing an agreement at La Uribe (Meta department) on 28 March 1984 for a ceasefire to begin on 28 May. It gained enormous publicity, and the country experienced the first round of the strains that were going to become familiar as the year went on. The publicity given to 'Don Manuel' and his camouflaged followers, who all along insisted that they would keep their arms and uniforms, was hard for the armed forces and much of bourgeois Colombia to take. But it was also the envy of M-19, which itself signed agreements at Corinto (Cauca) and El Hobo (Huila) on 24 August 1984, and thereby obtained its own wave of publicity. Agreements were also signed by EPL in a notorious champagne-and-machine-gun-spangled ceremony in Medellín on the same day.

To many commentators it all looked too good – or too bad – to be true. The armed forces expressed their disquiet principally by pointing out that the wearing of uniforms and the carrying of arms by these groups was unconstitutional – I would stress that it is significant that they should use this constitutional argument, and that they should accompany it by firm denials that they have any simplistic notions of a coup. Their point about arms and uniforms is undoubtedly correct, but equally correct on a different level is the argument that if the peace process is going to get anywhere, that article of the constitution must for a time be quietly ignored: the guerrillas insist on arms and uniforms for the moment, as they do not regard their signing the agreements as a surrender. Arms and uniforms are part of the show; the guerrillas are as conscious of this as any journalist, and the show is part of what they want. The government has to allow them to be spectacular until the spectacle pales. This is part of the demystification of the guerrilla, and it is not all to the guerrillas' advantage. They can occasionally be seen to be arrogant, simplistic, dogmatic, naive and inexperienced.

The ceasefire is to be followed by a more mysterious 'Great National Dialogue', a notion that derives more from M-19 than from FARC and one that it has not been easy for the government to translate into formal terms. Who is to talk with whom, where and what about? How are disagreements to be resolved? Are votes to be taken? What status are the results of these dialogues going to have? Congress has naturally declined to participate in any official fashion in these discussions. Yet peace is clearly about 'participation', on the guerrilla side and in the mind of President Belisario Betancur. The historical moment – and both the president and the guerrilla leadership are keen students of Colombian history – is judged to call for an opening of the system beyond the dominance of the two traditional currents of Colombian political life. That dominance has never been total, and it has, since the formation of the Frente Nacional, been exercised on the whole with flexibility and moderation. Both parties have always been permeable and anxious to recruit new political talent. But they have enjoyed a quasi-monopoly, they are privileged, they can exclude other currents, particularly at the local level. My impression is that 'participation' is M-19's central demand – not nationalisation, not agrarian reform – most of its adolescent urban membership can have little interest in that – nor any other specific reform (one searches the pronouncements of the leadership in vain for specific reforms: perhaps specific reforms do not dissolve well in a stew). FARC can also favour participation in its own way: the Colombian Communist Party is legal, and must see possible advantages in capitalising FARC's local organisation and its tenacity in at least surviving for so long.

Have results so far lived up to expectations? Just as no realist could have expected a surrender of arms and uniforms, it was unlikely that the ceasefires should have produced instant peace. There is a high level of criminality in Colombia, most of it unrevolutionary, and that will not respond to political overtures. Much crime is carried out on the fringes of subversion – it is frequently difficult to know for certain if a kidnapping or an assault on a bank is politically motivated or not. It is an illusion that all guerrillas are tightly disciplined. In some fronts FARC shoots anyone who steps out of line, but it is incapable of maintaining complete order in its 27 operations. It may be true that initially the government over-estimated the coherence of the enemy, and imagined that it was dealing with something like the Liberals under Generals Herrera and Uribe Uribe, who had signed the treaties of the USS *Wisconsin* and of *Neerlandia* that ended the War of a Thousand Days, after which tropical Appomatoxes everyone had gone home. One disconcerted government commentator told me: 'The first thing you have to realise is that the Colombian guerrillas are even more disorganised than the Colombian government.' They are less numerous than people think – there are far more lawyers in Colombia than guerrillas – but they are also not the models of organisation that they appear to be: it is easy for a guerrilla or a clandestine group to appear to be 'cleverer' and more coherent than the authorities, but this coherence is often only illusory.

Amnesties are rarely accepted by all they seek to embrace: the Colombian experience has been no exception in the past and it is no exception in the present. Not all groups will accept a truce: in Colombia the remnants of ELN and the dissident Ricardo Franco front of FARC are visibly unwilling to co-operate, but there are other less visible fragmentations. Those who continue to fight are logically the most aggressive; they are no longer under the control of the more political brains of their movements, and they are cut off from some of their old sources of funds. The amnesty may therefore have as a paradoxical immediate result an increase in violence as these factions assert themselves. One of the most disappointing aspects of recent months is the sustained high level of kidnapping. Colombia still has the highest rate in the world; many victims have not been released, and new victims have been taken. FARC and M-19 both confess to kidnapping in the past – and insist that kidnapping should be covered by amnesty and *indulto* – but they deny that they are continuing the practice.

Both movements need funds. They are less austere than guerrillas used to be:

> making the revolution costs a lot of money. In seven and a half years I think we have spent around 100 million pesos . . . at least 70 million pesos we invested in houses, cars, apartments which the army has taken. You can't have centralised accounting when you work illegally. . . . At the moment we are more or less well off [*estamos de plata como regularzongo*].

How is M-19 going to change in short order the habits of a decade? Even FARC confesses to some modernisation:

> The modern guerrilla wears faded blue jeans, smokes *Marlboro*, uses lavatory paper, listens to salsa, and some even listen to the piano concertos and symphonies of Beethoven, Mozart, Wagner and Brahms. When conditions permit they drink coca-cola and canned Clausen lager.

Arms, Brahms, it all costs money. FARC also pays regular sums to the families of its recruits. The connection between the movement and the cocaine trade is no invention of the US ambassador. It has made the guerrilla much wealthier than the party. Such connections are not lightly given up.

The Colombian government has not got the resources to give the amnesty programme a generous material underpinning. Amnestied guerrillas have been offered the minimum wage for six months – some US $90 a month. This will not keep them in the style to which they may have become accustomed. A rehabilitation programme is also no easy thing in these circumstances to devise, even if it could be paid for. Some guerrillas have agrarian interests, but by no means all, or even a majority. Many of them are too young to have any clear political ideas at all: they are something out of William Golding's *Lord of the Flies*, not the Sierra Maestra, not the Long March. A refusal to face this fact – when one states it, one is sometimes accused of *lèse-majesté* towards the revolution – does not make a solution of the problem any easier: effective compromises have to be based on realities, and it is not realistic to think that these elements represent much of a viable alternative government at *any* level. A military response has not only been unsuccessful so far: when one looks at a lot of armed 15-year-old-girls, that strikes one as inappropriate, but what is appropriate does not easily come to mind. Some tangible suggestions have been made: the guerrillas were to be equipped with taxis. This outraged taxi-drivers, and it was pointed out that it was not prudent to equip any recently-amnestied subversive group with such instant mobility. Some small municipal jobs have been given to beneficiaries of the amnesty, but there are not enough to go round, and many others have a claim on that patronage. Economic conditions are not good: unemployment is high and further austerities are probable.

Then there is the problem of physical guarantees. The shooting of Carlos Toledo Plata in Bucaramanga in mid-August 1984, either by the death-squad Movimiento Anti-Secuestros (the Anti-Kidnap Movement) or by some other group that wished to put a spoke in the wheel of peace-making, did not in the event prevent M-19 from signing the truce a week later, nor was it at the root of the movement's rising in Yumbo that immediately followed the killing. All the same, it showed what could happen to someone who took the amnesty too literally: Toledo Plata thought he could return to normal civilian life in a straightforward nineteenth-century fashion. It is an item of belief among many Colombians of the left that the somewhat radicalized Liberal leadership of the eastern lowlands that accepted General Rojas's amnesty of 1953-4 was thereafter eliminated. A similar belief could easily take root about the present amnesty, and the government has not got the resources fully to protect those who wish to take advantage of it. Their best protection lies in a change of atmosphere: many men with numerous enemies, many of those who had killed others during the *violencia*, changed their ways and survived under the Frente Nacional. A good measure of prudence and suspicion no doubt helped. The peace process has enough impetus behind it to survive one assassination like that of Toledo Plata, but it will obviously be threatened severely if there are many more.

The list of difficulties is long. It is not yet clear how 'dialogue' and 'participation' are going to be reconciled with existing political interests. In certain localities, with some of the new leaders, it is not impossible to visualise bargains being struck, but constitutional revisions require congressional approval by more than a simple majority. The country can afford a few more municipalities like Viotá, one of the quietest and most conservative regions of Colombia – governed now for decades by the Communist Party – but it is not easy to create new municipalities to hand over in that fashion and there are obvious limits to that sort of concession.

The balance of amnesty and ceasefire as of May 1985 could not easily have been foreseen by any of the parties involved. Incomplete success has lowered President Betancur's prestige from its previous heights (one should remember that they were exceptionally high, and he still gets a 30 per cent plus popularity rating) as he is seen to make humilating concessions to a deceitful and unworthy enemy. It is not possible to be precise about how prevalent this view is, but conventional Colombia is much larger, and popular support, beyond a vague tolerance, for revolutionary Colombia much smaller than most accounts convey. At the same time neither FARC nor M-19 appear likely to be able to sustain the interest and prestige that both movements momentarily obtained at the times they signed the truce. Government and guerrillas have mounted a shaky tandem on which neither cuts a convincing figure, but neither can get off, and both must keep pedalling away if they are not going to fall off. (In less elaborate forms this image of the bicycle is frequently used locally.) The prestige of the army has increased in political circles since its generals have been reduced to silence. The president's civilian critics grow in number, but they have no alternative policy to offer.

Whatever the deficiencies of the search for peace, the alternative may still be as General Matallana stated it: 'either we achieve peace or we are headed for a hecatomb of unforeseeable consequences.' It *may* only be thus, because Colombian political actors have long shown that they can evade the apparent logic of situations, and Colombia's years of intermittent subversive activity show that it can just go on and on and on. The evolution of the last two years has perhaps made the republic less vulnerable to developments in Central America. It has certainly made Colombia a far less attractive scene for that sort of international opinion that goes seeking a guerrilla movement with which to sympathise – in itself this is a practical gain.

What are the possible implications for Central America in these Colombian events? Are the differences everywhere so overwhelming that there are no parallels worth drawing, no lessons to be learnt? I think not, particularly in the case of El Salvador.

Colombia has had more practice at compromise, is a larger and more independent country, and has a particularly strong civilian political tradition. It has no equivalent to El Salvador's 1932 massacre, and Colombian anti-Communism, even in the armed forces, is not obsessive. It is not next door to Nicaragua or Guatemala, and it is further away from the United States. There has been no prolonged recent period of systematic repression in Colombia, as the biographies of M-19 leaders clearly show. These are important differences, but there are also similarities, and there are also Colombian experiences that are likely to be repeated in any peace-making process.

First, some similarities. It can be argued that Salvadoran guerrillas are not like Colombian guerrillas – they are proportionately more numerous, they are 'more ideological', they are more aggressive, particularly in sabotage. But in many ways they do look like Colombian guerrillas: their leaders frequently come from similar backgrounds to the politicians they oppose, the rank and file is much of it youthful and is probably no more ideological than its Colombian counterpart. Their aggression may be overstated – many parts of Salvador have not been much affected by the war, and its intensity is not so self-evident. As in most wars, in many places much time passes without anything much happening. As in Colombia, the line between guerrilla-held and government-controlled areas is a blur – the absence of the army may not necessarily mean the entire absence of government. The Salvadoran economy is more vulnerable to disruption than the Colombian, and has clearly been harder hit, but there is a case for applying to the Salvadoran guerrillas the same sceptical analysis that is certainly warranted in Colombia.

Then commentatators on both countries have at different times overstressed 'polarisation'. Colombia must have looked intensely 'polarised' in1952, but produced the Frente Nacional five years later. El Salvador is the scene of extreme antagonisms, but universal 'polarisation' is not quite the same as that. Are Salvadoran antagonisms more extreme than Colombian? There are more death-squads, but there is less *violencia*, by which I understand the sort of unrestrained banditry that Colombia suffered in the late 1940s, 1950s and early 1960s. It does not appear to be true that once a certain amount of blood gets into the system then there has to be some sort of unimaginable fight to the finish, and that compromise is impossible. The Colombians have been able to find compromises after fighting at least as intense as that which has been seen in El Salvador. Perhaps their leaders have been more political than the Salvadorans.

Some of the practical difficulties that the Colombian government has faced have been listed in this chapter. Many are bound to recur in Salvador, some more acutely: Colombian death-squads are not as numerous or as well-connected as the Salvadoran examples; the Colombian army is constutionalist – in no system can a coup be considered an impossibility, but the traditions, the rhetoric and the political sophistication – what would a coup solve? – of the Colombian army are notably different from what has until recently prevailed in Salvador. The strains in the political cycle of amnesty and *apertura* are likely to be similar in El Salvador and the politicians have less experience in taking them. The problems of rehabilitation, of reincorporating guerrillas into a normal life are more daunting: less space, a weaker economy. There is a better prospect of international assistance: El Salvador has attracted much more attention than Colombia. That is a disadvantage in the early stages of guerrilla war, but it may be a help when it comes to making peace. Those better acquainted with El Salvador than I may be able to draw further comparisons.

President Betancur wished to emphasise the national distinctiveness of Colombia's problems. The president of peace in Colombia was also necessarily the advocate of peace in Central America, and emphasised there the Central American essence of Central America's problems: they were not to be made a part of the wider conflict of East and West. As Fernando Cepeda has observed, by strenuously keeping Central America out of Colombia Dr Betancur began to risk getting Colombia into Central America: before the La Palma talks, the Farabundo Martí leaders requested that he be present at them as an international witness or guarantor. President Duarte, for the good of all, insisted that this was a Salvadoran affair. Like Belisario Betancur, he has played the nationalist card to some effect, and it is possibly an essential part of peacemaking. In excluding the Colombian president, perhaps he showed that he had learnt by the Colombian example.

Notes

The author wishes to acknowledge his debts to Fernando Cepeda, Universidad de los Andes, Bogotá, and to Laurence Whitehead, Nuffield College, Oxford, for their help with this chapter.

On the history of amnesty see Gonzalo Sánchez, 'Raices históricas de la amnistía o las etapas de la guerra en Colombia', *Revista de Extensión Cultural* (Medellín), no. 15 (1984).

Luis Villar Borda, *Oposición, insurgencia y violencia* (Bogotá, 1982).

Alfred Molano, *Amnistía y violencia* (Bogotá, 1980).

Hugo Ernesto Zarrate O, *La amnistía por los delitos políticos en Colombia* (Bogotá, 1984).

On the M-19, I have quote extesnsively from Patricia Lara, *Siembra vientos y recogeras tempestades* (Bogotá, 1982, January).

On FARC, I have used Carlos Arango Z, *FARC – Veinte años. De Marquetalia a La Uribe* (Bogotá, 1984).

General José Joaquín Matallana's reflections are published as *Alternativa del 84. Paz o Guerra* (Bogotá, 1984).

6 LAND, LABOUR AND DESPOTISM IN CENTRAL AMERICA

John Weeks

Introduction

Given the generality of the recent economic crisis in Latin America, it is tempting to interpret the conditions in Central America as part of an hemispheric economic collapse, resulting from the depressed level of primary product prices, restricted world liquidity and a debt burden accumulated over the past decade. But it would be a mistake to do so, for the Central American economic crisis is profoundly different from what brought other Latin American economies to the brink of catastrophe. It is the thesis of this chapter that the economic crisis was and is but a manifestation of the collapse of the Central American social formation, and this decade will witness the destruction of the old order and the emergence of a new one. Therefore, it is incorrect to postulate the recovery of the Central American economies or their reconstruction on the existing socio-economic basis.

This fundamental crisis of Central American society is the culmination of growing tensions and contradictions which can no longer be contained within the existing social order, and the present turmoil is a stage in the process of creative destruction. This interpretation, that the region is in the midst of an epoch-making historical disjuncture, has major implications for the present debate over United States policy towards the region. Much of this debate has centred over how normalcy or the status quo can be re-established, and as such is based upon counter-factual possibilities.[1]

Major structural transformations are imminent in the region; some of which, such as the overthrow of Somoza in Nicaragua, have already occurred, but others are in the offing and difficult even to anticipate. To develop our interpretation, we first analyse the nature of the 'old order' in Central America,[2] and how the process of commercialisation and integration into the world market strengthened the old order. We then argue that economic factors associated elsewhere in Latin America with modernisation, e.g. the inflow of foreign capital and industrialisation, were subsumed within the old order, further perpetuating it. We call this process in Central America 'development without modernisation'. The theme which ties our discussion together is that Central America's commercialisation has been based upon the power of landed property, and that the anachronistic regimes of the region persisted due to the reactionary character of landed property.

The Old Order in Central America

The Basis for US Hegemony

Since the nineteenth century, Central American history has turned on two axes: the power of landed property and domination by the United States. The first of these has its origin in the colonial period, while the second did not achieve its full expression until the first years of the twentieth century. These two central elements are not unique to Central America. Yet nowhere else in the hemisphere has either element been so overwhelmingly influential. The power of landed property is elaborated below. With regard to US domination, we can note that US troops have never intervened south of the Canal Zone, nor has a US government ever funded an insurrectionist army in South America, as it did to overthrow Arbenz in 1954, to invade Cuba in 1961 and now to remove the Nicaraguan government.

Both of these elements are closely related to the manner in which country-status emerged in the Central American region.[3] During the colonial period, Central America was administered from Mexico City via the Capitancy of Guatemala. The authority emanating from Guatemala City was always weak at best, and authority in the region decentralised around the provincial towns. The weakness of colonial authority in part reflected the wretched state of communications in the region, but the lack of roads and administrative infrastructure was itself a consequence of Central America's economic unimportance to the Spanish crown.[4]

The absence of major export products during the colonial period reinforced the parochial rivalries of the Central American landlord and merchant classes, rendering their economic interests competitive rather than complementary. The conflict among the provincial oligarchies centred on disputes with the elite in and around Guatemala City, which enjoyed the privileges associated with colonial administration. In South America, too, there were conflicts between the colonial capital and the provinces; e.g. the demand by the merchants of Buenos Aires for the end to Lima's monopoly of foreign trade. In South America, these conflicts for the most part reflected the economic development and growing importance of the provinces relative to Lima, and resulted in the eventual break-up of the colonial order and a coalescing of the dominant classes around regional centres. This process of fragmentation followed by coalescence resulted in the emergence of the modern states of South America, and was well underway by the time of independence.

In Central America, the conflicts between Guatemala City and the provinces derived from the stagnation and economic isolation of the latter. The end of colonial rule strengthened the tendency towards fragmentation rather than a process of coalescence. One province, Chiapas, split off permanently, not for independence but to join the Mexican union. The Central American Federation was founded in 1823 by five states, but this division into five parts was purely formal. These geographical entities had little cohesion or unique identity that coincided with the territories their governments formally claimed to control. The federation fell apart after 15 years of internal struggle, including a debilitating civil war from 1826 to 1829.[5]

But the collapse of the federation did not result in the formation of five cohesive countries. Guatemala was the only territory with a clear political identity, and for the rest of the nineteenth century it dominated the other areas, with the exception of Costa Rica, which was too far away and sparsely populated to make its domination tempting. Honduras had virtually no identity at all, and its presidents were imposed by Guatemalan dictators. The principal Guatemalan strongmen were Rafael Carrera and Justo Rufino Barrios, who together ruled their country from 1838 to 1885 with the exception of only eight years. These two regional strongmen also maintained subservient governments in El Salvador, so the 'Northern Triangle' of Central America lay under the domination of Guatemala City for half a century. During the same period Nicaragua was split by the rivalry between the upper classes of León and Granada, with no national government as such until the presidency of José Santos Zelaya during 1893-1909, who used the internal coherence he forged to dominate the region briefly himself.

Thus, Central America in the nineteenth century remained in the early stage of country formation. The political organisation of the region, whether it would be forcibly united by a local strongman or devolved into five countries, remained unresolved. This weakness of political organisation and institutions of state control left Central America uniquely vulnerable to outside intervention. During the nineteenth century the two major powers with designs on the region, the United Kingdom and the United States, were largely content to pursue their influence within the context of the domination of Central America by local dictators.

However, the last of these dictators, Zelaya of Nicaragua, manifested a nationalism unacceptable to the United States. The immediate contention was over the conditions for a canal route through Nicaragua. When Zelaya refused to accept US sovereignty over the proposed zone, Washington intervened with gunboats and troops to effect his overthrow. The fall of Zelaya and his replacement with a US client in 1909 created a power vacuum in Central America which the United States quickly filled. The dominant classes had not achieved effective and institutionalised control over their populations in any of the five states of Central America. This allowed for a degree of US hegemony in the area which would have been impossible in South America or Mexico.

Thus, it is a mistake to view Central America as merely within the US sphere of influence. This would be a correct assessment of US-South American relations, but Central America after the fall of Zelaya assumed protectorate status, a virtual semi-colonial relationship. The consequence for the evolution of the Central American ruling elites was profound. To a qualitatively greater extent than in South America, these elites were dependent upon Washington, and after 1909 their conflicts, within each state and among states, were mediated and directly resolved by US diplomatic (and undiplomatic) intervention. Nicaragua was the extreme case, militarily occupied by the US for 20 years, then ruled for another 45 by a family whose power had been created by Washington. In all five of the countries at least one government was removed or installed by US intervention during the period 1909 to 1945,[6] and few governments ruled without the consent of Washington.

The direct role of the US government in mediating intra-elite disputes and often imposing solutions gave a particularly reactionary and anti-popular character to the regimes in Central America (with the exception of Costa Rica). Since Washington placed certain groups in power and demonstrated its willingness to use force to keep them there, the regimes felt little pressure to take accommodating steps to satisfy the demands of the middle and lower classes for reform or even nominal political participation. This, in turn, complemented the system of land tenure and labour coercion which had emerged during the coffee boom of the mid-nineteenth century.

Land Tenure and Labour Control

In the colonial period, the vast majority of the Central American population lived in Guatemala and El Salvador. Agricultural production was based on large estates with semi-feudal social relations that tied the peasantry to particular landlords. Even in the early nineteenth century, land ownership was highly concentrated. Indeed, in 1811, an organisation of merchants in Guatemala City identified land concentration as the colony's major economic problem and recommended a land-to-the-tiller agrarian reform.[7]

The most important aspect of the land question in Central America has not been the concentration of ownership, however, but the social relations governing the occupancy and use of land. In colonial times, semi-feudal social relations characterised the more densely-occupied areas of Central America. Royal land grants entitled the Spanish landlords not only to land, but also to rights to the labour of the peasantry occupying that land.[8] Such arrangements were common in Spanish America, from Mexico to Chile, and the system as it evolved in Central America up to the middle of the nineteenth century was probably no more coercive than elsewhere.

During the early years of the Central American Federation, Liberals controlled the central government, and their ideology derived from the Cádiz Constitution of 1812, stressing anti-clericalism and economic modernisation. Economic modernisation in the contemporary context called for the alienability of land and the abolishment of servile labour systems. The federal government sought to implement these reforms, but quickly confronted strong opposition from landlords and the peasantry.[9] The landlords accepted the alienability of land, since in practice it implied the elimination of the peasantry's traditional rights to common lands. However, landed property resisted reform of the servile labour systems, which would have caused a drastic change in both its political power over the peasantry and the economic organisation of its production. The opposition of the peasantry to the reforms was even stronger, since commercialisation of land implied dispossession and landlessness. The result of the Liberal programme to modernise the countryside was alienability – rendering land a commodity – without significant alteration of the servile labour systems.

The superficial and incomplete nature of reform laid the basis for the rigidification of traditional land tenure systems. In the 1840s coffee production spread rapidly through Costa Rica, Guatemala and El Salvador, bringing Central America into international trade. Until the development of banana production at the end of the century, coffee would be the region's only export of importance, marking the years

1850-90 as the era of the 'coffee republics'. The label is singularly appropriate. In the three states where coffee boomed, this export crop would not only determine the economic health of the economies, but also political power and the nature of the state.

Particularly in El Salvador and Guatemala, governments served as the direct agents of landed property, and the repressive role of the state reached into the day-to-day operation of the large estates.[10] Once the profitability of coffee production made itself evident, landed interests used the state to force the peasantry off land suitable for the cash crop and onto marginal plots of low productivity. This process of forcible dispossession of the peasantry in El Salvador and Guatemala tended in itself to generate the labour required for the large estates. Reduced to tiny holdings, a large portion of the peasantry could no longer sustain self-sufficiency. However, with its power virtually unchallenged, landed property in these two states was not content to let the pressure of poverty and deprivation generate an adequate supply of field labour. In order to ensure a permanently-available supply of labour at the lowest possible cost, landed interests employed the state to adapt the traditional servile labour systems to their new commercial coffee production.

Perhaps nowhere in the western hemisphere since the abolition of slavery has personal freedom been so restricted in the interests of landed property as in Central America. Forced labour had been formally abolished in 1823 by the Liberal government of the Federation, but it persisted in practice, and with the coffee boom took the form of debt peonage. Under this system, a debtor was legally required to work for his creditor until repayment could be made, and failure to do so was a criminal offence. Coffee-planters employed a variety of methods to ensure continual indebtedness by labourers and, in any case, the state authorities tended to accept the testimony of landlords on the state of repayment.

During the latter part of the nineteenth century the coffee oligarchy introduced 'vagrancy' laws to strengthen the coercive character of the labour system. These laws required peasants to work as wage labourers a number of days during the year, and failure to do so could bring criminal prosecution. In 1934, the Guatemalan government formally abolished debt peonage, but the same 'reform' law more strictly codified the legal obligation to engage in wage labour. The constitutions of El Salvador and Guatemala retained clauses making 'vagrancy' a criminal offence into the 1960s.[11]

Thus, the relationship between land tenure and authoritarianism in

Central America is quite clear cut. To facilitate the cheap production of coffee, landed property introduced a coercive system of labour relations which precluded any process of democratisation or popular political participation in any form. This gave the regimes in Central America their uniquely despotic and anachronistic nature. While these regimes can be called 'conservative', it is more correct to view them as anti-democratic, based on a political philosophy which pre-dates the age of liberalism, a throwback to feudal despotism. In South America and Mexico, political systems evolved in the twentieth century based upon the liberal-nationalist principle that governments rule by the consent of the governed. In practice this principle has been violated more than it has been sustained, but political philosophies that explicitly deny the principle have largely been on the margin of the body politic.[12] In Central America, the principle of oligarchic rule, rule by the few with the acquiescence of the many, remains a mainstream political philosophy to this day.

That this reactionary, pre-modern political philosophy and practice has its basis in the system of land tenure is clearly shown by contrasting Costa Rica to the rest of the region. Many explanations are offered for Costa Rica's uniquely pluralistic society, from the implicitly racist argument that the country is populated almost exclusively by Europeans, to the allegation that the distribution of wealth and income is considerably less unequal in Costa Rica than elsewhere in the region. The true explanation lies in the nature of land tenure and the way in which capitalism developed in Costa Rica.

Because of its remoteness from the colonial centre and the absence of an indigenous population of any significant size, Costa Rica had few attractions during Spanish rule. The lack of an indigenous labour force made land grants of little value to Spanish upper-class settlers, so the area of the Central Valley was occupied by smallholders, using family labour. Thus, during colonial times peonage and forced labour were of no significance in Costa Rica. In the middle of the nineteenth century, coffee production spread rapidly, and the commercialisation of peasant life generated a rapid process of economic and social differentiation. Land prices boomed, and the cycle in coffee prices generated indebtedness. The combination of rising land prices and accumulating indebtedness resulted in a powerful process of land concentration, creating on the one hand a wealthy coffee aristocracy and landless labourers on the other.[13]

This, of course, is the 'classic' class differentiation which commercialisation of peasant life generates, with the rural population stratified among large capitalist estates, 'yeoman' farmers and landless labourers. In the absence of coercive labour relations, as well as the existence of an open frontier in the southwest to which the landless could migrate, coffee wages were relatively high. The combination of a residual independent peasantry and a relatively prosperous rural working class provided the basis for Costa Rica's pluralistic institutions. It should be stressed, however, that Costa Rican society is characterised by great inequalities – a study of land distribution in the 1970s revealed that the concentration of ownership of agricultural land was as high in Costa Rica as in El Salvador or Guatemala, and Costa Rica is a country in which the landed oligarchy continues to monopolise political office.[14]

However, because of the capitalist nature of rural transformation in Costa Rica, it has not been possible for the oligarchy to impose despotic rule. In the rest of Central America, the landed oligarchy used its power to maintain pre-capitalist land systems while fostering the development of agro-export economies. It is in this sense that we earlier used the phrase 'development without modernisation'. The coffee boom commercialised Central America, provided the incentive and revenue for development of infrastructure and lent a veneer of material prosperity. At the same time, except in Costa Rica, the propertied classes blocked any attempt at political modernisation, constructing their agro-export economy upon a pre-capitalist system of labour exploitation which required the forcible repression of the popular will.

Capitalist Development and the Old Order

Central America commercialised in the nineteenth century on the basis of landed property, which adapted to the coffee boom by rigidifying pre-capitalist land tenure and labour-control systems. Through the nineteenth century, Central American society was despotically ruled by a tight alliance of the coffee aristocracy and urban merchant and financial groups closely linked to the export trade. The entry of foreign capital into Central America, rather than being a force for modernisation, tended from its arrival to reinforce the power of landed property and 'reactionary despotism'.

The first major incursion of foreign capital occurred via the banana companies in the last decade of the nineteenth century. The banana companies did not themselves employ forced labour systems. However, the narrowly-based, oligarchic nature of the regimes in Central America complemented the economic interests of the companies. The coercion of the peasantry allowed wages for coffee-pickers to be extremely low,[15] and this in turn ensured a virtually unlimited supply of labour for the banana companies, whose wage levels were considerably higher.

Further, the lack of popular support for the oligarchic regimes made them easily dominated by the banana companies. In this century perhaps no governments in the hemisphere were so closely allied with narrow corporate interests as those in Central America, and particularly the governments of Guatemala and Honduras. While the banana companies were capitalist enterprises, their operations had little modernising effect on Central American society. The modernisation of Central America would have required the destruction of the power of landed property, followed by a land reform which would lead to the type of class differentiation which occurred in Costa Rica. Through this differentiation peasant life would have been monetised and commercialised, generating a domestic market for industry. This in fact was the Arévalo-Arbenz programme for the modernisation of Guatemala.[16] Land reform, however, threatened the banana companies as well as the traditional oligarchy, so the two groups were united in opposition to the keystone of any modernisation programme.[17]

The banana era, 1890-1940, transformed Central American society relatively little. For the most part, the plantations were located on previously unused land, and production had few linkages, other than financial, to the rest of the economy. In consequence, the companies proved the ideal ally for the old order, generating a spillover of wealth for the local elites, but creating few contradictions with the anachronistic system of labour coercion.[18] Much more important in transforming social relations in a capitalist manner was the development of cotton production after the Second World War. The spread of coffee production in the nineteenth century had involved the forcible dispossession of the peasantry from lands suitable for the export crop, except in Costa Rica where economic factors achieved the dispossession. This dispossession did not, however, result in the expelling of the peasantry from the land, but rather pushed it onto marginal, sub-self-sufficiency plots, creating a part-time labour force for the plantations.

A second great wave of dispossession occurred after the Second World War, in the Pacific lowlands of Nicaragua, El Salvador and Guatemala, to create large cotton estates. This second wave did result in expelling peasants from the land, creating a large class of landless rural workers. The cotton plantations were from the outset based on wage labour, without the servile labour systems or antiquated land tenure relations of the coffee zones. Thus, the growth of cotton production, unlike the expansion of coffee and bananas, transformed rural society in the zones where it developed. Coffee had transformed neither labour relations nor the tenure of land; bananas had transformed labour relations, but in previously unoccupied lands, leaving land tenure elsewhere unaffected.

But again, the cotton boom was based upon landed property and exports, which created a strong commonality of interest between the cotton capitalists and the traditional coffee oligarchy. With few exceptions, the two groups did not compete over land, since coffee and cotton thrive in different ecological zones. Since cotton production based itself upon large-scale enterprise and landless labourers, land reform threatened the cotton capitalists as much as it did the coffee aristocracy. And because all cotton was exported, capitalists had little interest in reform of land tenure outside the cotton zone which would commercialise peasant life and expand internal markets.

Thus, the particular way in which capitalism developed in Central America from 1890 to the middle of the twentieth century tended to strengthen the rule of the old order. Reactionary despotism in Central America, strong in the nineteenth century, grew even more powerful in the twentieth, based on a *troika* of landed property – the coffee oligarchy, the banana companies and the cotton capitalists. The first significant source of productive wealth not based on landed property emerged in the 1960s, with the formation of the Central American Common Market (CACM).

Nationalists in Central America have attacked the CACM as a vehicle for multinational capital (particularly US) to dominate the economy of the region.[19] This is not a very compelling argument. Prior to the formation of the CACM, in no area of the hemisphere of comparable size was US capital as hegemonic as in Central America, and it is unclear what advantage foreign capital gained as a result of regional economic integration. It is clear, however, that the CACM was implemented in a manner that minimised any conflict between regional integration and the agro-export economy upon which the power of landed property was based. First, the regional tariff protection granted to industry was quite moderate by Latin American standards, maintaining the relative openness of the five economies.[20] While the import-substitution industries created could not have been viable without tariff protection and are now in ruins due to the collapse of the regional agreement, studies show that the differential between intra-CACM prices and world prices was relatively modest.[21] As a result, relative profitability of production for extra-regional export and intra-regional trade did not alter dramatically.

Second, steps were taken to ensure that the fostering of intra-regional trade would not drain resources from the agro-export sector. It is this conflict over credit, foreign exchange and state expenditure on infrastructure which brought export-producers and capitalists oriented to the internal market into conflict in a number of South American countries. Within this conflict over scarce resources lies the struggle for economic modernisation, since export sectors have characteristically been dominated by pre-capitalist landed oligarchies.[22] The growth of import-substitution industries in Central America produced no such modernising conflict. Domestic credit allocation in the four northern Central American countries continued to favour agro-exporters, both in quantity and 'softness' of conditions. Foreign capital played its role by providing the financing of new industries so that the growth of manufacturing did not conflict with the credit demands of the agro-exporters.

Foreign exchange is a resource over which exporters and capitalists oriented to the domestic market have struggled in Latin America. Characteristically, exporters earn foreign exchange and domestic industry consumes it, for intermediate inputs and machinery. The struggle by domestic industry to redistribute foreign exchange tends to generate qualitative foreign exchange controls which make the national currency in effect non-convertible except through the state. But in Central America, every currency remained freely convertible throughout the effective life of the CACM. The agro-exporting oligarchy never allowed serious restrictions upon the monetary form of their revenues nor upon the movement of those revenues in and out of the region. The Central American states are the only under-developed countries in the hemisphere to have pursued an import-substitution policy with freely-convertible currencies.[23]

A third aspect of the subsumption of the CACM strategy to agro-export interests involved the extensive complementarity between agricultural and manufacturing production. Regional manufacturing growth was not merely tolerated by the old order, but assumed a pattern which directly benefited it. A number of industries developed behind the tariff wall which used by-products of the agro-exports or the low-quality output of those products as inputs. In the cotton-producing states (Guatemala, El Salvador and Nicaragua), new factories rendered cotton seed into cooking oil for the regional market. Throughout the region low-grade coffee beans, unsuitable for the world market, provided the input for domestic instant coffee. Cattle-ranchers – the Somoza family being one of the largest – benefited by selling hides to the protected shoe industry, again with high-quality hides exported and the lower grade for domestic demand. Not all manufacturing development within the CACM benefited the agro-export producers. For example, the protected fertiliser and insecticide sectors replaced cheaper imports with higher-cost domestic production. But overall, the organisation of the CACM reflected the dominance of landed property and its orientation to extra-regional trade.

Thus, the commercialisation of Central America through coffee, the entry of foreign capital via bananas and the emergence of cotton as a major export all served to strengthen and solidify the hold of landed property over the economic and political life of the region. When industrialisation came to the region, it was managed and directed in a manner subservient to landed property, and the modernising effect of industrialisation was minimised. Certainly, in no part of Latin America has the landlord class been so successful in holding back political modernisation as in Central America.

Challenges to the Old Order

Until now, we have considered the development of the 'reactionary despotism' of the old order in Central America as if it progressed smoothly through the nineteenth and twentieth centuries. In this century, however, the rule of the landed oligarchy faced major challenges, but proved able to overcome and crush them until the general crisis of oligarchic hegemony in the 1970s. The most important of these challenges were Sandino's rebellion, the Salvadoran peasant revolt of 1932 and the reformist regimes of Arévalo and Arbenz.

Our purpose is not to recount these events, but to identify their long-term impact upon oligarchic rule in the region. Prior to the 1930s, the armies of the Central American states had been ill-trained, poorly-armed and rather incohesive bodies. These armies played minor roles in internal politics, pawns in the political game rather than makers and breakers of governments. Sandino's rebellion and the Salvadoran insurrection of 1932 permanently altered the role of the military. US troops were stationed in Nicaragua beginning in 1912, but their primary role for the first ten years was to prevent intra-oligarchic struggles from erupting into civil war. In 1925 the troops withdrew, only to return a year later and play a considerably expanded role. In response to popular outrage over what was now an occupying army, Augusto Sandino launched a guerrilla war which eventually drew in several thousand US troops, supported by air power. By any objective judgement, Sandino defeated the occupying army and forced its withdrawal from Nicaragua.[24]

Sandino's insurrection demonstrated forcibly to Washington the limits to a policy of direct military intervention in Central America. The expense of the intervention and opposition to it within the United States prompted a shift in policy towards creating professional, US-trained armies to maintain the established order. This policy was applied with great success in Nicaragua itself, with the creation of the National Guard. In other countries of the region (and elsewhere in the hemisphere) the policy was also pursued, expanding dramatically after the Second World War. One consequence of the policy was to create armies in Central America which had the cohesion and power to impose themselves upon the political arena. This, in turn, resulted in a militarisation of political life and an institutionalising of armed terror as the basis of the stability of oligarchical rule.

Coinciding with the shift in US policy from one of direct military intervention to fostering local armies was the Salvadoran peasant revolt of 1932, which shook the confidence of the landed oligarchy throughout the region. The Great Depression brought economic hardship to El Salvador, particularly falling wages and unemployment for coffee workers. A mildly reformist president, Arturo Araujo, won election in 1930, and proved too tolerant of dissent for the taste of the coffee oligarchy. In late 1931, the oligarchy encouraged the army to depose him, and he was replaced by his vice-president, Maximiliano Hernández Martínez. Hernández Martínez himself was a general, though the army had little independent political power at the time.

A few months later, a general insurrection broke out in the countryside. The insurrection never posed a serious threat to the oligarchy, with the victims of the wrath of the peasantry numbering only about 30. However, the rebellion threw the landed oligarchy into a frenzy of repression, and the army retaliated by massacring from 15,000 to 20,000 peasants.[25] The effect of the insurrection was to transform profoundly Salvadoran politics.[26] Subsequently, the landed oligarchy lived in fear of a resurgence of popular rebellion. Obsessed by this brief challenge to its despotic rule, the oligarchy ceded to the military considerable freedom of action, and after 1932 the military controlled political succession in El Salvador.[26]

But also in Honduras and Guatemala the combined effect of US military aid and fear of mass insurrection made the army the controlling force in political succession. This combination of the oligarchy and a strong military, maturing in the 1950s, further closed political systems which were already rigidified anachronisms. Indeed, defeat of the military and its dismantling had become a pre-condition, not just for revolution, but for modernisation and reform.

In the four northern states of Central America, the first serious attempt to reform the old order came immediately after the Second World War in Guatemala. In 1945, the long-reigning dictator, Jorge Ubico, fell to a coup of young, progressive military men, who then passed power to Juan José Arévalo, who gained a landslide victory in Guatemala's first free presidential election. By hemispheric comparison, the reforms of the popularly elected Arévalo and Arbenz governments (1945 to 1954) were quite mild. Both presidents were explicit in their goal of transforming Guatemala into a modern, pluralist and capitalist society, and this project attacked the basis of oligarchic rule. In the 1950s in Central America the development of liberal capitalism presented itself as revolutionary as the same development had been in Western Europe 200 years before. But in Guatemala, the alliance based on landed property, along with considerable help from Washington, overthrew the reformist coalition and restructured society in even more despotic form. The crucial importance of the Guatemalan military in precipitating the resignation of Arbenz cast doubt on the possibility of peaceful reform.

In several Latin American countries over the last 40 years the military has demonstrated a tendency to play a nationalistic and modernising role: the Velasco government in Peru is perhaps the best example. In Central America, the events of the 1930s forged a powerful, cohesive alliance between the military and oligarchy, backed without qualms by Washington, and this combination proved an impressive bulwark against modernisation. Except for very brief moments, only in Guatemala has a reformist faction emerged from the ranks of the military, and there the reaction of the oligarchy was brutally fierce. Thus, reformers could hold out little hope that the military would acquiesce in their project. This cohesive reactionary role of the military not only precluded reform through election, but implied that it could only be achieved through the extreme and catastrophic vehicle of civil war.

Reactionary Despotism Runs its Course

In an insightful observation, Baloyra-Herp comments that what is surprising about Central America today is not that the old order is collapsing, but that it managed to endure so long.[27] Indeed, this is the analytical issue, and while we have described the nature of the old order, we have only partly accounted for its persistence in Honduras, Guatemala and El Salvador. Obviously, it persists because of its strength, and particularly the close alliance between the oligarchy and the military. But landed oligarchies elsewhere in the hemisphere had equal zest to survive and failed to do so.

We suggest two explanations for the hardiness of reaction in Central America, economic adaptation and what Baloyra-Herp calls *regimes d'exception*. Earlier, we traced the commercialisation of Central America through coffee, bananas and cotton, and argued that economic development never broke free from a landed property basis. Perhaps the primary source of survival for the oligarchy was its success in preventing the development of economic power divorced from the ownership of land. As a consequence, major conflicts of economic interest did not emerge among the dominant classes. However, of equal importance over the last 50 years has been the involution of each of the four northern countries into grotesquely deformed political systems, each unique and a virtual parody of itself. The landed oligarchy has held back modernisation in each country only by generating deformed vehicles of political control and succession.

Nicaragua until the fall of Somoza was the most grotesque case: a country ruled by a family with presidential succession based on kinship. The other unique characteristic of Somoza's Nicaragua was the role of the military establishment, which served not even as the army of the elite, but as the personal army of the dictator. While the Somoza family was aggressively capitalist in the way it used the state as a vehicle for private gain, its form of rule was profundly anti-modern. The personalised character of the dictatorship blocked the development of pluralism even among the elite as well as the development of political institutions through which portions of the middle and lower classes could be coopted into political life. Obviously not a democracy, Nicaragua under Somoza was not even a republic of the oligarchy.

In Honduras a unique system also emerged, though its character has been partly concealed by the façade of electoral politics. Since the turn of the century, Honduras has been ruled by the banana companies, and while the control of governments by foreign capital has not been rare in Latin America, in Honduras this has been so overwhelming and foreign capital so monolithic that the relationship defies comparison.[28] The extreme deformation of political life in Nicaragua and Honduras – rule by a family in the former and by a product line in the latter – reflects in part the weakness of the oligarchies in both states. In Guatemala and El Salvador, the cohesion of the oligarchies precluded a personalistic dynasty or overt domination by narrow corporate interests (though United Fruit was extremely powerful in Guatemala). The exceptional nature of the Guatemalan political system has since 1954 taken the form of institutionalised state terrorism, in which the oligarchy via the military has waged open warfare against all reformist elements. While state-directed repression has been at least an occasional characteristic of almost all Latin American countries since the end of the Second World War, in no other country has it been systematic and virtually continuous. In part this reflects the character of the military-oligarchic alliance, which a CIA report called 'the most extreme and unyielding in the hemisphere'.[29] This intransigence itself arises to a considerable degree from the strength of the reformist movement during 1945-54. In effect, all-pervasive state violence has been a largely successful attempt to roll back reform, rather than co-opting it along conservative lines.

The exceptional nature of the Salvadoran political system has been less of a deformation than a pure anachronism. Here, the landed oligarchy managed to maintain a hold on political and economic power unique even in Central America. In consequence, El Salvador in the 1960s probably represented the last Latin country in the hemisphere with a predominantly pre-capitalist agricultural sector. In 1961, only 19 per cent of tenant farmers paid their rents in cash, and while the proportion rose over the next ten years, it was still less than one-third according to the agricultural census of 1971.[30]

The process of commercialisation and capitalist development tends to generate a class differentiation of society which calls forth the political ideology of liberalism, with its secularisation of a state nominally based upon the principle that governments rule by the consent of the governed. The tension between the principles of eighteenth-century liberalism and the concentration of economic power inherent in capitalist society has been a motive force in the political evolution of Latin American countries out of their feudal Hispanic heritage. By the end of the Second World War, the elites of Latin America had generally conceded the principles of liberalism while seeking to undermine them in practice.

Not so in Central America. Here, the oligarchies still rule in Guatemala and Honduras, have yet to concede defeat in El Salvador and hope for a triumphant return to Managua. Even as abstract principles, the ideals of the French Revolution or of the more conservative North American Revolution remain radical doctrines. This astounding anachronism was maintained north of Costa Rica by an almost pathological deformation of political life in four countries: dynastic succession, foreign corporate domination, systemic terror and a hegemonic pre-capitalist landed oligarchy. But in 1979, mass insurrection transformed Nicaragua, and now Salvadoran society is collapsing under the weight of civil war. Throughout the region, landed property can no longer hold back the tide of accumulated contradictions. Only massive US military intervention can sustain these profoundly anachronistic regimes, for oligarchic rule in Central America has run its course.

US policy towards the four northern states of Central America has for the last decade been based on the presumption that social reform and political accommodation could be managed within the parameters of the old order. For example, in 1979, the Carter administration sought a solution to the Nicaraguan crisis which would have involved the resignation of the last Somoza, but the maintenance of the National Guard. Such a solution was as unacceptable to the moderates as to the revolutionaries. In El Salvador, a similar strategy has been followed: social reform and electoral politics within the context of a state and military establishment which exists to maintain oligarchic rule. As in Nicaragua, the pre-condition even for reform is the total reorganisation of civil and military authority, if not the complete destruction of that authority. In Nicaragua and El Salvador it was not a question of events having progressed to a point that it was 'too late' for peaceful reform, but that the nature of the military-oligarchic alliances always precluded peaceful reform.

The US policy failures in Nicaragua and El Salvador, with more to come in Honduras and Guatemala, reflect a mistaken conceptualisation of Central American history. Policy-makers, and many of their critics in the United States, view Central American history on the presumption that they are facing forward, with the future unfolding before them, capable of anticipating and managing that future. It would be more correct to recognise that in Central America we are looking back, at the most recent manifestation of a reactionary past, with the future bearing down on us from the blind-side, unseen, perhaps catastrophic in unanticipated ways.

Notes

1. Most notably, the Kissinger Commission Report. See United States Government, *Report of the National Bipartisan Commission on Central America*

(New York: Macmillan, 1984).

2. Our characterisation of the 'old order' in Central America has much in common with the analysis of Baloyra-Herp, who uses the term 'reactionary despotism' to describe the regimes of the region. See Enrique A. Baloyra-Herp, 'Reactionary Despotism in Central America', *Journal of Latin American Studies*, vol. 15, no. 2 (1983).

3. 'Country-status' is used in place of 'nationhood', because we refer to control of territory, independence of governments and state institutions, as well as the development of national identity.

4. Surveys of the colonial period may be found in Woodward and Parker. Ralph Lee Woodward Jr., *Central America:A Nation Divided* (New York: Oxford University Press, 1973); and Franklin Parker, *The Central American Republics* (New York: Oxford University Press, 1965).

5. The process by which Central America gained independence and the subsequent formation and collapse of the federation is analysed by many writers writers. See Thomas Karns, *The Failure of Union: Central America, 1824-1960* (Chapel Hill: University of North Carolina Press, 1981).

6. These interventions are given in Walter LaFeber, *Inevitable Revolutions: The United States in Central America* (New York: W.W. Norton, 1983).

7. The manifesto of this group, *El Real Consulado*, is discussed in Mario Rodriquez, *The Cádiz Experiment in Central America* (Berkeley: University of California Press, 1978).

8. For an excellent discussion, see Martinez Pelaez, *La Patria del Criollo* (San Jose: EDUCA, 1979).

9. The collapse of the federation was the direct result of a peasant insurrection, allied with upper-class Conservatives. See Mario Rodriquez, *Central America* (Englewood Cliffs: Prentice-Hall, 1965), Ch. 2; and Woodward, *Central America*, Ch. 4.

10. See Chester Lloyd Jones, *Guatemala: Past and Present* (Minneapolis: University of Minnesota Press, 1940); and Parker, *Central American Republics*, pp. 120ff. The process of dispossession and rigidification of the coercive labour system was well advanced by the 1870s. See Baloyra-Herp, 'Reactionary Despotism', pp. 297-8.

11. See Parker, *Central American Republics*, p. 125; and on page 194, where he quotes from the constitutions of Guatemala and El Salvador.

12. The current regime in Chile is an exception.

13. This process of land concentration is described in Mitchell A. Seligson, *Peasants of Costa Rica and the Development of Agrarian Capitalism* (Madison: University of Wisconsin Press, 1980).

14. Based on 1970 data, the Gini coefficient for land distribution for all of Central America was .59 and .62 for Costa Rica. Banco Inter-Americano para Desarrollo, Instituto para la Integracion de America Latina (BID/INTAL), *El desarrollo integrado de Centroamerica: desarrollo agricola* (Buenos Aires: BID, 1973), p. 82. On political control by aristocratic families, see Seligson, *Peasants of Costa Rica*, p. 45.

15. A study in the 1950s showed that wages for coffee-pickers in El Salvador were lower than in the Ivory Coast by 20 per cent, even though per capita income was higher in the latter country and Salvadoran coffee commanded a higher price on the world market. Cited in Alastair White, *El Salvador* (New York: Praeger, 1973), p. 123.

16. See Stephen Schlesinger and Stephen Kinzer, *Bitter Fruit* (Garden City: Doubleday, 1982), Chs . 2 and 3. Even pro-US writers describe the reforms of Guatemala's two freely-elected presidents as 'moderate'. For example, Rodriquez,

Central America, p. 142.

17. Commenting on Guatemala, Parker observes, 'when Ubico was president, the government and United Fruit worked hand-in-hand, both profiting at the expense of the laborer in the fields'. Parker, *Central American Republics*, p. 117.

18. The eventual growth of trade unions on the plantations did challenge the despotism of landed property, particularly in the case of a major strike in Honduras in the mid-1950s.

19. See Tomas Borge, et al., *Sandinstas Speak* (New York: Pathfinder Press, 1982).

20. See John Weeks, *The Economies of Central America* (New York: Holmes and Meier, 1985), Ch. 4.

21. See BID/INTAL, *El desarrollo integrado de Centroamerica: desarrollo industrial integrado* (Buenos Aires: BID, 1973), pp. 28ff.

22. For an analysis of this conflict in Peru, see Elizabeth Dore and John Weeks, 'The Intensification of the Attack against the Working Class in "Revolutionary" Peru', *Latin American Perspectives*, vol. 3, no. 2 (1977).

23. The exchange rate between the dollar and the currencies of Guatemala, Honduras, El Salvador and Nicaragua remained the same from the end of the Second World War until a devaluation of the Nicaraguan cordoba in early 1979. The Costa Rican colon was devalued during this period, but remained freely convertible.

24. Sandino's insurrection is described briefly in Woodward, *Central America*, and the definitive work on the Nicaraguan nationalist is Gregorio Selser, *Sandino* (New York: Monthly Review Press, 1981).

25. For a thorough presentation of the revolt, see Thomas P. Anderson, *El Salvador's Communist Revolt of 1932* (Lincoln: University of Nebraska Press, 1971).

26. See White, *El Salvador*, p. 95.

27. Baloyra-Herp, 'Reactionary Despotism', pp. 314-15.

28. See LaFeber, *Inevitable Revolutions*, and Philip L. Shepherd, 'The USS *Honduras:* United States Policy and the Destabilization of Honduras' (Miami: Florida International University, unpublished ms, 1984).

29. Quoted in LaFeber, *Inevitable Revolutions*, p. 171.

30. For a discussion of land tenure in El Salvador, see Weeks, *Economies of Central America*, Ch. 5.

7 BRIDGE OR BARRIER? THE CATHOLIC CHURCH AND THE CENTRAL AMERICAN CRISIS

Margaret E. Crahan

Introduction

Conflicting stereotypes of the Roman Catholic Church have tended to obscure the actual role of that institution in the present crisis in Central America. Over the past 25 years scholars, politicians, the media and others have variously described the church as a support of the status quo, champion of centrist reformers and the defender of revolutionaries and subversives. Churchpeople have themselves been described as right-wing reactionaries, liberal reformers and Marxists. Much of the confusion results from the fact that historically the Catholic Church in Central America pursued a strategy of elite insertion, or cultivation of the bourgeoisie, in order to achieve its goals which were not only aimed at the salvation of all, but also at institutional preservation. This strategy emphasised identification with political, economic and social elites in order to ensure influence and resources for ecclesiastical projects. Such tactics tended to distance the church from the largely poor majority in Central America. However, by the 1950s, clerical and lay leaders began to engage in wide-ranging reassessments of church strategies, particularly in the face of increasing inroads by secular and religious competitors, such as political parties, labour unions, student groups and Protestant missionaries from the US. The initial response was to focus on revitalising the traditional source of Catholic support, the bourgeoisie, and evangelising those who previously had not been targeted, primarily urban slum-dwellers and the rural poor. In the face of escalating socio-economic pressures, particularly from the lower classes in post Second World War Central America, and increased political experimentation, this strategy propelled the Catholic Church into the centre of political struggle.

While some clerical leaders and a good proportion of the laity felt some misgivings over this, the reformist/self-preservationist impulse of the church took on a dynamic of its own and gained ground in the late 1960s and 1970s, reinforced by the second Vatican Council (1962-5) and the Latin American bishops' conference at Medellín, Colombia, in 1968. These two gatherings, which were intended to better equip the institutional church and its personnel to deal with the challenges of the modern world, tended to stimulate the more progressive sectors in the church to undertake theological, spiritual and political experiments that catapulted the Catholic Church squarely into the centre of political strife, particularly in societies that were highly conflictual. The impact of such developments on the Central American churches was strongly felt. This was in part a consequence of the presence of large numbers of foreign clerics, particularly Jesuits, Maryknollers and Capuchins. Exposed via their international networks to theological, pastoral and political innovations in other areas, a minority of priests and religious began in the late 1960s and early 1970s to establish base Christian communities (CEBs), workers' co-operatives, social welfare programmes, student groups and other organisations infused with the emerging theology of liberation.

In its earliest versions, this theology strongly challenged certain elements of the traditional Catholic strategy of elite insertion in favour of exercising a preferential option for the poor. Identification with the poor at a time of growing political and economic demands by the popular classes, led to the categorisation of the church as subversive by defenders of elite dominance. This resulted in the beginnings of repression of churchpeople and the first disappearances, torture and assassination of priests, religious and lay preachers known as Delegates of the Word. In the face of such repression, political, theological, pastoral and doctrinal divisions within the church tended to decrease as churchpeople united to denounce gross violations of human rights. This contributed to a growing tendency of the Catholic Church in Central America to support broad-based societal change. Agreement over the nature of this change and how to accomplish it was not achieved by churchpeople. Hence the apparent contradiction of support for insurrectionary movements such as that which toppled Nicaragua's Somoza in 1979 being followed by increasing criticism and sharpening attacks on the Sandinista leadership once it was in power. This clearly demonstrates that while the church has become more committed to change, there are limits to the type and degree of change the church is willing to accept. This is largely determined by the carry-over of historic Catholic attitudes and positions.

The stereotype of the revolutionary Catholic Church consequently ignores continuities in theology, social doctrine and bureaucratic processes. In spite of the oft-expressed preferential option of the poor, the institutional church and its membership reflect a variety of progressive, centrist and conservative stances with respect to how to accomplish societal change to benefit the poor in Central America. The image of the church as a unified institution bears little resemblance to its reality today. What is true is that in societies in which institutions with a national presence have traditionally been largely absent, the church plays a unique role. In addition, it possesses a degree of moral authority unmatched by other Central American institutions. While the church is more present in the daily lives of the faithful, it has not abandoned many of its traditional principles, including a commitment to a vision of society as non-conflictual, acceptance of Western liberal democracy and capitalism, albeit reformed, and a strong residue of anti-Marxism. All these have influenced the responses of the church to the Central American crisis.

The interplay of these continuities, together with the on-going definition of new positions within the church, has contributed to sometimes contradictory actions. It has also fuelled the expression of opposite positions by different sectors within the same national churches. Given these contradictions and divisions, the question arises whether the church can play a major role in solving the present crisis. The answer lies in an examination of what contributions the church has already made to the search for non-violent solutions to conflict in El Salvador, Nicaragua, Guatemala and Honduras.[1] This chapter analyses the strength of the church in each country in an effort to evaluate its capacity to be a major influence on the contending parties. In addition, the strategies used by the church in dealing with the crisis will be examined in order to establish their efficacy. Finally, the objectives of the church in each country will be explored to establish whether they are consonant with the working out of pragmatic political solutions to the crisis.

El Salvador

The role of mediator between the government of President Napoleón Duarte and the opposition Democratic Revolutionary Front (FDR) and Farabundo Martí National Liberation Front (FMLN) currently being played by the leadership of the Salvadoran Catholic Church is one which it has sought for some time and is consonant with the support of San Salvador Archbishop Arturo Rivera y Damas for the Christian Democratic government of José Napoleón Duarte. The mediating efforts of the episcopacy are also a response to the increasingly popular demands for a national dialogue and the church's own historical view of itself as a peace-maker. Given the moral bankruptcy of most institutions in Salvadoran society, the bishops are virtually the only leaders with the national reputation to exercise some moral suasion. Divisions with the church as a result of varied political commitments, as well as distrust of churchpeople, particularly by the extreme right and extreme left, limit their impact. Whether the church contributes substantially to the resolution of the Salvadoran crisis will depend on its capacity to mobilise public sentiment in favour of specific options. The fact that the leadership of the church is split, however, limits the church's role in any process of mobilisation of the public in support of a particular option.

The identification of the most influential of the Salvadoran bishops with the Christian Democratic Party (PDC) has its roots in the post Second World War search by clerical and lay elites for reformist rather than revolutionary solutions to increasing societal pressures and conflicts in El Salvador. In this context, the attraction of Christian Democracy for the Catholic Church lay in its espousal of non-violent evolutionary reform and commitment to traditional values. In the 1960s and 1970s, such an orientation had particular appeal for many clerics and lay Catholics.[2]

The difficulties of effecting sufficient change to still popular demands in a society as unequal and repressive as Salvador's became increasingly obvious to a fair number of church activists during the course of the 1970s. As early as the 1970 elections, some church activists became discouraged about the possibilities of change via the PDC. These included a number of Christian Democratic Youth, some of whom joined with Communist Party members and independent leftists to form the Revolutionary Army of the People (Ejército Revolucionario del Pueblo – ERP). Others determined to work within the PDC to revamp it and make it more directly responsive to the needs of the popular classes.[3] Both these trends were reinforced by reformist impulses generated by Vatican II and Medellín which were increasingly felt in El Salvador.

Increasingly, the detention, torture and assassination of priests, religious and Delegates of the Word, among others, prompted the church leadership to become more vocal in denouncing repression. The level of the repression directed against the church is evidenced by the fact that between 5 January 1980 and 27 February 1981, there were some 300 attacks against the church, including 39 assassinations, 19 bombings and 43 attacks on church buildings.[4] Denunciation of attacks against the church, and of gross violations of the rights of the general populace, have sometimes been interpreted as meaning that the church was united with the opposition to the government. This was not, and is not, the case. In fact, the Catholic Church in El Salvador continues to reflect the full spectrum of political opinion in that country, which suggests that if it were to attempt to promote a specific option, it would exacerbate divisions within the church.

The hierarchy itself is split, with Bishops José Eduardo Alvarez (San Miguel), Pedro Arnaldo Aparicio (San Vicente) and Marco René Revello (Santa Ana) holding considerably more conservative views than Archbishop Arturo Rivera y Damas, and Bishops Gregorio Rosa Chavez and Ricardo Urioste of San Salvador. The former tend to have an hierarchical view of society, leading them to emphasise respect for political and episcopal authority and rejecting experimentation whether it be in pastoral forms or socio-economic structures. The majority of the priests under their authority reflect their views. Hence, progressive clerics are concentrated in the Archbishopric of San Salvador and particularly at the Jesuits' Central American university, José Simeon Canas (UCA), which is the other principal Catholic actor in El Salvador.

Established in 1966, UCA rapidly became the epicentre of progressive theological and pastoral currents in El Salvador. By 1970, it was championing agrarian reform and condemning repression and exploitation of the poor. By 1975, it had become the target of rightist attacks and in 1977 the Jesuits were given notice by right-wing elements to leave El Salvador or be killed. This precipitated an international uproar that succeeded in reducing the threats against the Jesuits and UCA. It also persuaded the Jesuits to adopt a more discreet *modus operandi*. This has led them since 1977 to emphasise research and analysis together with refugee work. Hence, while they constitute an important sector of the intellectual and ecclesiastical elite in El Salvador, they are not an active force for conflict resolution in El Salvador. Furthermore, their political orientation is generally more progressive than the most liberal of the bishops, which suggests that they are unlikely readily to accept their lead in supporting a specific political option. Within the Salvadoran Catholic Church, then, the principal actors – the divided bishops and the Jesuits – are not in a position to unite and mobilise broad-based popular support for a particular option.

What is more likely is that the Archbishop of San Salvador and his colleagues, Rosa Chavez and Urioste, reflecting the popular demand for peace and their historical closeness to that sector of the Christian Democratic Party led by Napoleón Duarte, will continue to encourage and facilitate the peace talks. There is no indication at this time, however, that they are playing, or will play, a substantive role in those conversations. Hence their capacity to influence is limited to reinforcing and giving voice to the general desire for peace and an end to repression. While they can help bridge the gap between the FDR/FMLN and the Duarte government, it does not appear that they have much control over the success or failure of negotiations.

Nicaragua

The Catholic Church in El Salvador, in spite of its limitations, has substantially more opportunities to serve as a bridge between the government and the opposition than the church in Nicaragua. The bishops have limited credibility among the Sandinistas and the Archbishop of Managua, Monsignor Miguel Ovando y Bravo, is the most outspoken critic of the government within the country. Hence when the episcopacy, on 22 April 1984, called for thc initiation of dialogue between the Sandinistas and the US backed counter-revolutionaries, the suggestion was sharply rejected by the former.

Interior Minister Tomás Borge characterised the bishops' call for talks as criminal on the grounds that it encouraged the armed opposition.[5]

Both the bishops' position and that of Borge reflect the substantial gap which has developed between the episcopacy and the Sandinistas since the overthrow of Anastasio Somoza in July 1979. Just prior to that event the hierarchy had dealt a substantial blow to the legitimacy of Somoza's government by supporting the insurrection on the grounds that the government had engaged in gross violations of civil, political rights and socio-economic rights. The bishops' support for the insurrection, they cautioned, was not a *carte blanche* for any form of government. Rather, the hierarchy stated any new government must strive to maintain political pluralism and promote popular participation.[6]

Immediately after the overthrow of Somoza, the bishops amplified their cautionary words, while at the same time publicly expressing their support for the new Junta de Gobierno de Reconstrucción Nacional (Governmental Junta of National Reconstruction, JGRN). In a 30 July 1979 pastoral the hierarchy warned all Nicaraguans to beware of foreign 'imperialisms' and to concentrate on building political and social structures rooted in Nicaraguan needs. The latter were to reflect human values that promoted authentic liberation and opposed state idolatries. Special care was to be taken to avoid the 'massification' of society, a word which has traditionally been used by the Catholic Church to refer to the building of a one-party Marxist state.[7]

By the autumn of 1979, fear of Marxist inroads and radicalisation of the Sandinista revolution prompted Catholic clerics and laity to criticise the government. In a 17 November 1979 pastoral letter, the bishops demonstrated their growing preoccupation with the possibility that the creation of Sandinista mass organisations and programmes such as the literacy campaign would encourage atheism and the abandonment of the church by the people.[8] Such fears tended to underline the importance of maintaining a unified church position *vis-à-vis* the government, which led to some ambiguity in official church statements. While the bishops were expressing some disquiet over the direction of the revolution, they accepted the incorporation of over 20 priests into the government, five at the ministerial level, in order to facilitate Catholic influence over the revolutionary process. The presence of priests in public office flowed out of the high level of clerical support for the insurrection,[9] and the fact that in 1979 less than 1 per cent of Nicaraguans had a university education. Priests and religious were members of a very small group with any preparation for high office.

The initial receptivity of the institutional church to priests in government eroded as the hierarchy became more and more alienated from the Sandinistas. After a two-day meeting in July 1981, it was agreed by the priests and the Nicaraguan Episcopal Conference that the former would retain their public offices, but would not use their clerical status to support the government. However, their very presence in government, particularly as relations between the bishops and the Sandinistas worsened, tended to focus attention on a church engaged in sharp political and ideological struggle. The result was an increasingly divided church in which a visible progressive minority helped legitimise the Sandinista government as the bishops were attempting to delegitimise it.

As early as 1980 the Sandinistas had tried to respond to the preoccupations of the episcopacy by preparing a position paper that affirmed the government's intention to respect religious freedom and the role of the Catholic Church in Nicaraguan society. The Sandinistas did, however, assert government authority to decide if political parties or individuals were attempting to convert religious activities into political events. The bishops reacted negatively, issuing a detailed criticism of the Sandinista statement. It reflected fear of the emergence of a single-party state that promoted atheism.[10] Growing tensions between the episcopacy and the Sandinistas increased divisions within the church, as indicated by the criticism of the bishops' statement by a number of CEBs, youth and student organisations, the Jesuits, CONFER and some social action and study groups.[11]

Such groups constitute the core of the progressive sector of the church, headed by the Central American Historical Institute at the Jesuit-run Central American University and the Antonio Valdivieso Ecumenical Centre. Both these institutions, together with some parishes, CEBs, youth and student organisations, Jesuits, Maryknollers, Capuchins and others, constitute the progressive axis that serves as a counter-weight to episcopal criticism of the government. Neither the progressives nor the bishops are totally united and the majority of Nicaraguan churchpeople appear disinclined fully to accept either position. Hence, while the general populace has a high degree of loyalty to the church, the divisions within the church have left them unsure of which direction to follow. This decreases the possibility that either the bishops or the progressive churchpeople will mobilise the populace behind a single political strategy.

The distance between the progressives and the bishops was highlighted during the 1983 visit of John Paul II to Nicaragua. In León, John Paul insisted upon the right of parents to determine the type of education they desired for their children and the right of Catholic schools to be free from governmental interference.[12] This speech was prompted by widespread Catholic resistance to the government's attempts to reform elementary and secondary school curriculums in both public and private schools. The latter are partially funded by the government: 25 to 30 per cent of all Nicaraguan students attend Catholic schools. In a 8 December 1982 pastoral letter the hierarchy expressed concern that the new curriculum would promote a conflictual interpretation of society that would heighten tensions between classes. The bishops also thought it would undermine Christian values. The Sandinistas responded that under the new curriculum private schools would actually have more opportunity to incorporate their own materials than previously.[13]

The other issue on which John Paul focused was the exercise of authority within the church and the obligation of the clergy and faithful to accept episcopal teaching on doctrine and morals. He specifically criticised the 'popular church' constituted by progressive and pro-Sandinista Catholics. John Paul's criticism was rooted in the belief that the existence of a 'popular church' diminished the authority of the bishops, undercut doctrinal orthodoxy and opened the church to Marxist inroads.[14]

The level of church-state tension in Nicaragua in 1983 was clearly demonstrated by the uproar that occurred during the Pope's open-air mass in Managua, where pro-government chanting occasionally drowned the Pope out. This incident has been variously interpreted. The progressives criticised the Pope's speeches on the grounds that they

> seemed admonishing and negative, lacking any connection with the people he addressed. In its religious aspect the language was political. The theological subjects dealt with were beyond the scope of comprehension . . . of the great majority of the people.[15]

Opponents of the Sandinistas within the church rejoiced. The *Washington Post* reported:

> 'The Pope has helped us a hell of a lot,' said a wealthy business opponent of the government. 'That's the best thing that could have happened to us.'
>
> His comment reflected a widely held assessment that the church hierarchy increasingly could become the focus of political opposition in this overwhelmingly Catholic country. Under Ovando y Bravo's uncompromising leadership, it is considered more able to attract mass following than the alliance of conservative parties and business groups that constitutes the Sandinistas' tolerated political opposition.[16]

Coming as it did after an upsurge in military attacks across the Honduran border by anti-Sandinista forces, the visit and the Pope's statements appear to have bolstered conservative elements within the church and the country. The visit increased rather than decreased polarisation. The hierarchy followed the Pope's lead and became more critical not only of the government, but also more active in attempting to impose episcopal authority on progressive clergy and laity, including the priests serving in government.

Without doubt the visit weakened attempts by progressive elements to insert the church into the revolutionary process. The sense that the church and the Sandinista revolution are antithetical was heightened; competition between the government's mass organisations and episcopal-sponsored groups increased. Local conflicts have occurred, pitting Sandinista youth against Catholic school students in some instances. An expanded religious offensive calling into question the legitimacy of the Sandinista leadership was undertaken in 1983. The bishops had already initiated a series of social welfare programmes, aimed at diminishing the impact of similar government efforts.[17]

In September 1983 the bishops directly challenged the legitimacy of the Sandinista government in a pastoral letter criticising the implementation of universal military service. Calling the Sandinista army an extension of a political party rather than of the nation, the episcopacy deemed the call to universal military service illegal. Since that time individual prelates have challenged the legitimacy of the government on other bases, particularly in terms of respect for civil, political and religious rights. Progressive church sectors have challenged such attacks.

In July 1984, after the Nicaraguan government expelled ten foreign priests accused of anti-government activities, episcopal and Vatican spokespersons described church-state tensions as 'extremely grave'. The expulsions appear to have consolidated clerics who had urged episcopal and Vatican support for Ovando y Bravo's hard line on the Sandinistas. Months later, the head of the Nicaraguan Bishops' Conference, Pablo Antonio Vega, issued a wide-ranging criticism of the government which charged that Sandinista ideology 'promotes and institutionalizes violence' and attempts to impose 'systems that the people have not accepted or chosen'. Furthermore the prelate asserted that:

> After five years of euphoric illusions, revolutionary myths and painful deviations, Nicaragua is now a living lesson for the entire continent. Once again, it is proven that ideological dogmatisms and materialist schemes do not meet human needs. They are mechanisms for domination, plans that disregard the fundamental rights of the people. They see man as nothing more than an instrument of labor, one more 'soldier' for their goal of world domination.[18]

With respect to the November 1984 national elections, Vega held that free elections were unlikely when citizens have 'lost their sense of freedom': 'free expression means being able to say yes or no, not just yes'. He concluded by asking why, if the Sandinistas 'are truly seeking unity, peace and self-determination . . . they rely so much on spreading "internal hatred" among Nicaraguans, and move from submission to one imperialism to another that is no less degrading?'[19]

Coming as it did after the 6-7 September 1984 meetings of a delegation of Sandinista officials and Vatican representatives in Rome, the statement seemed to confirm reports that little had been accomplished by the exchange. The chief issues discussed in Rome were the expulsion of the ten foreign priests and governmental authority and church autonomy. The head of the Nicaraguan delegation, René Nuñez, secretary of the Sandinista National Directorate, stated after the meetings that it was clear that the Vatican believed the Sandinistas were persecuting the church. A Sandinista proposal that a bipartisan church-government committee be formed to study the rights of the church in Nicaragua was rejected by the Vatican as a violation of the church's autonomy.[20]

In spite of worsening relations with the Sandinistas, the church leadership did join in late October with 32 other opposition groups, including political parties, unions and business organisations ranging from the far right to the far left, in a 'national dialogue' with the government to reduce differences on major political and economic issues.[21] The conversations were clearly an attempt to reduce political polarisation and increase the legitimacy of the government. The Sandinistas were however adamant that no conversations with the armed counter-revolutionaries would be initiated as the bishops had urged. In early 1985, conversations between the government and the episcopacy were resumed, but no major improvement in church-state relations was forthcoming.

Meanwhile, the church was moving ahead to impose penalties on priests holding public office. Monsignor Pablo Vega warned in September of 1984 that if the four priests still holding ministerial office (Miguel D'Escoto Foreign Minister, Ernesto Cardenal, Minister of Culture, Fernando Cardenal, Minister of Education and Edgard Parrales, ambassador to the Organisation of American States) did not resign their political posts they would be laicised and possibly excommunicated.[22] Parrales resigned the priesthood in late 1984 and Miguel D'Escoto, Ernesto Cardenal and Fernando Cardenal were laicised. The latter was also dismissed from the Jesuits, but similar action was not taken by the Maryknollers with respect to D'Escoto. There is no strong evidence that such ecclesial actions have had a major impact on Nicaraguan public opinion.

Given the extraordinary gulf which currently divides the episcopacy and the Sandinista government in Nicaragua today, it is highly unlikely that the Catholic Church could play an effective mediating role. In fact, since the hierarchy is clearly identified with the opposition to the government, it has contributed to the further polarisation of Nicaraguan society and the lack of inclination of the Sandinistas to consider proposals such as the bishops' April 1984 call for dialogue with the counter-revolutionaries. In addition, the deep split between pro- and anti-government sectors within the church suggests that the church does not have the capacity to unite and mobilise the general populace in favour of a specific option. Rather, it appears that the conflicting positions of churchpeople and the actions flowing from them constitute a barrier to a resolution of the Nicaraguan crisis. It is likely that elements within the church – including the bishops, priests in government, the Jesuits, Maryknollers, Capuchins, the Antonio Valdivieso Centre and Central American Historical Institute – will continue to play visible roles in the conflict. It is unlikely, however, that they will come together in support of a single agreed political solution.

Guatemala

On 12 October 1984, approximately 700 relatives of the disappeared, as well as labour leaders, students and religious marched from San Lucas Sacatepequez to Guatemala City.[23] This was the first public demonstration against political detentions since 1 May 1980, and a major breakthrough for human rights activists. The organisation of the march was made possible, in part, because of the recent repositioning of the Catholic Church in Guatemala under the new Archbishop Próspero Penados del Barrio. Under his predecessor, Cardinal Mario Casariego, church policy had emphasised accommodation with the government even to the extent of co-operating in the expulsion of progressive clerics. Since his assumption of the archbishopric in January 1984, Penados has increasingly served as an intermediary between human rights activists together with other democratic elements and the government.[24]

The new policy of the church leadership has its roots in changes that began in the 1950s, particularly in the aftermath of the 1954 CIA-backed coup that overthrew the elected government of Jacobo Arbenz. During this period the Catholic Church initiated pastoral work aimed at reanimating the loyalty of the faithful and reducing the inroads of both secular and religious competitors. The purpose was to promote rededication to Catholicism and the institutional church by traditional bourgeois supporters of the church. Special efforts were made to point up the threat of communist inroads among the urban and rural poor. New dioceses and parishes were created, and bourgeois Catholics were encouraged to assist the poor via social welfare projects. The 1950s also witnessed the organisation of political parties influenced by Catholic social doctrine, including the Concordia Social Guatemalteca, Acción Social and Democracia Cristiana Guatemalteca (Guatemalan Social Concord, Social Action and Guatemalan Christian Democracy).[25]

Such initiatives greatly increased social and political awareness within the church, which served as fertile ground when Vatican II and Medellín called for an increased emphasis on socio-economic justice, human rights and peace. The mission of the church in Guatemala was increasingly conceived of as recreating the Kingdom of God on earth via the elimination of poverty, exploitation and injustice. New methods of evangelisation and organisation were developed which emphasised greater grassroots autonomy and empowerment. Such developments did not, however, result in the total revamping of the church or its personnel. As one analyst has noted, 'Although an important sector of the clergy was politicized – particularly the religious ones – the majority maintained conservative positions due to the absence of a political project which would articulate the objectives of the pastoral work with the interests of the popular masses.'[26]

The 1960s was a period of ferment both within and without the church, with liberal developmentalism dominant. By the 1970s, however, increasing numbers of Catholics had lost faith in developmentalist solutions to Guatemala's problems and began incorporating themselves into more radical movements. This resulted in increased governmental suspicion and repression of the church. The 1970s also witnessed a substantial increase in the activities of lay preachers known as Delegates of the Word, pastoral and leadership training centres, base Christian communities and youth groups. These groups facilitated network building, particularly in rural areas. Not all church groups abandoned the developmentalist strategy. Their calls for societal change, however, came to be regarded by the government as just as suspect as those of more radical groups.

By the late 1970s state terror had become so serious that in June 1980 the Guatemalan episcopacy, conservatives and liberals alike, felt compelled to issue a pastoral letter condemning the persecution of the church by the kidnapping, torture and assassination of catechists, Delegates of the Word and other churchpeople. Accusations that the church had been penetrated by and was serving as the dupe of atheistic communism were rejected with the reassertion of the church's claim to be non-partisan and neutral. The hierarchy urged dialogue among all the contending factions within Guatemala and argued that peace would come only through the acceptance by all of the true message of Christianity, that is, justice and equity for all. Such statements on the part of the bishops, together with the activities of liberal and progressive churchpeople, helped convince the military that the Catholic Church was an ally of the guerrillas, and repression increased. With the coming to power in March of 1982 of a fundamentalist Protestant, Colonel Efraín Ríos Montt, relations between church and state reached a low point.

Representing the fastest growing religious denomination in Guatemala,[27] Ríos Montt believed that Catholicism had become so corrupt that it opened the way for Marxism. The new sects, such as his own *The Word*, represented a purer form of Christianity that would resolve societal problems through emphasis on individual probity. Ríos Montt's brother, Mario Enrique Ríos Montt, the Catholic bishop of Escuintla, had a different view. His preoccupation was with the consequences of manipulation of the religious sentiments of the Guatemalan people in an atmosphere made volatile by acute inequalities and guerrilla warfare. Bishop Ríos Montt also regarded the growth of Protestantism as:

> part of a larger design, conceived in the United States. 'Don't forget the United States was founded by Protestants,' he says. 'The Catholic Church south of Texas is regarded as too large, too strong. Because we cannot be confronted or fought directly, we must be weakened and divided otherwise. Of course, the Church struggle is not new. Protestants and Marxists are both against it – Protestantism as the arm of conservative capitalism; Marxism as the arm of atheist communism.'[28]

This view is not unique among Guatemalan Catholics, reflecting a widespread sense of the church as under attack from a variety of quarters. This view led, until the advent of Archbishop Penados, to a tendency on the part of the church leadership to follow a cautious strategy of avoiding conflicts with the government and with the most influential groups within Guatemalan society. There are some indications, however, that the Catholic Church in Guatemala will increasingly assume a prophetic role in support of human rights and social justice in Guatemala. This is likely to reduce the government's already limited receptivity to the church's role as mediator between the present military government of General Mejía Victores and the guerrillas. If the 1985 elections result in the coming to power of a moderate civilian government, the possibilities of the church playing a role are increased, albeit not guaranteed. Under Penados the church is increasing its credibility with democratic sectors and reducing the gap between the episcopacy and progressive clergy. The majority of both bishops and clergy, however, are not progressive and rather fearful of both the extreme right and extreme left. This inclines the church towards centrist options of the sort represented by Vinicio Cerezo and the Christian Democratic Party. (Editor's note: assumed the Presidency in January 1986.) If such an inclination is pursued it could alienate both conservative and progressive sectors within the church, thereby increasing internal divisions and undercutting the strength of the church as a political actor. Hence the potential of the Catholic Church to play a major role in the search for pacific solutions to conflict in Guatemala is limited by factors internal and external to the church. The probability is that the church will play a role, albeit a circumscribed one.

Honduras

The Catholic Church in Honduras has not played as large a role in politics as have the churches in El Salvador, Nicaragua and Guatemala. This is, in part, the result of its limited human and financial resources which makes it institutionally the weakest of all the Central American churches. In 1973 there were 211 priests in Honduras, 170 of whom were foreigners. This resulted in a ratio of one priest for every 10,327 inhabitants as compared to one for every 5,215 in Nicaragua and one for every 3,738 in Costa Rica. Ten years later the number of priests had increased to only 255, of whom 175 were foreign, with a ratio of one priest per 15,111 inhabitants.[29] In addition, with the lowest per capita income in the western hemisphere outside of Haiti, Honduras has few material resources for church activities. This has encouraged a considerable degree of caution on the part of the church leadership, who have been generally disinclined to pursue policies that would cause a serious rupture of their relations with political and economic elites.

Nevertheless, since the 1950s the Honduran church has undergone some of the same changes as the churches in El Salvador, Nicaragua and Guatemala, resulting in more social and political consciousness among the clergy and laity, greater identification with the poor, and an inclination to denounce socio-economic injustice and violations of human rights. The Honduran church has also experimented with a variety of strategies to maintain its moral leadership in the face of modern problems.

In the 1950s, reformist groups such as Catholic Action were organised, but had little appeal to young, urban, bourgeois Hondurans. There was, in addition, considerable preoccupation with combatting the inroads of communism: this stimulated a certain revitalisation of the church which was given expression via such events as a national crusade in 1959 and anti-Cuban demonstrations. In 1961 16 radio schools began providing basic education and spiritual direction. These, together with the Honduran Popular Cultural Action Movement, focused on the needs of the rural population and served as a stimulus for peasant organisations which had been initiated in the 1950s under secular auspices. Emphasis was on 'Christian developmentalism', that is, the promotion of individual realisation within the context of community betterment. By the late 1960s a Christian Democratic Party had emerged incorporating a good number of church activists.

Increased labour tensions, particularly in rural areas in the 1970s, made the church leadership more aware of rural conditions and more involved in efforts to improve them. Some priests and religious became closely identified with peasant groups facilitating networking and community organising. The concentration of the military government that came to power in 1972 on rural problems caused church people to become more heavily involved in social welfare. One of the targetted areas was Olancho, where some clerics were exceptionally vocal in denouncing exploitation of the peasants. In mid-1975 20 individuals were assassinated in Olancho, including two priests and several agrarian leaders. This and other repressive acts caused a retreat on the part of the institutional church and the departure of some clerics from the area.

While the episcopacy denounced these acts and excommunicated those responsible for the massacre, they were also conscious of the need not to provoke a full-scale attack on the church. There was a retreat into spirituality on the part of some Catholics who became involved in the charismatic movement, which encouraged withdrawal from the world. Others used it as an opportunity to turn their attention to fortifying the church internally, in order to make it more effective in promoting change over the long term. Still others were attracted to fundamentalist groups, including the Assembly of God, the Cenacle and the Moonies, which have reinforced anti-communist sentiment. The tendency towards quiescence on the part of Catholic activists working at the grassroots level was supported by Pope John Paul II during his 8 March 1983 visit to Honduras.[30]

The Catholic church in Honduras is not, at present, in a position to play a major role in resolving societal tensions. Rather, it has opted to attempt to revitalise its membership spiritually and educationally, although it does speak out sometimes to denounce repression and violations of human rights by government authorities as threats to democracy.[31] The progressive sector is not substantial and the episcopacy continues to be linked to traditional political and economic elites. With the worsening economic situation and widespread corruption under Roberto Suazo Cordova's government, the possibility that much greater demands will be placed on the spiritual and material resources of the church is good. If that happens, then it is possible that the church might emerge as an opponent of the current political elite rather than as a bridge to bring contending forces together.

The Vatican

The Vatican under Pope John Paul II has taken a special interest in the Central American crisis. The Pope has been particularly active in denouncing foreign interference in regional problems and those who encourage class struggle, including churchpeople. He has suggested that the widening economic gap between rich and poor nations and the wealthy and the poor within nations is at the root of the present conflicts.[32] Rather than follow the theology of liberation, the Pope has called for a new theology of 'social liberation', which foresees bringing 'social liberation to the masses of have-nots . . . in a line of fidelity with the Gospel, which prohibits recourse to methods of hate and violence.' It emphasises individual conversion to the cause of justice, rather than structural change.[33]

Coming after the Vatican's September 1984 critique of liberation theology and John Paul II's own criticism of 'popular churches' and priests in politics, the Pope's proposal represents a new offensive against progressives within the church. This suggests that internal struggle within the church will be heightened in the near future, thereby reducing the capacity of the church to play a critical role in conflict resolution in Central America. That does not, however, eliminate the possibility of ecclesial leaders serving as mediators between centrist governments and guerrilla movements in El Salvador and Guatemala.

In Nicaragua, where the church is severely divided, the support of the Pope for Ovando y Bravo, the most outspoken critic of the Sandinistas, has virtually eliminated the church as a mediator. The church in Honduras is already following the less political, more evangelical path that the Pope has recommended. For those within the church who believe that individual moral conversion is not sufficient to ameliorate Central American problems, the possibility of increasing disaffection with Rome is high. A church divided internationally and within nations is not likely to make a major contribution to the resolution of the Central American crisis.

Conclusion

The presumption that the Catholic Church can play a major role in conflict resolution and democratisation in Central America rests on a belief that the church is a powerful, united institution. While within the context of the Central American societies, the Catholic Church has been a relatively powerful institution, its material and personnel resources are limited. In addition, in recent years there have been increasing differences of opinion within the church over how best to achieve its stated mission of the salvation of all. The emphasis on the preferential option for the poor has led some sectors of the church to move away from the traditional universalistic thrust of the church's mission towards a more conflictual view of society. This has been reinforced by the societal analysis of the theology of liberation and increased direct political involvement of clerical and lay Catholics. Today the Catholic Church in Central America is unified in its condemnation of terror by both the extreme right and left. It is sharply divided over how socio-economic justice can be brought to societies that are deeply riven by poverty and exploitation. There is no clear agreement on political, economic or even pastoral and theological strategies. The lack of unity and programmatic coherence is clearly seen in an analysis of the specific situation of the church in El Salvador, Nicaragua, Guatemala and Honduras.

In El Salvador the Catholic Church is currently playing the role of facilitator of the peace talks initiated at La Palma on 15 October 1984. It is not, however, taking a substantive role in those talks and there does not appear to be a particular church position that might be put forth. Essentially, the church is responding to the strong public sentiment in favour of national dialogue, as are Duarte and the FDR/FMLN. Lack of political unity within the church is indicated by the fact that while some bishops have long-standing links with that sector of the Christian Democratic Party led by President Duarte, others are strongly opposed to him. In addition, other influential actors within the Salvadoran church, most notably the Jesuits and the faculty at their Central American University, are not convinced that Duarte and his allies have the capacity to democratise El Salvador. The prospects are, consequently, that the church will continue to facilitate the present exchanges, but will not have a substantive role in the conceptualisation of specific agreements.

The close identification of Monsignor Ovando y Bravo, the Archbishop of Managua, with the opposition to the Sandinista government and the increasing support he has received from his fellow bishops and the Vatican for that position, militates against the church mediating the present conflict in Nicaragua. The ideological and political struggle in that country is currently focused, in large measure, in and on the church, making it a partisan rather than neutral actor. Hence, it would be virtually impossible for the Sandinistas to accept the institutional church as a mediator. Rather, the episcopacy has clearly identified itself as an important element of the opposition. Efforts by the Sandinistas to have the Vatican intervene to lessen church-state tensions have been unavailing as the Pope strongly supports the hierarchy's criticism of the government. Of all the Central American churches, the Nicaraguan is the most seriously divided, with an influential progressive sector strongly at odds with the bishops. Neither the bishops nor the progressives appear, however, to have the loyalty of the majority of Catholics, who fear the consequences for themselves and their country of the increasing political and ecclesial polarisation. At present the Nicaraguan church is serving as a barrier to conflict resolution.

The Guatemalan Catholic Church under the leadership of the new Archbishop Próspero Penados del Barrio has recently embarked on a more activist, less cautious course than the one it traditionally pursued. Increasingly outspoken on behalf of human rights, the church leadership can provide some legitimation and protection for democratic elements. Advances in this direction are contingent on progress towards the establishment of a civilian government that will be able to consolidate itself sufficiently to deal with the socio-economic conditions and repression that have given rise to guerrilla warfare. There are substantial barriers to that and the church does not have major resources that could be brought to bear to overcome them. What the church could do is to help to create an atmosphere of support and receptivity for democratic government. However, there are a wide variety of opinions within the church about how best to democratise Guatemala which will no doubt be more strongly expressed once civilian government is re-established. At most, the church can serve to reinforce redemocratisation, if civilian politicians are successful in strongly initiating the process.

The weakness of the Honduran church has traditionally circumscribed its political role. Lack of personnel and material resources limits its presence throughout the country and has made it unwilling to abandon its links to political and economic elites. Past experience with social activism by progressives within the church has led to serious repression and reinforced caution. Pressure from Rome has encouraged emphasis on evangelisation and spiritual regeneration rather than political activism. The Catholic Church in Honduras is somewhat marginal politically.

Throughout Central America, the Catholic Church is playing a variety of roles in the resolution of the present crisis and promotion of democracy. Given national circumstances and divisions within the church, it is serving variously to facilitate peace talks and exacerbate political polarisation. Hence it is currently playing the role of both bridge and barrier to a peaceful solution of the present Central American crisis.

Notes

1. The role of the Catholic Church in Costa Rica and Panama will not be dealt with in this chapter as those societies do not suffer from the level of conflict experienced in El Salvador, Nicaragua, Guatemala and Honduras. In addition, space does not permit an examination of the role of the Protestant churches, whose membership is substantially less than the Catholic.

2. Stephen Webre, 'The Politics of Christian Democracy', in Marvin E. Gettleman et al, (eds.), *El Salvador: Central America in the New Cold War* (New York: Grove Press, 1981), pp. 99-100. See also Webre's *José Napoleón Duarte and the Christian Democratic Party in Salvador Politics, 1960-1972* (Baton Rouge: Louisiana State University Press, 1979).

3. Jorge Cáceres Prendes, 'Revolutionary Struggle and Church Commitment: The Case of El Salvador', *Social Compass*, vol. XXX, nos. 2-3 (1983), pp. 266-7.

4. Tommie Sue Montgomery, 'The Church in the Salvadoran Revolution', *Latin American Perspectives*, vol. X, no. 1 (Winter 1983), p. 81.

5. Bernard Debusmann, 'Sandinista Official Assails Bishops Bid for Talks', *Washington Post*, 26April 1984, p. A25.

6. Conferencia Episcopal de Nicaragua, Presencia Cristiana en *La Revolución: Dos Mensajes – Momento Insurreccíonal 2 de junio 1979, Iniciando la Reconstrucción, 30 de julio 1979* (Managua: Cristianos en el Mundo, Comisión Justicia y Paz, Documentos, 1979), pp. 4-8.

7. Ibid., 30 July 1979, p. 14.

8. Nicaraguan Conference of Bishops, 'Pastoral Letter', 17 November 1979, p. 2.

9. It was estimated in June of 1979 that 85 per cent of the priests in the country, plus a majority of nuns and other religious, supported the insurrection. Sergio Mendez Arceo, Bishop of Cuernavaca, Mexico, 'Introduction to Pastoral Letter of the Episcopal Conference of Nicaragua', 17 November 1979, Managua, p. 2.

10. 'La iglesia en Nicaragua', *CELAM*, vol. XIX, no. 158 (January 1981), pp. 11-21.

11. National Catholic News Service, 7 November 1980, p. 1.

12. Juan Pablo II, 'Laicado y Educación' (4 March 1983), León, Nicaragua.

13. Central American Historical Institute, 'Greater Resources for Education in Nicaragua: The New Curriculum Stirs Public Response', *Update*, vol. 2, (no. 3

3 March 1983), p. 2.

14. John Paul II, Letter to the Nicaraguan Bishops, 29 June 1982 (Rome) and 'Threats to the Church's Unity', *Origins: NC Documentary Service*, vol. 12, no. 40 (17 March 1983), pp. 633, 635-6.

15. 'Christian Reflection on the Pope's March 4 Visit to Nicaragua by a Theological Reflection Group', Translated from 'Imperialismo, Enemigo del Pueblo y la Paz Dicen Intelectuales Cristianos', *El Nuevo Diario*, 6 March 1983, pp. 1-2.

16. Edward Cody, 'Tension Grows in Nicaragua: Sandinistas Take Harder Line', *Washington Post*, 5 March 1983, pp. A1;A10.

17. Ana Maria Ezcurra, 'La jerarquía católica nicaraguense y U.S. contra la Revolución Sandinista', *Testimonios y Documentos* (21 February 1983), pp. 8-10.

18. Stephen Kinzer, 'Leading Nicaraguan Bishop Says Sandinista Impose "Oppressions" ', *Los Angeles Times*, 25 October 1984, pp. 1; 4.

19. Ibid., p. 4.

20. John Lantigua, 'Church-State Tension High in Nicaragua', *Washington Post*, 1 October 1984, pp. A1; A10; 'Nicaraguans Meet Vatican Aides', *New York Times*, 7 September 1984, p. 4; Sari Gilbert, 'Nicaragua, Vatican Seen Still at Odds', *Washington Post*, 14 September 1984, p. A31.

21. Robert J. McCartney, 'Sandinistas Begin Talks with Opposition', *Washington Post*, 1 November 1984, p. A32.

22. Stephen Kinzer, 'Sandinista Priests Told They Could Be Defrocked', *New York Tmes*, 29 September 1984, p. 4.

23. 'Guatemala Marchers Spotlight Missing Relatives', *Los Angeles Times*, 14. October 1984, p. I-8.

24. William R. Long, 'New Guatemalan Archbishop Challenges Government on Human Rights', *Los Angeles Times*, 14 September 1984, p. I-A-3.

25. Oscar Rolando Sierra Pop, 'The Church and Social Conflicts in Guatemala', *Social Compass*, vol. XXX, nos. 2-3 (1983), pp. 323-4.

26. Ibid., p. 328.

27. Protestant and Mormon groups claim 22 per cent of the total Guatemalan population. Fundamentalist groups are reported to be growing at 15 per cent annually. Marlise Simons, 'Latin America's New Gospel', *New York Times Magazine*, 7 November 1982, p. 47.

28. Ibid.

29. Pablo Richard and Guillermo Meléndez (eds.), *La iglesia de los pobres en América Central: Un analísis socio-político y teológico de la iglesia centroamericana (1960-1982)* (San José, Costa Rica: Departmento Ecuménico de Investigaciones, 1982), p. 322; Alan Riding, 'Honduran Lay Preachers Hear the Pope', *New York Times*, 9 March 1983, p. 4.

30. Ibid.

31. 'Bishops of Honduras Denounce New Violence', *New York Times*, 29 October 1982, p. 5.

32. 'Pope Assails Foreign Intrusion in Latin America', *Los Angeles Times*, 14 October 1984, p. I-4.

33. Don A. Sehanche, 'Pope Offers His Own Plan of Latin Social Liberation', *Los Angeles Times*, 12 October 1984, p. I-1; 20.

8 GUATEMALA: BETWEEN AUTHORITARIANISM AND DEMOCRACY

Mario Solórzano Martínez

Introduction

Since the establishment of the liberal-oligarchic regime in Guatemala (1871), Guatemalan society has presented a distinctive type of authoritarianism. Liberal governments have always tried to give the appearance of promoting a democratic society, founded upon constitutionalism and including the freedom of political parties competing in regular elections. Without exception, all oligarchic dictators prolonged their presidencies either by reforming the constitution or through electoral means. This 'preoccupation' with a democratic appearance has continued into the recent past, particularly during regular presidential elections. During such 'elections' a democratic ritual is enacted and the political stage is suitably embellished with discourses and the appearance of political parties. Should the vote confirm the candidate previously agreed upon by the ruling groups, the choice is respected; if, on the other hand, public opinion proves unreliable, fraud takes place. In this manner, the candidate endorsed by the oligarchy is imposed upon the nation, generally with the assurance of military support (see Table 8.1).

The least observant viewer of Guatemalan affairs must recognise that this is the manner in which the power structure operates. Nevertheless, the struggle against authoritarianism has also been present in the country for a long time. Throughout this time significant intervals of democracy have existed in the political life of the republic, as well as periods of passive resistance against the authoritiarian display put on by those in command.

However, the authoritarian regime has succeeded in establishing mechanisms of control, resting primarily on violent coercion, to obtain the community's obedience. The use of coercion, force and terror has given rise to forms of political relationships marked above all by their violence. As a result of this, the struggle for power, even within the ruling sectors, is characterised by violent confrontations. A logical consequence of this authoritarian ascendancy, which fundamentally rests upon the use of force, has been the emergence of a high level of

Table 8.1: Forms of Accession to Power in Guatemala between 1948 and 1982

Name	Term	Method	Personal Background
Jacobo Arbenz	1950	Elections	Military
Carlos Castillo Armas	1954-7	Imposed by counter-revolution	Military
L.A. Gonzalez Lopez	1957	Succeeded Castillo when the latter was assassinated	Civilian
G. Flores Avendano	1957-8	Chosen by Congress	Military
M. Idigoras Fuentes	1958-63	Elections	Military
E. Peralta Azurdia	1963-6	*Coup d'état*	Military
J.C. Méndez Montenegro	1966-70	Elections	Civilian
C.M. Arana Osorio	1970-4	Elections	Military
K. Laugerud García	1974-8	Elections (fraud)	Military
R. Lucas García	1978-82	Elections (fraud)	Military
E. Ríos Montt	1982-3	*Coup d'état*	Military
H. Mejias Victores	1983	*Coup d'état*	Military

political polarisation and the use of violence not only by the dominant elite in order to maintain itself in power, but also by the excluded sectors of Guatemalan society.

The historical alternative to the self-perpetuating violence would be the construction of a democratic society. This possibility is not foreign to the Guatemalan people. On the contrary, it has been a constant factor in the aspirations of the populace in general and within the middle sectors and even within the upper classes. The democratic regime which emerged during the 1944-54 period provides the best historical reference point. This democratic interlude established a national-popular conscience which remains part of the political beliefs and influences of society to this day.

Subsequent democratic experiments in Guatemala have met with little success, although they have shown the existence of important opportunities for struggle. The reactionary ideology of the ruling groups, influenced not only by enduring oligarchic values, but also strengthened by the effects of the Cold War and by ideological-political conceptions of counter-insurgency, has taken its toll on society as a whole.

The guerrilla struggle in Guatemala was launched prematurely in November 1960 as an outcome of the radicalisation of bourgeois groups who had been inspired by the Cuban Revolution. This completed the consolidation of authoritarian political culture, where reactionary oligarchic tradition helped turn counter-insurgency into the primary public and political concern of the Guatemalan state.

The political violence which has been developed over the last few decades has affected society as a whole and has blocked all hope of economic, social or political transformations. Worse than that the endemic violence has produced a progressive degradation of society. Institutionalised violence not only failed to resolve the problems of the country, it has aggravated the conditions that have afflicted Guatemala since its earliest days as a republic and perhaps made those deficiencies even more acute. If one were to diagnose Guatemala's political climate in clinical terms, one would describe an exhausted patient who shows clear tendencies towards a further deterioration in health.[1]

Can a remedy be found through an effort at democratisation which will at least allow Guatemala to reach some civilised minimum in its political relationships? This chapter will try to identify those options which would allow us to find the way towards a democratic transformation of Guatemalan society. A return to democracy would require a decisive change in power relations, so that political strategies and tactics would have to be clearly defined, social alliances would require definition, a new political philosophy of tolerance breaking with authoritarian culture would be needed. Several factors can be adduced in favour of a democratic alternative, namely the weakening of traditional ways of thinking; certain changes within key centres of power; and above all, the will of the Guatemalan people to continue the struggle.

The Regional Setting

This section seeks to place the debate over the possibility of a democratic alternative in Guatemala in its regional context. The events of the last six years, since the overthrow of Somoza, must be taken into account when seeking realistic solutions to Guatemala's problems.

Since the Sandinista revolutionary triumph (1979), the Central American political process has gone through two distinct phases. The seizure of power by the Sandinista Liberation Front produced a massive wave of sympathy among all political groups from the centre leftwards. It was a moment of optimism, and of militarist triumphalism. Political analyses, already highly ideological in character, found evidence in the wake of the Nicaraguan triumph that a revolution in El Salvador would follow, and, close behind it, that the success of the Guatemalan revolutionary process would also be assured. The prospect of seizing political power through military means clouded political judgements.

This idealised vision of a region-wide political transformation mirrored unconsciously the very crude position adopted by the Kissinger Commission. Kissinger believed that if the domino theory could be applied anywhere, it was in Central America, and that owing to the Sandinista success in Nicaragua, Marxist-Leninist revolutions would soon spread throughout the region, thus threatening US national security. However, the power relations both within the region and external to it are such that this analysis, whether made by left or right, stems from false assumptions and cannot be applied in the Central American context, because of the qualitative differences between the various republics.

The period from 1979 to 1982 constitutes the first phase of the revolutionary process in Central America, particularly in Nicaragua, El Salvador and Guatemala. The principle events which occurred at this juncture can be summarised as follows: (i) the triumph of the Nicaraguan Revolution; (ii) the development of the Salvadoran and

Guatemalan revolutionary movements; and (iii) the strengthening of international solidarity with the revolutionary cause in Central America.

After 1979, political life in both El Salvador and Guatemala became more militarised. In the former, the impressive growth of the mass movement was characterised by popular mobilisations, the takeover of embassies and government ministries, The collapse of the Salvadoran junta which took office after the 1979 *coup d'état* was the culmination of the development of the mass movement in that country. The following year marked the climax of popular mobilisation in the republic. In March 1980 the Democratic Front was established, anticipating the appearance of the Revolutionary Democratic Front (FDR) in April 1980, followed by the founding of the Farabundo Martí National Liberation Front (FMLN) in September. By the end of 1980, the popular movement was seriously demoralised and was being driven from the political scene because of the violent escalation in repression by the security and armed forces.

In Guatemala, the development of a popular movement began in 1976 and lasted until 1980. Although the Democratic Front against Repression (FDCR) had clandestine origins, it had gone public by February 1979. The FDCR was made up of a large number of organisations, which did not in themselves aspire to form a new government. Nevertheless, the FDCR aspired to unity and dedicated itself to the organisation of such demonstrations as were allowed and to protests at the continuing acts of repression. Repression was not new in Guatemala, but it became increasingly institutionalised after 1978.

At the international level, solidarity was expressed by several international organisations and political parties who lent their support to the revolutionary cause in Central America. Among these were the Franco-Mexican declaration; the Mexican-sponsored regional grouping of Latin American and Caribbean nationalist and Social Democratic parties known as the Permanent Conference of Political Parties of Latin America (COPPAL); the development of solidarity committees and widespread activity by human rights organisations and Christians from the Catholic and Protestant churches. During this time, the Socialist International, principally led by European Social Democratic parties, made important statements concerning the Nicaraguan case, as well as those of El Salvador and Guatemala.

All of this helped to reinforce an optimistic and triumphant attitude on the left concerning the revolutionary process. On the other hand, it also forced the oligarchies seriously to consider the possibility of defeat and induced them to cede more political initiative to their respective national armies in the hope of maintaining the status quo.

The election of Ronald Reagan to the US presidency in 1981 heralded a more aggressive strategy towards Central America. Concern with human rights was downgraded and primacy was given to the need to block the revolutionary process in Central America, no matter what the cost. This shift in US politics towards the right has decisively affected the political dynamics of Central America and has had effects which will be described below From 1982, the variables which make up the current political situation in the region began to appear.

The Military Offensive and North American Politics

The present US administration believes that it is facing a problem of a global character, which can ultimately be seen as an East-West confrontation. Therefore, the Nicaraguan government is viewed as a political-ideological enemy of the West and is considered part of a Soviet-based strategy implemented through Cuba. It is from Managua that logistical support derives for the Salvadoran and Guatemalan revolutions. Thus, it is essential for North American interests to destroy the Sandinista Revolution.

This belief has been put into practice through a series of policies, among which the following should be mentioned:

US economic, political and military support for the Nicaraguan counter-revolution;

The military blockade of Nicaragua, as well as the presence of US warships on Central American coasts and the decision forcefully to subvert the Sandinista government in Nicaragua and to thwart any possibility of a Salvadoran triumph. For some, the US invasion of Grenada had all the markings of a dress rehearsal for the Central American situation;

Honduras has become the United States' new strategic buffer state on the Isthmus. Military agreements with the Honduran government were made which led to the establishment of American bases in that country, as well as the training of the Honduran and Salvadoran armies, and the supply of geographic and political support for the Nicaraguan counter-revolution. This creates a threat of military invasion of Nicaragua on the part of the Contras based in Honduras, thus creating further ill-feeling and politico-military friction between both countries;

Generous economic, political and military support by the US government to the Salvadoran government. Because of this, the military and logistical capabilities of the Salvadoran army have been sufficiently strengthened at least to maintain a stand-off with the insurgents;

The establishment of better relations with the Guatemalan government, particularly with the army, which until recently has not been on good terms with the US;

The development of a diplomatic offensive with the appointment of the ex-Senator, Richard Stone, as a presidential envoy to deal with the Central American region. American diplomacy also began to make use of its mechanisms of co-operation and alignment in relation with the other countries in the region in order to isolate and pressurise the Sandinista government.

Finally, this diplomatic offensive also reached Europe, seeking to obstruct European support for the Central American left, particularly that of the Socialist International.

Elections as a Political Solution

This arises in part from the strategy of Washington, which in theory favours a democratic solution over a military outcome. Nevertheless, this approach also corresponds to the interests of many political groups within Central America itself. This applies, for example, to Christian Democratic currents not only in Guatemala, but also in El Salvador and Nicaragua. Some traditional parties too, such as the National Liberation Movement (MLN) of Guatemala, for instance, also insist on the holding of elections and demand that the military government establish an electoral timetable. One way or another, elections are being held throughout the region and the results are likely to prove revealing, particularly in Guatemala and Salvador. More will be said about the Guatemalan case below.

The Military

Three events are worth mentioning in this respect:

1. The opening of a battle front on the borders of Nicaragua and the overt support given by the US government to the Contras.
2. The strengthening of the Salvadoran army through US support, thus averting the disintegration of that army and stabilising the civil war.
3. The Guatemalan government's military offensive, which has driven the guerrilla groups into retreat.

The Socialist International and the Contadora Group

Two initiatives must be mentioned here. There is, on the one hand, a European initiative, expressed mainly through the Socialist International and by certain Social Democratic European nations, and on the other hand, a Latin American initiative taken by Mexico, Colombia, Venezuela and Panama.

In Latin America, the growing possibility of a military confrontation between Nicaragua and Honduras was particularly disturbing because of US involvement in the region. In 1983 the prospect of a regional war led the Contadora countries to urge a negotiated solution. To date the Contadora group has helped to avoid a military confrontation by providing an acceptable arena for discussion of the regional crisis by the governments affected. It does not communicate with the political forces inside each country. In theory, almost everyone supports the Contadora approach, and its stated objective of finding a democratic alternative to the armed confrontation.

The emergence of the Contadora group, and the widespread support it enjoys, has led the Socialist International and Social Democratic governments to endorse it as a political formula. The Contadora initiative envisages the adoption of national conciliation, free elections and the observance of human rights as a solution to the present crisis. Contadora also stresses the need for economic reform, stressing the need for a fairer distribution of wealth in Central America.

This approach has gained momentum since 1982, and has helped to promote a more realistic outlook in place of the initial triumphalism, obliging contending forces to consider what sacrifices are needed in order to bring about a democratic solution, about the demands made by the political parties, and also about the way in which dominant groups might be willing to make some concessions.

Undoubtedly the dynamics of this search for an *entente* differ radically from one country to another. In Nicaragua, the central problem is the need for a serious dialogue between the Sandinista government and the Reagan administration. This is imperative if a negotiated solution is to be reached. In El Salvador, talks must be held between the main political protagonists, namely the FMLN-FDR coalition and the Salvadoran government. Since the current Salvadoran government has close links with the US government, it will indirectly be representing American interests should a dialogue be established. In Guatemala, there is a very special situation in which the effort to achieve a democratic outcome cannot centre on a direct agreement between the government and the insurgents, since the latter have been so severely weakened. For the time being, at least the government shows itself unwilling to carry on a dialogue, be it with the rebels in arms or with the democratic left.

We shall now attempt to establish certain important considerations which are necessary if a democratic system is to be established as a politically viable regime in Guatemala.

Authoritarianism

Throughout Guatemala's political history, whether under conservative or liberal rule, the country's class structure has remained basically authoritarian in character. The establishment of the oligarchic political regime in 1871 imposed an economic system based on a mono-export crop, with productive relations characterised by the use of violence against the Indian majority of the population. The shift to a coffee economy during this time provided an opening for adjustments in the Guatemalan power structure. The cheap labour force of the Indian communities was essential to the republic's 'modernisation' and further integration into the world market. In this period, a system emerged by which the state openly co-operated with landowners in order to force a majority of the indigenous population to work. In this manner the Indians were subjected to the institutionalised violence of an emergent police state.

To great extent the triumph of the Liberal revolution led by García Granados and Barrios represented by the ascendant class of coffee-growers, whose intention was not completely to displace the old *criollo* elite, but rather to incorporate it. The Catholic Church, however, considered a bastion of conservatism, was viewed unfavourably by the new Liberal government. As a result of increased, centralised state power, dictatorship, repression and generalised terror became the norm for all but the ruling class and foreigners.

The principal characteristics of the economic model which emerged with the Liberal revolution are:

1. The rise of coffee production which resulted in the strengthening of the latifundio system at the expense of church holdings and the seizure of communal Indian lands. From this emerged the latifundio-minifundio system which we know today.
2. The development of a system which guaranteed a permanent supply of the cheap labour required by coffee-growers and foreign investors.

As the Indians were dispossessed of their lands and forced to depend on the plantations for work, a series of laws were instituted in order to institutionalise an enduring sytem of debt peonage.

3. The insertion of Guatemala into the international economy, a process which marked the beginning of the republic's economic development and dependency.
4. The outward orientation of the national economy eventually imposed rigid limitations on the expansion and development of the internal market, which ultimately created serious obstacles for the independent industrialisation of the country.
5. All of this seriously impeded the formation of a genuine capitalist bourgeoisie and a modern proletariat.

Liberalism, with its aspirations for modernity, required the establishment of an oligarchy which could guarantee Guatemala's agro-exporting status. Guatemala's entry into the world market was closely linked to North American capital, particularly after the beginning of the twentieth centiry. The construction of railroads and the development of the banana trade ensured that the Guatemalan economy would be tightly aligned with foreign interests. Characteristic of this was the dependent relationship which emerged between the Guatemalan bourgeoisie and foreign interests. From this alliance there emerged a political regime which tried to give the appearance of constitutionality on the one hand, while on the other it operated through an authoritarian and dictatorial system.

The political pattern established by Barrios during his presidency became the norm throughout the period of oligarchic dominance. The distinctive features of this political system can be summarised as follows:

1. A series of personalistic dictatorships such as that of Justo Rufino Barrios (1873-85), Manuel Estrada Cabrera (1898-1920) and Jorge Ubico (1931-45).
2. A system of restricted and exclusionary participation in politics.
3. Authoritarian and repressive governments despite a legal-administrative structure of the republican type including a division of powers, the existence and holding of elections, and a form of liberal-bourgeois discourse.

Although Guatemala underwent certain important changes during the 1944-54 decade, these were incomplete and far from institutionalised at the end of this period. Substantial progress was made in instilling a sense of political consciousness and establishing patterns for democratic political behaviour in the future, but the progress was not sufficient to eradicate traditional oligarchic ways of thinking.

The defeat of the 1944 revolution ten years later meant the re-establishment of the old alliance between the coffee-growing oligarchy and North American capital. This coalition promoted a new socio-economic scheme based on reviving the traditional latifundio-minifundio system. Although this political project was firmly established on oligarchic foundations, it nevertheless extended the process of agricultural diversification which had been launched during the 1944-54 decade. The new regime also engaged in a process of industrialisation under the aegis of the newly-created Central American Common Market (CACM).

In the political sphere, the regime once again adopted an authoritarian form of government. This was particularly true after 1963, when the military took control of the government. Since then, the army has been a fundamental factor in national life. It is important to note that the type of regime which was established in Guatemala after the 1963 *coup d'état* differed from the so-called bureaucratic-authoritarian regimes of the Southern Cone countries of South America in many ways. The first and most obvious of these differences is that the South American military seized government control in order to hold power indefinitely. During the 1970s it became customary for such regimes immediately to suppress all aspects of a constitutional regime and to disregard constitutional laws, thus abolishing elections and political parties.[2]

In Guatemala, on the other hand, a subtler political game can be observed under the military regime. Here, use is made of certain democratic processes which are applied in a unique manner, announced publicly and formally accepted as law, thus appearing to offer a semblance of political freedom and guaranteeing the electoral process. In practice, however, the power depends entirely upon the will of the armed forces and their economic allies.

Restrictions on political participation impose severe limitations on political and popular organisation. Only those parties which are acceptable to the regime are permitted to participate in national elections. In this manner, Social Democratic and Communist parties have been banned and barred from taking part in elections. Therefore, the model only admits the presence of traditional groups from the right as far towards the centre as the Christian Democratic Party. Concomitant to this, both formal and very real barriers obstruct the institutional organisation of the popular movements in general, particularly unions, marginal groups, etc.

National elections are held every four years, although the results are not necessarily respected. When the electoral results conflict with ruling interests, the vote is overturned.

Finally, the Guatemalan government operates a highly repressive political system based on counter-insurgency ideology. This was the case even during the 1970-4 period, at a time when insurgency had been completely defeated. The government viewed all those groups or persons who opposed or questioned its authority as national enemies, regardless of whether these persons were undermining public order through passive or violent means. This policy of indiscriminate repression involves permanent and gross violations of human rights.

Consequently legitimacy does not function through the channels usual in a democratic system. On the contrary, the regime has sought legitimation of a corporatist nature, with the army seeking direct support from the centres of power, such as private enterprise, the Catholic Church, the legal political parties and the media. In this manner, the army has become the fundamental source of power, while conceding direct responsibility for running the government to various socio-economic groups.

The roots of this 'façade democracy' are to be found partly in the polarised political situation following the 1954 revolution, greatly reinforced by the experience of armed insurgency during the 1960s. The activities of the guerrilla groups have provided an objective basis on which the existence of this counter-insurgency theory has been justified.

However, the regime which began with the 1963 *coup d'état* has now become inoperative. Among the various reasons for this, the weakening of the government's centres of support should be considered. The critical political situation in the rest of Central America has also played its part. Does this mean that the Guatemalan state is undergoing a fundamental change? What is evident is that, as the present political system has deteriorated, reformist alternatives have emerged within the right. These endeavour to generate a new model of domination as the solution to the country's crisis. Certain political forces which have support within the popular movement are also joining in this effort for political renewal.

Modifications on the National and International Scene

The Emergence of New Social Forces

If a democratic alternative is to emerge, major realignments must occur in the social alliances that have hitherto underpinned the authoritarian regime. Traditional ways of thinking, which serve the present hegemony, must be challenged and displaced so that a new democratic approach to politics and government can emerge. For a democracy to be consolidated it will be necessary to supplant existing reactionary ways of thinking and to establish a new system of social alliances. Currently, several developments are underway that could prove crucial for the construction of a more democratic regime.

Development of an Urban Popular Movement

In the course of the last 30 years, the relationship between urban and rural dwellers has changed in Guatemala. Central to the proletarianisation of rural and urban sectors has been an inadequate industrial development and the inability of peasant families to maintain rural self-sufficiency. Large numbers of urban workers have swelled the ranks of the unemployed and have begun demanding that the government helps them find adequate housing and provides them with basic medical care and a minimum of education. This relatively new sector has become part of the popular struggle, by challenging the government. Since 1976, it has become increasingly important.

The Development of Peasant Consciousness

A peasant movement first emerged in Guatemala during the 1940s. However, this was brought to an abrupt end in 1954. Since then a more radical peasant movement has developed, which is viewed with apprehension by the government. Their demands now go beyond the question of agrarian reform, raising other major national issues, such as the historical grievances underlying the Indian-*ladino* contradiction. The Indian majority have developed their socio-economic demands and linked them to their cultural and racial experiences giving rise to a high level of politicisation. In many areas, they have even joined the ranks of the armed struggle, thus strengthening the guerrilla movement.

The peasant movement now expresses itself in three ways:

1. In demands for transformation of the system of land tenure, i.e. agrarian reform.

2. In demands for wage increases, which have given rise to mobilisations and strikes throught the countryside.
3. In political demands in which peasant organisations have taken a revolutionary stance, pressing not only for radical new political arrangements, but also for a change in the nature of the state itself.

The Emergence of the Working Classes and the Urban Popular Movements

The industrialisation which began in the 1960s produced a small working class that eventually began to organise itself and to make demands of the economic and political system. These organisations were basically under Marxist-Leninist leadership and soon attracted other sectors to their side, some of which had little or nothing to do with the working classes – marginalised groups, together with university and high school students and others who wished to challenge the ruling classes. This movement was able to mobilise impressive numbers of workers, the unemployed and urban marginals.

The Emergence of the Middle Classes

In general, the modernisation of the economy and of the Guatemalan state produced a high level of growth within the middle classes. These sectors soon made their socio-economic demands apparent. Civil service strikes, student movements and the struggles of their incipient political parties and organisations, brought them into increasing conflict with the established regime.

The events of recent years demonstrate that the present political regime is incapable of responding to the emergence of the new social forces outlined above. The inefficiency of the present economic model has resulted in the growth of rural and urban poverty and has led to further economic polarisation in the country. The 'façade democracy' has proved incapable of articulating the social demands of the emergent groups, and has allowed such severe economic polarisation that it has spilled over into the re-emergence of armed struggle and generated a further cycle of violence.

Fissures in the Power Structure

Lately divisions and splits have appeared within the centres of power which until recently underpinned the authoritarian regime. Among these the Catholic Church, various political parties, employers' associations (*cámaras patronales*) and the military must all be considered. Traditionally, at critical moments they have always chosen to preserve the status quo and to present a united front. It could be argued that these groups, though consisting of different centres of power, in fact share a similar outlook with regard to national politics, even though their reasons may differ. The current rupture within this coalition, however, is a major departure from formerly prevalent norms of Guatemalan society. The new ways of thinking have not yet crystallised into a dominant ideology for society, but it is nevertheless apparent that a certain sector of the oligarchy is aware of the bankruptcy of the present authoritarian regime and of the need to find a quite different solution to the crisis.

Liberation theology, the new current of Catholic thought that has become widespread in Latin America, has likewise become a force for change within the Guatemalan Catholic Church. Liberation theology has led to a process of *concientización* at all levels of society, especially with regard to social and economic inequality. It has also allowed the church to become further involved with marginal rural communities and other neglected groups. As a result, the church now faces internal contradictions. One sector with close ties to the oligarchy wishes to maintain the status quo, whilst another demands radical measures in order to bring about change. Faced by contradictory views within its own ranks, the church has chosen to make concessions to both the traditional and the progressive sectors. In public, the church denounces terror and violence and demands that all groups involved respect human rights. It also recommends a search for a democratic alternative. This final point brings the church into conflict with the existing authoritarian system, particularly with the militarist strategy that has been its recent hallmark. Thus, the oligarchy runs the risk of losing a basic pillar of support and of social control.

Although the legal parties have not performed a major role, they have operated within the limits allowed by 'façade democracy'. The monopoly of expression enjoyed by these groups in the last 20 years has allowed them a certain margin, sufficient at least to develop and renew themselves. Between 1966 and 1982, Guatemala's political arena was limited to four political parties, three of which – the National Liberation Movement (MLN), the Institutional Democratic Party (PID) and the Revolutionary Party (PR) – assumed the reins of office during certain periods. Athough the Christian Democratic Party has not yet been given the opportunity to govern, it nevertheless has had its share of the power exercised by Congress.

After the 1982 *coup d'état*, the structure of the political parties changed, and new political forces emerged, although for the most part these were of little significance. At this time, three important developments occurred. First, the traditional parties such as the MLN, the PID and PR were weakened. In the case of the MLN this was not because of any fall in its electoral potential; although it experienced no quantitative growth during the last constituent election, it nevertheless finished third. Rather, what has weakened it and the others has been the emergence of new currents of political expression inside the dominant parties themselves, a phenomenon without precedent which indicates a turning-point in the way of thinking of the dominant social groups. Secondly, there has been a strengthening of the political parties of the centre. The 1984 election indicated a shift towards the political centre, represented by the Christian Democrats who for the first time participated in a fair election and who took first place. Also at this time another political force made its appearance, namely the National Centre Union (UCN). This political organisation reflects the outlook of the modern entrepreneurial class. Thirdly, the high proportion of blank and nul votes cast indicates the lack of confidence the Guatemalan public feel towards the electoral process (see Table 8.2).

All this has broken the monopoly of power formerly enjoyed by the traditional parties who were accustomed to negotiate their quotas of representation directly with the military, and who in exchange cooperated in electoral fraud.

Concerning the various organisations of the private enterprise sector there are two noteworthy points:

1. This sector now expresses its institutional opposition to any continuation of a system in which the military assume total control of the government. There are several reasons for this opposition, including the problem of corruption arising from 'disloyal' competition between military sectors and private entrepreneurs. This group feels that the existing problems of polarisation and armed conflict cannot simply be resolved by military means. Above all it feels (and sometimes even explicitly states) that the army is to blame for the country's economic difficulties and that the fall in business profits is basically due to bad administration by the military. Finally, the army has failed to put an end to the problem of insurgency.
2. The other fact worth stressing is that the 'private enterprise' sector appears willing to support centrist options. It encouraged the creation of the UCN as a managerial alternative and the Christian Democratic Party has also been known to receive support from certain sectors of private enterprise. A change is also evident in the discourse

of the parties traditionally allied with the right, indicating a shift within their bases of support towards the political centre.

Table 8.2: Official Results for the 1984 Constituent Assembly Elections

Party	Total Votes	Percentages
Christian Democracy	318,300	15.5
Union of the National Centre	269,372	13.1
Nationalist Liberation Movement		
The Authentic Nationalist Central Party	245,514	12.0
Void Vote	428,068	20.9

Source: Table prepared by the author and figures quoted from Miguel Angel Reyes in: 'Guatemala: Elementos para comprender la jornada electoral', *Polemica*, vol. 14, no. 15 (March-June 1984).

The 1982 *coup d'état* was the result of a contradiction within the army concerning the present political situation. Broadly speaking, this division was between those sectors which support a process of a restrained *apertura democrática*, or democratic opening, and those seeking firmly to maintain a strictly military option.

The Position of the United States

The Guatemalan case has acquired a special significance for the United States because of the very independent attitude taken by the Guatemalan military. During the Carter administration, the Guatemalan government reacted assertively to the prospect of US pressure, particularly in regard to its human rights record. President Lucas García ignored most external criticism of his government, whether the complaints came from the US government, from human rights groups or from other democratic regimes. As a result of this, all US military aid to Guatemala was suspended.

Since 1980 terrorism and repression have continued to define Guatemalan politics. The Reagan administration has had to deal with this, as well as the relatively independent position the Guatemalan government takes in Central American politics. Recently it seems that a better understanding has been reached between the two administrations, with economic and military aid being restored to Guatemala. Now that the Guatemalan government appears to espouse a so-called *apertura democrática*, the US government seems eager to help.

With less armed conflict in Guatemala than in neighbouring El

Salvador, US support for democratic elections could produce more effect. Some 73 per cent of the electorate voted during the last constituent assembly election, which demonstrates a high electoral turnout. This vote also showed that the army was capable of respecting a popular choice. In the Guatemalan case, the United States seeks to create and to encourage a broader political opening than the one which exists in El Salvador. The US recommends that previously banned political parties should be allowed to take part in the electoral processes.

It would appear that the present US policy is similar to that espoused by those centrist political forces attempting to bring about a programme of democratisation. If so, the US would be relegating its traditional alliances to a subordinate position. The Reagan administration appears willing to deal with such centrist political groups as the Christian Democratic Party and the National Central Union.

Some Basic Issues Concerning Democratisation

The most basic issue concerns the concept of democracy itself. What is to be understood by democracy? How far are political parties able to agree on a concept of democracy, and how tenable a system is it? These questions are not unfamiliar ones, particularly since the struggle for democracy in Guatemala has a long history. Nevertheless, the various uses of the term have created confusion, and have distorted the essence of democracy itself. Thus, in Guatemalan discourse the concept of democracy appears to be an elastic one, but ultimately certain factors and values cannot be ignored if a true democracy is to be established.

Democracy consists of 'a combination of norms (the so-called rules of the game) which directly or indirectly allow the greatest possible freedom and guarantee the full participation of citizens in political deeision-making, i.e. in deciding those questions that affect the welfare of the community'.[3] This concept implies the existence of a system of political parties, without exclusions for ideological resasons. It requires universal suffrage and respect for the voters' choices, and it would permit divergent political alternatives to exist, each with the possibility of attaining political power if elected through a majority. Finally, it would ensure respect for minorities.

Obviously we have here a narrowly political definition of democracy, and would not wish to claim that these conditions exhaust the possibilities. They do however constitute minimum requirements for the existence of a democracy. Underlying this concept, the respect for human rights and tolerance of a broad spectrum of political opinions are part of the spirit of democracy and are essential elements of the struggle being waged against authoritarianism in Guatemala.

A further matter which should be clarified concerns the *proyectos* – the proposals, schemes or designs – which the various political parties have put forward. In many cases it is difficult to refer to concrete political programmes. Nevertheless three alternative political projects can be identified at present:

1. Reformism of the centre-right, notably the Christian Democrats and the Union of the National Centre.[4]
2. Reformism of the left, as represented by the Social Democratic Party.[5]
3. Armed struggle to overthrow the present system. This effort is headed by National Revolutionary Unity (URNG), a coalition of the country's guerrilla groups.

The reformist sectors of the right offer proposals which reflect upper-class and also middle-class standpoints. Their principal proposals concern respect for human rights and a broadening of the political arena. On the economic front, they advocate modernisation rather than social reform. In brief, they envisage the establishment of formal democracy.

Social democracy propounds freedom, equality, social justice and solidarity as its basic premises. The Social Democratic Party focuses on the principles of liberty and social justice and believes that socialism is impossible without democracy. It also stresses the need to promote political, social and economic democracy at all levels. Finally, the party sees itself as an expression of the working class in its broadest sense.

Whilst the parties of the reformist right have been able to operate within the political framework imposed by the oligarchy, the Social Democratic Party has had to adopt a position of non-violent resistance. Until 1985 it was forced to operate clandestinely.

On the left, the struggle for change by military means is defined in Marxist-Leninist terms. This view proposes a global transformation of society through a popular revolutionary war. The guerrilla coalition created in January 1982 proposed respect for human rights, freedom of political expression and organisation (including free and fair elections) and a foreign policy of non-alignment.[6]

Reviewing these proposals, one can say that the reformist right offers a short-term solution, that is, the formation of a political regime of a democratic-liberal nature. By contrast, social democracy propounds the need to move forward through peaceful means, thus permitting the establishment of conditions for a democratic development by proposing the struggle for socialism as the long-term objective. This is a gradualist view which consists of beginning with the establishment of a regime which respects human rights and allows widespread participation, and which will initiate fundamental economic reforms. The construction of a socialist and democratic society is viewed as an ultimate goal. The insurgent groups claim that such gradual reform is impossible. They believe that military struggle and a seizure of power is the only way to change society.

Setting aside any ideological-partisan focus, the concrete situation dictates that no transformation of Guatemalan society can be accomplished overnight. In fact, a transformation began some time ago and a continuing dynamic ensures its perpetuation over time. In this sense, the construction of democracy must be viewed as a long-term endeavour, although important developments can occur conjuncturally to facilitate a social pact aimed at accelerated democratisation. It would be utopian and romantic to believe that the background and culture of authoritarianism will disappear in the near term.

The Need to Overcome Traditional Ways of Thinking

A manichean vision of society has long united the Guatemalan oligarchy. This group sees the world in black and white terms, divided between communists and anti-communists, engaged in deadly confrontation between East and West. They also feel the need to mount an unconditional defence of private property against those who would promote a fairer distribution of wealth. As has already been mentioned, they view all those who dissent from their reactionary and closed *Weltanschauung* as enemies of the system. Their use of coercive methods for remaining in power has resulted in a highly polarised and authoritarian type of government. Until recently this authoritarian system succeeded in enlisting the support not only of the oligarchy, but also of other important sectors such as the medium and small proprietors, the church and sections of the military.

On the international front, the US has played a significant role in propping up the status quo. This has been the case since 1954, when the US became directly involved in Guatemalan politics. Throughout this period American support has been decisive in the construction and institutionalisation of Guatemala's authoritarian regime. At present, however, owing to the fissures within the internal power structure and to the regional crisis, the US may have begun to redefine its policy towards Guatemala.

Moreover, internal opposition has become entrenched, as indicated by the persistent struggles of Indian peasants, non-Indians (*ladinos*), urban and rural workers, as well as those marginal sectors of urban areas and indeed the middle sectors. All this suggests that the forms of government which traditionally dominated the country in the past are currently eroding and that the oligarchy is rapidly losing its cohesive force.

The Question of Establishing a Broad Social Pact

Daily experience indicates that convergence between the many sectors of society that desire to attain social peace is a real possibility. Extremely high levels of violence and the unfettered repression by the government has produced a state of social disintegration. Wide sectors of society, including the widows or relatives of those who have disappeared, condemn these barbaric violations of human rights. All reformist political parties agree that terror and violence are unacceptable as a means of social control. This belief has brought many political groups together, with the aim of ending this polarisation and restoring social peace. These groups range from the university intelligentsia to the church, in its different guises, as well as a variety of political parties and social organisations. Tacit understanding between these groups is, however, insufficient: to be effective it needs to be organised. A formal alliance is, however, unlikely because of the level of polarisation between competing ideologies in the present political struggle and because of the inability of important political parties to break away from traditional ways of thinking.

Consequently it should not be expected that a convergence can be brought about by means of agreement in advance among the organised groups. The Guatemalan process has not yet reached such a level of development. More likely would be a gradual strengthening of co-operation under the pressure of events and in response to the demands of society at large. Other possibilities for attaining political convergence may emerge from the process of social and political struggle itself.

In this sense it is essential for those political parties who wish to construct a democratic system to subordinate their ideological principles and to give highest priority to a campaign for the observance of human rights and an end to terror and repression. They should also press for a broadening of political participation in order to achieve minimum working agreements on practical steps towards a 'solution' to the present crisis.

The Question of Economic Reform and a Fairer Distribution of Wealth

Democracy must aim to provide better living conditions for the majority of the population. In order to reach this goal, there will have to be a gradual advance aimed at addressing basic needs, promoting economic development and bringing an end to the current crisis. Those groups who have most benefited in the past will have to make financial sacrifices on behalf of the rest of the population, something which until now they have refused to do.

Even if there were a total restructuring of society, these objectives could not be reached in the short term. It is nevertheless essential to begin an economic reform if democracy is eventually to be created in Guatemala. Economic reform is essential if we are to bring violence and authoritarianism to an end and permit democracy to develop in the long term.

The Role of the United States

Given Guatemala's strategic position, and the strong links between certain sectors of the society and the US, some consideration should be given to the role played by US foreign policy. Throughout the twentieth century, the United States has taken a strong interest in political developments in Guatemala. As early as 1920 the United States played a part, with the country's Unionist and Liberal Parties, in ousting the dictator Manuel Estrada Cabrera. In 1944 the bargain struck between the 'revolutionaries' and the representatives of the Ponce dictatorship occurred under the auspices of the US embassy. Better known than these cases was the active role taken by the American government in ousting the 'revolutionary' government in 1954, its involvement in the 1963 *coup d'état*, and finally in the transfer of the presidency to Julio César Méndez Montenegro in 1966. In each of these cases, the United States imposed its perception of the issues at stake, and its views usually coincided with those of the traditional elites.

More recently, the crisis in Central America has intensified US concern about the outcome of local events. The establishment of a democratic government in Guatemala will be conditioned by the nature of the relationship with the US. The insurgent forces have understood this and have therefore adopted a policy of non-alignment. Nevertheless, this seems insufficient given the American response to Nicaragua and US policy regarding El Salvador. Unless the US modifies its policies and seeks to influence the country's ruling elite in favour of a democratisation, the authoritarian and traditional groups will continue polarising political life, and the possibility for democracy will be minimal. Carried to extremes, a militarist vision would force all political sectors into reliance on force, and could create a military conflict of regional dimensions.

The Problem of Internal War

It must be stressed that the internal war in Guatemala, like the war that is continuing in the rest of Central America, is not a product of the East-West confrontation. The current crisis is due to appalling living conditions, high levels of exploitation and the extreme poverty which are the legacies of authoritarianism. The present warfare is a desperate attempt to bring about social and political change. The struggle is directed at a small economic, political and military elite who oppose the establishment of democracy and refuse to relinquish their powerful positions.

Conclusion

Throughout this chapter we have attempted to describe the sources of Guatemalan authoritarianism, the present regional context and the ways in which it affects the possibilities for democratic government in that country. Some attention has also been given to internal developments within Guatemala's political life and to the US position on Guatemala.

Although it has been possible to identify some encouraging points for the possible establishment of democracy, the polarising effects of the war still over-ride all other considerations. Ultimately a democratic alternative can only be seen as a long-term objective, but the first steps can and should be taken now. This might permit a gradual alleviation of the situation, opening the way to more extensive political and economic reforms.

It is at present impossible to envisage the establishment of a direct dialogue between the contending political forces in arms. As has been mentioned above, the process of understanding will first require the displacement of traditional ways of thinking; the creation of appropriate conditions so that opposition parties can openly participate in public life; a halt to repression and the observance of human rights; and finally, important economic reforms to satisfy at least partially the most immediate needs of the poor. What is required is a process of national convergence that accepts the political and economic changes necessary for the construction of a lasting democracy. Only this can bring the present state of violence to an end.

Notes and References

1. This is backed up by the evidence provided by human rights groups, particularly concerning the extreme use of violence in the instituionalisation of repression. It can also be seen in the growth of delinquency and the type of violent crimes now perpetrated on a daily basis. The Archbishop of Guatemala City told the Spanish newpaper *La Vanguardia* (25 July 1985); 'it is very symptomatic of our problems that even in the midst of an election campaign the violence is on the increase.' He also noted that it was not possible to open an office for the defence of human rights; 'they would make them disappear, or kill them, each and every one'.

2. Enzo Faletto, 'Estilos alternativos de desarrollo y opciones políticas. Papel movimiento popular'. *América Latina: Desarrollo y Perspectivas Democraticas* (San José: FLASCO, Colección 25 Aniversario, 1982).

3. Norberto Bobbio, 'Qué alternativas a la democracia representativa', *El Marxismo y el Estado* (Barcelona, 1978), pp. 49-50.

4. The UCN maintains contacts with the Liberal International.

5. Two Social Democratic parties exist in Guatemala: the United Revolutionary Front (FUR) and the Social Democratic Party (PSD). In addition to these, other small groups identify themselves with the democratic left. However, the only political party which is recognised by the Socialist International is the PSD, which has belonged to the SI since 1980 [and is currently led by the author of this chapter – Eds].

6. 'Proclama Unitaria', *Nuevo Diario* (Managua), 10 February 1982.

9 NICARAGUA: ONE STEP FORWARD, TWO STEPS BACK

Rodolfo Cerdas

Background, Importance and Role of Nicaragua in Central America

The Somoza regime was more than a contemptible and criminal dictatorship. The dynasty, or *somozato*, was nothing like the Hernández Martínez government in El Salvador. While sharing the same tyrannical and criminal methods, the *somozato* presented a characteristic which was doubly original: on the one hand, a very strong internal consolidation which, on the other hand, allowed it to play an often decisive role in the rest of Central America. This regional role in turn reinforced the regime's domestic position.

These two aspects – the domestic and the external – relate to the peculiarities of Nicaraguan historical development, its situation in the Isthmus, its desire for a canal and its specific political evolution.

This is why Somoza's Nicaragua had a part to play in the problems suffered by the government of Teodoro Picado in Costa Rica during the civil war of 1948; in the 1949 and 1955 invasions against the José Figueres governments; behind Castillo Armas in Guatemala; and even in the preparations for the Bay of Pigs in 1961.

For this reason, the Somozas seem to have been a dynasty of guardians, rather than guardians of a dynasty.

But guardians of what? Obviously of interests which essentially corresponded to the political, economic and strategic needs of the United States as supreme regional power and was itself responsible for the birth, consolidation and development of the Somoza regime. Nicaragua's interests, as defined by Somoza Garcia – that is, his own interests – corresponded without much difficulty to the interests of the United States.

This sacrifice of Nicaragua's interests in turn revealed the essentially national liberationist character of any serious movement against the *somozato*, since a foreign presence has historically been a basic political fact in the Nicaraguan political scene, throughout the nineteenth century and more especially in the twentieth century.

Use of Nicaragua by Foreign Powers

Nicaragua has had a long history of foreign interventions, on the pretexts of protecting lives and capital, ensuring domestic order and inter-oceanic traffic, the recovery of loans, or even of lending disinterested and fraternal assistance to patriotic forces fighting for national liberation or for liberty and democracy.

The tale of interventions promoted by the strategic interests and perceptions of international capital, whether American, French or British, has been told repeatedly. And much attention has recently been paid to the anti-Sandinista actions co-ordinated and supported by the United States and its regional allies. This is an aspect which must be borne in mind in our analysis – but one should not over-emphasise it, and ignore the other side of the coin: namely, increasingly diverse domestic social and political configurations; the inheritance of a Liberal-Conservative confrontation, replaced in the final period of the *somozato* by a confrontation with self-proclaimed Marxist-Leninist guerrilla groups; an additional but decisive interest taken by the powers, bringing in their train the East-West conflict; and a present governmental political orientation, nationally and especially internationally, which converts the Nicaraguan situation into an axis of regional and possibly of world tension, to the extent that the confrontation transcends local actors and affects the global interests of competing superpowers. All of which merely confirms once again that the Nicaraguan problem is essentially national and political.

As early as 1927 the Communist International defined its policy in Central America, identifying the Nicaraguan probem as a typical case of national liberation, and that of El Salvador as social in nature, involving the move from a backward society to an advanced socialist society which, with the possible help of the dictatorship of the Soviet proletariat, would avoid the capitalist stages.

That was how the international communist movement began to take an interest in Central America in general and in Nicaragua in particular. However, even during the earliest days of that interest, it was clearly the aim of the communist movement to reduce the Nicaraguan problem to a pre-eminently profitable event in its global confrontation, which was of greater historical and political moment and which developed from two basic state interests, identified in its ideological discourse with the international communist movement's general interests and principles; the second – complementary to the first – was the possibility of weakening the Soviet Union's main ideological adversary. The specific interests of the Nicaraguan people came a very poor third.

In fact, Sandino's tragic struggle presents an easily forgotten aspect which not only exonerates Somoza Garcia and his US mentors, but which also provides the full dimension of the tragedy of a people whose national interests, for reasons of ideology or convenience, are sacrificed in a supposedly world revolution which actually served the state and national interests of a new great power.

Faced with US intervention and Somoza's National Guard, Sandino was accused by the Comintern of being a petty bourgeois nationalist, incapable of becoming a truly revolutionary social reformer imbued with the spirit of proletarian internationalism. He refused the different positions which the Comintern offered him in order to make him more useful to its political designs – situated, significantly, in Europe, where the communists wanted to send Sandino as a propagandist of anti-imperialism. As is well known, the Nicaraguan's refusal led to his expulsion from the Anti-Imperialist League, his anathemisation as a traitor who sold out to American imperialism for $66,000 and to his description as a petty bourgeois *caudillo* whose sole ambition was to be president of Nicaragua.

General Sandino's greatest mistake, in the eyes of the international communist movement, was his inability to transform the struggle for national liberation into a revolution capable of constructing a socialist society in Nicaragua.

Without wishing to go over all of that and the concept held at the time of the type of revolution appropriate to a country like Nicaragua in the first third of this century, it is useful to point out that such an interpretation of the political events unfolding there contributed not only to the abandonment of Sandino to his fate, but also to the consolidation of the American project under the aegis of the founder of the *somozato*.

Somoza, Strongest Link in the Chain

The make-up of a political power so unquestioned as *somocismo*, despite the rearguard actions fought by some of the surviving ex-Sandinista generals who tried repeatedly but always unsuccessfully to overthrow the dictatorship, lies in the special nature of the Nicaraguan political system under Somoza Garcia's leadership, a factor which was missing in other political systems in the region, whether authoritarian, as in Guatemala and El Salvador, or liberal-democratic, as in Costa Rica.

The various distributions of landownership, capital and labour/work in the different regions of Central America placed the dominant elites in different positions within their respective political systems. In the north, especially in El Salvador and Guatemala, an abundance of productive resources made the economically dominant elites inclined to concentrate on properly economic and lucrative activities. In the south, however, particularly in Costa Rica, the shortage of resources forced the oligarchy to turn to politics and involve themselves directly in the national political system.

The consequences of delegating the political system to the military, in the first case, and of direct participation, in the second, produced completely different characteristics of structure and function in each system. While for the north's dominant elite the military guaranteed the absence of bothersome political demands which could upset the peaceful workings of productive activity – the more closed the system, the more functional that system appeared to the economic elite to be – in the south the complete opposite occurred. There, with political power and the title to it contested, cousins belonging to the same conquistador dynasty were in opposition: to settle their quarrel, they had to seek social support which would back up their conflicting desires to exercise political power in the name of the supposed general interest. Social sectors initially alien to the tiny elite were invited to participate in government, to express their aspirations and alleviate their discontents through political alliances, and to contribute to the establishment of rules of the game to regulate the family rivalries of the elite. This is the context in which the electoral system of Costa Rica has been developed and refined.

In both cases – in the north and the south – the political systems appeared strong for different reasons, but enshrined political practices which could make them unviable in the medium and long term.

As far as the closed political system of northern Central America is concerned, the population's demands were systematically rejected or merely satisfied temporarily, with no real attempt to respond adequately to the needs of those societies whose structure, differentiation and development were becoming ever more complex. All this blocked off the process of legitimising the system, which would have enabled it to respond to the demands of the population, and thereby to stimulate a supportive civil society. Instead there was first a gradual deterioration, followed by an accelerated loss of legitimacy not only for the traditional elites but even for the political system itself. Last-minute attempts to give such systems a spurious responsiveness are not only insufficient and rather incredible but go against the existing relations of power in the very state structures of those societies. They also reveal that it is not a matter of implementing policies which make concessions to the population's demands, but of radically restructuring the political and social system so that those demands, the response to those demands and the subsequent feedback, become the very essence of its working. Although that, of course, presupposes a substantial modification and displacement of the traditional structures of economic and social power, in particular the delegation of political power in the hands of the military. In other words, it assumes an authentic national democratic revolution, in the specific context of those societies – mere expressions of goodwill and promises of good behaviour by the military and the oligarchy will not suffice, for everyone would know that they were simply waiting for their moment of revenge.

In the south, the system's weakness derived from its excessive openness and from the indiscriminate and demagogical way in which popular demands had been met without regard for the requirements of production and accumulation. These demands were not simply accepted, but actually stimulated beyond any limits of prudence; given the productive structure, and in the absence of any real model of development other than the traditional system, the demands of the different social sectors were met through constant expansion of the state apparatus, which became increasingly difficult to manage and control as it mushroomed in size. Once its course of development had been set, the Costa Rican state grew under its own inertia both in aggregate and in terms of each of its various institutes and branches. With only traditional sources of production, together with the derivative import-substitute industrialisation created by the Central American market, and with an agricultural frontier which was exhausted and a population undergoing sustained growth – although at a slower pace than in the 1950s – the state became a source of political booty, a major employer, and moved successively from being an interventionist state to a managerial state and finally – to use the words of José Figueres when commenting on some of its excesses – a hand-out state. To the dependent structure of the economy – where, according to official reports, a grain of coffee contains 60 per cent imported components – there was added a giant state, a chronic fiscal deficit, indebtedness totally disproportionate to the country's exports and its capacity for payment, a reduction in its exports because of the world economic crisis, and a slowdown in its rate of GNP growth. To this has been added not only sustained demands by the population and a channelling of those demands in an undifferentiated way within the political system, but also a redistribution of the system itself to respond to different pressure groups – industrial, business, labour, bureaucratic, political, etc. – which have accumulated enough force to counter the initiatives of others but lack the muscle to realise their own projects. This creates a political-institutional paralysis which has particularly serious consequences at a time of world and regional crisis, together with the collapse of its social structure, for which the dynamism of the country's political system can scarcely compensate.

In these circumstances, the foregoing considerations can be summarised by saying that while in the north the political system was weak because of its closed nature and its unresponsiveness to the demands of the population, in the south it was weak because of its excessive openness and its tendency to take on board every type of demand, even the most bizarre, beyond the objective limits imposed by its underdeveloped and dependent productive system. In the first case, the economic elites remained relatively uninvolved in the direct exercise of political power; in the second, they involved themselves in politics to such an extent that they practically abandoned the characteristics of an *economic* elite. In the first case the participation of newly emergent social forces was rejected; in the second, not only the title but whole areas of power were shared with the newcomers and gate-crashers, with unexpected consequences for the initial strategy of compromise and conciliation.

In Nicaragua the presence of foreign interests gave rise to a situation unique in Central America. With its power and regional interest opposed by Sandino's guerrillas, the United States tried to resolve the problem directly as it had done in that same period in other Caribbean nations: the intervention of the marines. When this, and the attempt to hold elections under the supervision of the US military failed, the US established a trustworthy military force, able to take on the responsibility of a war between Nicaraguan and Nicaraguan. In that way, the US localised the fight against Sandino, creating the National Guard. It was no accident that the methods used by the US in Nicaragua were subsequently applied in China and Vietnam many years later.

The important thing is that in the case of Nicaragua the leader installed by the US – Anastasio Somoza – united, both in his own right and through his marriage to a Debayle, not just military power but also the traditional economic power of the principal families who had inherited the colony. To both of these factors he added undisputed political power, especially after the assassination of Sandino and, decisively and fundamentally, the privileged position of being the most trusted interlocutor of the United States in Central America.

Somoza's power was, then, fourfold: military, economic, political and regional. Somoza's regime in Nicaragua was not just one more tyranny established with the diligent help of the United States, but an authentic power axis which was stable, permanent, lasting and which had all the political flexibility required to carry out its role in the region.

The Strongest Link Becomes the Weakest

In stark contrast to what Somoza and his acolytes in Nicaragua and, abroad, his allies in the United States and Central America have tried to present as the result of an international conspiracy – the process of weakening, military and political resistance, crisis and fall of the regime – the collapse was the result of a complex process of internal differentiation in the social and economic spheres of Nicaragua and the emergence of middle social sectors, employers, intellectuals and politicians, for whom the regime was incompatible not just with the possibility of development but with their real needs.

The notable increase in the production and export of cotton in the mid-1940s, and the subsequent liberal-conservative convergence enabled Nicaragua to postpone a political realignment of the type characteristic of the immediate post-war period. The subsequent development and diversification of the Nicaraguan economy in the 1950s, and especially in the 1960s, produced a range of new social sectors which, although initially able to progress and develop under the patrimonial control of the *somozato*, soon experienced first friction and then outright conflict with a system which not only seemed to obstruct their full economic, social and political development, but even threatened them with retrogression in those fields. This sense of threat arose from the regime's systematic policy of monopolising, cartelising and annexing to its own advantage all sorts of initiatives, particularly in the economic and financial fields.

The regime, which had helped to unite traditionally antagonistic groups through the economic impulse of cotton and by virtue of the political tutelage of the United States, gradually became an obstacle to the political and economic development of the new Nicaragua which was coming into being despite the shackles which the *somocista* regime was imposing on it.

To the inspiration of the Cuban Revolution, which had provided the impulse for the actions of Carlos Fonseca Amador and José Benito Escobar, were added attempts to construct fronts of civil and political struggle, beyond the traditional political formations, such as the United Popular Movement which united the Nicaraguan left, the National Patriotic Front which combined forces of the petty and middle bourgeoisie, as well as outstanding individuals representing the most powerful fractions of national capital, and who were in another sense a clear expression of the political fact that Nicaragua's new social, economic and political realities went beyond the narrow limits of its political system and the traditional party formations.

The *somocista* regime, then, not only had to deal with a challenge from young guerrillas inspired by the Cuban Revolution and in more than one sense opposed by other forces of the traditional left, whom they accused of playing Somoza's game and of betraying the forward march of the revolution, but also with deeper social, economic and political processes. Only with difficulty could these processes be contained through the traditional methods of brutal repression, terror and corruption with which the regime had fought previous threats: they were not just rearguard actions from the preceding period, they obeyed development forces and impulses which aimed at the future of Nicaragua. They were not the last gasps of a dying movement, but the beginning of something new, which had an irresistible momentum.

In this sense, both Somoza and the United States remained committed to the use of the traditional political formulae, and were willing to revert to the old methods which had produced such favourable results for them in the recent past. Thinking only of what was familiar to them and unable to understand the profound democratic aspirations that were stirring in the souls of the Nicaraguan people, they continued relying on their traditional practices, and as recently as mid-1978 could see no possibility of change.

As a result, the United States not merely failed to influence the process of change in Nicaragua but, as on other occasions elsewhere, they ensured that change occurred without them and against their wishes. That is why not just the most radical sectors of the Sandinista Front, traditionally anti-imperialists and ideologically Marxist-Leninists, but also important bourgeois and business elements firmly and justifiably rejected US policy. It was not just their anger at US complicity in the origin, development, consolidation and maintenance of the Somoza regime for so many years; it was also their response to the substantial inability of the designers of US policy to recognise real changes, to take in the decadence of the old and the emergence of the new in developing societies and change in Central America and particularly in Nicaragua.

Paradoxically, Nicaragua's domestic developments, which militated against the regime and from which *somocista* greed sought to profit, gradually turned the strongest of the regional systems of domination and the most secure base of support for US policy in the Isthmus into the exact opposite. *Somocismo*'s growing isolation; the obsolescence of the regional military pacts in the light of conflicts such as the El Salvador/Honduras war; the generalised instability of all the other military regimes; the indecision and the moral and political crises within the United States; and the deterioration of the economy after 1975 were all important factors in precipitating the political crisis. The presence of a corrupt regime and a repressive apparatus, personified in an individual who represented a black period in the history of United States-Latin American relations, an ill-fated relic from the era of the Trujillos, the Carías and other tyrants, strengthened the international prestige of the democratic struggles not only in those countries which had traditionally been anti-Somoza, such as Mexico and democratic Venezuela, but also even within the area of United States public opinion.

The strongest link in the chain became the weakest; the axis of regional power which arose from the conjunction of political, military, economic and social power, assimilated as the chosen instrument of United States foreign policy for the region, became the source of instability for an authentic democratic, national, socially advanced revolution affirming the sovereignty and self-determination of the Nicaraguan people.

The Nature and Methods of the Nicaraguan Revolution

The regime's repressive and anti-democratic nature gave rise to a Nicaraguan business sector which was dynamic and able in business but totally inexperienced and traditionally uninterested in politics, in which, for their own peace of mind, they preferred not to meddle. And it was precisely there, in the key matter of their lack of practical political experience at a time when the system of domination was entering open crisis, that the bourgeois business sectors were too weak and too inexperienced to claim for themselves the vanguard of a movement whose characteristics, extent and vicissitudes were extremely difficult for them to assimilate. The strategy for Nicaragua of '*somocismo* without Somoza' was totally unviable, given the basic demands which had to be taken into account and which had caused the decomposition of the *somocista* regime from within in the first place. This decomposition was not, then, in my view, purely political: it was social and economic; and superficial or cosmetic modifications were not enough to stop its collapse not just with respect to Somoza's domination, but as a patrimonial state and type of socio-economic organisation at the service of the Somoza family, its parasitical hangers-on and especially the US scheme of domination in the region.

Nicaragua, like El Salvador – although for different reasons – was at this later period facing not a change of political regime but an authentic national democratic revolution, a global and coherent restructuring of its productive structure, social organisation and political system as well as its role, under those conditions, in the already critical context of Central American societies. It was a matter of adjusting the political system not to the United States' external control and security needs within the Isthmus, or to the insatiable appetites of the Somoza family or of its parasitic caste, but to the existing and ongoing transformations in the productive structure of Nicaraguan society and its corresponding social organisation.

For the purpose of this analysis, all of the foregoing is important because it throws light on a decisive political fact: the real, objective possibility of the FSLN being in the van of the revolutionary process and the clear difficulties facing the FSLN's only possible rivals, the businessmen and sectors of the national bourgeoisie, in taking that task upon themselves.

For that very reason, it was not only from a US security standpoint that Nicaragua appeared as the weakest link in the Central American chain of domination. This was also how it appeared from the viewpoint of those who hoped to transform the first stage of the revolution uninterruptedly into a triumphant socialist revolution.

It was this very standpoint that had dominated the thinking of the FSLN from its inception. The Sandinistas had always considered the Nicaraguan bourgeoisie easy to neutralise and eventually to dispense with once the process of revolutionary mobilisation had developed sufficiently to make possible a socialist regime, in the Marxist-Leninist sense of the term.

The Sandinistas' political scheme had original aspects, some of which had emerged spontaneously in the aftermath of the Cuban Revolution:

the Cuban practice and interpretation of Marxism had an enormous influence on the Sandinista leaders, who were trained with the direct help of Ernesto Che Guevara.

The matter of the route the revolution would take was the most important topic in political discussions of the 1960s. There was an intransigent defence of the theory that the only way to get rid of *somocismo*, to push forward the revolution and prevent US and bourgeois manoeuvres, which could and did occur in the shape of somocismo without Somoza, was through armed popular struggle.

This theory, and its discussion in the Nicaraguan case, highlighted the other peculiarity of the process: the fact that it took place, as far as the armed struggle is concerned, not only *without* the participation of but *against* the opinion and political attitude of the communist movement directed by the Soviet Union. This movement, more inclined to negotiation and compromise, and with a long tradition along those lines, not only mistrusted guerrilla methods, but openly repudiated them and instead promoted the traditional orientation of first creating the party, basing itself on the workers, forging alliances, etc. The use of terms like 'pseudo-Marxists', 'reformists, revisionists' and eventually traitors who had to be not just neutralised but 'rejected and smashed' (FSLN communiqué of 24 July 1978), arises precisely from this problem of the route to revolution; however, in another sense, these terms point, by omission, to a full agreement, or at least a basic concordance in relation to the ultimate objectives: national liberation and socialism.

The Sandinistas' whole policy of alliances was framed within the classical Marxist perspective of forming a broad front of forces to combat a common enemy. This broad front of popular and democratic forces, as they are usually defined, must first overthrow existing power, which is the political expression of traditional domination. Later, as the revolutionary dynamic deepens and attempts to keep the revolution within the framework initially accepted by the different allies according to their own perception of the process emerge, those who oppose the orientation of the movement begin to be displaced; and thus begins a speedy radicalisation whose domestic key lies, above all, in ensuring that the breakaways are as gradual as possible, in order to avoid uniting in a single front all the adversaries, present and future, of the revolution.

The stages of the revolution, for their part, maintain a dialectical relationship between the maturing of the consciousness of the revolutionary masses, their degree of organisation and capacity to fight and mobilise (the subjective element), and the degree of concrete development of the economy, production relations, technological level and financial situation (the objective element). The latter cannot be changed arbitrarily and, despite and perhaps because of the possible political radicalisation, since this raises the threat of voluntarism, it is the frame of reference in which the revolution must be situated. Within this frame of reference we must evaluate the goals put forward, the driving forces which will enable those goals to be attained and the political nature of the party organisation and the leadership; here too we must weigh up the real degree of confidence it merits as a revolution.

We are not dealing here with irrelevant theoretical matters. For example, the Soviet reading of these revolutions and their more-than-cautious attitude, as has been observed, when weighing up the socialist enthusiasms and especially the self-descriptions as Marxist-Leninists of the leaders of these revolutions, find a strong political, ideological and categorical basis in this type of appreciation, whether dealing with Cuba in the 1960s, Grenada in the 1980s, Mozambique, Angola or Nicaragua at present.

For that very reason, the stage immediately after the triumph followed in Nicaragua with a policy defined as anti-imperialist, nationalist, or a mixed economy, pluralist *within* the revolution, repressive outside of it; and organised on the basis of increasing control by ever more sectarian and intolerant organisations at the popular level, and the constant refining of police-repressive structures and control of political dissidence. This was not now on the level of defeated *somocismo* but of potentially disaffected sectors, possibly capable of betraying the revolution and of going over to the enemy. The political form in this degree of development of the popular revolution is the revolutionary dictatorship of the workers and peasants and their allies from the radicalised petty and middle bourgeoisie.

Who are these disaffected people who swell the ranks of the inevitable counter-revolution? They are clearly predetermined and it is only a matter of time before the predictions are borne out in reality.

The Sandinistas, with great political acumen, calculated the role which their anti-*somocista* national bourgeoisie would have to play. But they failed to calculate with equal accuracy the consequent reactions from outside, given a US regional hegemony which was strategic and not tactical in nature. In particular, they failed to assess the long- and not just the short-term aspects of this reaction. Because of that miscalculation they conceded too little to their bourgeois allies, and this hastened the demise of their alliance strategy and undermined its benefits for them. Instead they attempted to 'skip stages' – not so much with regard to economic policy (where they had no choice), but in the political realm. As we shall note below, official Soviet doctrine indicates that the best way to defend a revolution may be to accelerate the process of political consolidation and control.

Nicaragua's Domestic Policy: Some Features

The Sandinistas' triumph opened up an exceptional possibility for profound transformations in Nicaragua's social reality and productive structure. The distinctive feature here, as in the Dominican Republic, lay in the fact that the dictator was not simply a puppet of an oligarchic class closely linked in its economic affairs with foreign capital, but was of a quite different type, a type more conducive to social transformation after its overthrow. In effect, the Somozas had established a family patrimonial state, surrounded by concentric circles of parasitic elements who shared in the spoils of power. In such a case, the rise is possible of a revolutionary group supported by the middle classes, enjoying the approval of international public opinion and committed in advance to the expropriation of the assets of the dictator and his acolytes. This point of departure permits an enlargement of the public sector and the acquisition of fundamental productive resources by state-managed enterprises (not fully socialised enterprises, for they would require conditions which do not yet exist in Nicaragua), without all the tension, friction, irritation, reactions and pressures which acconpany every other type of nationalisation. The percentage of productive property held by Trujillo was particularly high, and there derived from this a Dominican state with a presence in the economy which was also particularly high. The same applied in Nicaragua.

On this point, I think it is valid to say that it has not been the domestic economic and social reforms – I deliberately exclude the political orientations – which have provoked increasingly intolerant responses in the US that now seem to be culminating in an open policy of encirclement and confrontation. Rather, it has been an irresistible rhetoric and certain specific anti-democratic measures adopted by the Sandinista leadership and endorsed by their friends, which have distorted and profoundly damaged the Nicaraguan Revolution. That rhetoric and those policies have confirmed the worst fears of increasingly broad sectors of regional, and particularly US, public opinion.

Legitimately laying claim to an independent foreign policy, there emerged in many international forums a rather provocative Nicaraguan policy revealing an inexcusable under-estimation of the United States. Support for the Soviet invasion of Afghanistan, a repeated testing of the limits of US concession and acceptance, and a risky self-perception as being responsible for the Central American revolution, provoked Nicaragua's representatives into expressions like 'now it's El Salvador's turn and later Guatemala's', which coincided exactly with the FMLN's calls to regionalise the struggle in El Salvador and other inflammatory and provocative speeches, such as that made by Bishop, also calling for the 'liberation of the other Central American countries'. Dangerous and irritating alliances, such as those with the PLO and Gaddafi, for example, might have satisfied the enthusiasms proper to the triumph, but they also alienated foreign opinion, which was beginning to view with suspicion what was happening in Nicaragua. Most important, however, is that all of this, including the matter of the image projected, reduced the margin for internal alliances and fostered domestic social support for the external opposition.

This factor is particularly important because it combines a double political phenomenon: ideologically, disaffection is viewed as predictable; since it is foreseen, it is finally encouraged to occur. But this runs the risk of allowing the emergence of a social, possibly political base (since *somocismo* had literally disappeared), from which those sectors most intransigently opposed to change in Central America can try to constitute an opposition structure able to face up to the new regime, and can create 'siege' conditions. These in turn feed the process of 'defending the revolution against its foreign and domestic enemies', a process which justifies every excess, including direct foreign intervention.

Although it is, of course, impossible to know how to lead a revolution without having led one – that is, as a matter of practice rather than of theory – the truth is that the main internal problems facing the Sandinista leadership seem more a product of their own verbal excesses, their provocative attitudes and their growing inability to face up to objective realities, than to the important social and economic changes which have been attempted in the country. An excessive romanticism has not been accompanied by that intellectual coolness which Lenin recommended in order to discern the real regional and international balance of forces, namely the stage of recovery and nascent offensive in which the United States and the present Nicaraguan administration find themselves; the policy of defence and self-preservaation of the Cubans and the Cuban Revolution; and the prudent detachment of the Soviet leadership, which encourages the process, and even contributes economically and militarily to it, but does not assume political responsibilities which might in any way affect its own prestige or compromise its foreign policy beyond those minimum limits.

On the contrary, the Sandinistas, not content with overthrowing Somoza, with deriving a certain initial, albeit reluctant, benevolence from the USA, together with the advantages mentioned above that came from painlessly confiscating Somoza's holdings, chose to turn their guns on the United Sates, first making verbal attacks and then engaging in political initiatives which provoked and seemed to confirm every conceivable prejudice against them. They turned on allied sectors, mocking their political influence and their lack of a mass social base, as if this were really the important thing in the conditions prevailing in the country, so limiting not only their domestic and foreign social support but also the audience for their discourse and the credibility of their tactical retreats. The Sandinistas have provoked an unnecessary and very dangerous confrontation with the Catholic Church, first in their own country and later, with the brutal and unjustified attack on John Paul II during his visit to Nicaragua, with the Catholic Church in the whole of Central America. Finally they have pursued a dangerous, violent and hasty policy with respect to the Miskita minority, only recognising at the very last minute that it would have to be substantially and urgently modified.

There can be no denying that some aspects of Sandinista policy have been successful, despite the usual criticisms of their handling of economic management. In my opinion, their successes have been sufficient to secure for them a decisive amount of support from the popular sectors, making their over-controlled and even brutal management of the electoral process quite unnecessary, even from their own point of view.[1] However, the extent of their domestic support is not decisive in the political circumstances at hand, because here it is a question of foreign intervention and counter-revolution rather than the restoration of internally displaced classes. To use one of the analogies dear to Marxism-Leninism, it is not that the *ancien régime* threatens to return by means of a 'Fronde' (as in the French Revolution), but that the armies of the Holy Alliance are preparing to march against their revolution.

In this sense, the continued pursuit of a pre-established strategy and the stubborn adherence to objectives derived from the stage theories of classical Marxism-Leninism in Nicaragua, are more than a tactical or theoretical problem, involving the political prestige of the leadership and the rights of a people. Rather, they are a political problem. And for that reason it is a dilemma which reveals the objective international conditions in which the process must unfold and the subjective and objective internal conditions which taken together render the proposed political project viable or unviable.

For that very reason, if one is to evaluate the Sandinista regime, the mixed nature of the economy is relatively unimportant. This could hardly be changed to complete state control, for such a system would not survive for long, if the Russian experience of the introduction of the NEP is anything to go by – and Nicaragua is an even weaker case. The important level of discussion is what may properly be described as the political realm. This makes it both possible and desirable to find solutions and mechanisms which will avoid definitive military confrontation that would drag Central America, not into a bloodbath through a supposed extension of the war, but into a long period of militaristic and fascistic reaction from which recovery would be extremely slow, even in Costa Rica. (A region-wide bloodbath is not as imminent as some believe, because wars are not extended at will: the Salvadoran guerrillas are not extending their country's war because they cannot do so, and the Nicaraguans will have enough to keep them occupied in their own country without thinking of opening formal and extended war fronts while they face the prospect of a US invasion.)

The tendency to strengthen state controls over freedom of expression and of the press; the concentration of power and political intolerance, whether through the *turbas divinas* (divine mobs)[2] or through the Committees for the Defence of the Revolution; the combination of army, party and government; the tendency to monopolise the union movement and to divide the country into friends and enemies on the basis of total solidarity, pushing potential allies into the arms of an opposition which is already reconstituted and constantly strengthend; all form part of a systematic under-estimation of Nicaragua's concrete reality which goes beyond the very objective limitations of its economy and society and is located within a regional context which includes not just the other Central American countries but the United States itself.

Outside observers can hardly fail to note that such developments coincide exactly with Soviet recommendations to revolutionaries in those countries. In effect: in addition to the 'stage theory' approach to revolution already enshrined in the 1928 congresses, Soviet academic circles have observed how the Sandinistas were able to avoid errors such as those committed by Allende's government, because they were the only political force to emerge from the ruins of *somocismo*. However, sticking with the Soviet scheme alluded to, those same Soviet sources reinforce the coincidence in question with their affirmation that the Sandinistas have 'understood that the question in Nicaragua is not the breadth of economic reforms but the securing of all power as tightly as possible', as S. Mikoyan wrote in the Soviet journal *Latinskaia Amerika* in July 1982.

For this reason the matter of internal liberties, effective pluralism and objective restrictions through censorship and social and institutional intolerance towards dissidents cannot easily be dismissed simply as the inevitable result of the state of siege against the Sandinistas' revolutionary citadel. They are that: but they are also the expression of a clear policy aimed at consolidating power, structuring that power and keeping it at all costs in a revolutionary perspective which will eventually – when it is in the interests of the world revolution (read the Soviet Union) – create a point of support right on the American continent in the East-West conflict.

It is on this real, objective base that the Nicaraguan question has developed from a national and regional problem to become a more important conflict. It has become necessary to ask whether what is now at issue is not the appropriateness or goodness of such a political scheme for the construction of a Cuban-Soviet type of society, but whether, given the difficulties of Nicaragua's objective and subjective domestic and external conditions, such a scheme is realistic. My answer is that it is not. It was not realistic in 1928 when the sixth Comintern Congress approved it, and it is not realistic now. The real nature of societies like Nicaragua makes such a Marxist-Leninist historical project fail over a more important problem than taking power: the very character of the revolution in dependent, under-developed countries which are within the United States' sphere of direct interest.

The chances of a negotiated outcome to the conflict depend on the recognition of this basic fact. In my view, as long as no serious and coherent attempt is made to redirect the process, objectives and methods of the Sandinista regime along the lines of the programme of national reconstruction and the formal duties acquired within the Organisation of American States at the time of the final crisis of the *somocista* regime, and if the regime does not abandon its dogmatic and unrealistic goal of establishing in Managua a Marxist-Leninist Cuban-Soviet style political regime, then the whole process is travelling on a clear collision course – to the detriment not only of Nicaragua's democratic future, but that of Central America as a whole.

The US Reconstruction Plan and the Chances of a Political Solution

As we have seen, the problem of the Nicaraguan Revolution is indissolubly linked both to domestic and to foreign matters, which, in Nicaragua's case more than in others, become fundamentally confused. In Nicaragua, historically, the foreign element has been projected regionally and has occupied a place in the United States' strategies for Central America. Consequently it is not simply a problem of favourable or unfavourable external conditions affecting the achievement of the final goals of the Marxist-Leninist scheme. It is something much more complicated which, in my opinion, highlights the real possibilities and the unrealistic objectives of Nicaragua's political scheme and decisively marks the projection of that revolution's problems onto the whole region.

From the United States' point of view, the problem is much more complex than whether or not to tolerate a Marxist-Leninist regime in its so-called backyard. It is not simply a matter of a regime ideologically committed to the global strategies of the Soviet Union and potentially subordinate to the tactical aims of the leaders of the Communist Party of the Soviet Union or of the Cubans. This, although important in itself because of the supposed threat to US security and for reasons of ideology and national prestige, acquires a greater dimension in a regional context, because such a situation requires the United States to reconstruct, with Nicaragua in mind but also in more general Central American terms, the axis of power which disappeared with the Somoza regime and on which certain basic aspects of US regional security policy rested.

Just as some guerrilla movements promote the idea of 'regionalising the armed struggle', of creating a popular army of Central America, of eventually establishing a socialist federation of the region, etc., so historically Central America's military sectors, clearly encouraged by US policy-makers, have promoted a military, ultra-conservative, clearly anti-democratic alternative on a regional level. And for that reason, the prospect of a basically military alternative to the regional crises effectively precludes the chances of democratic development and social transformation which the oppressed social structures of Central America require as a matter of urgency.

The attempt to turn Honduras, especially its armed forces, into a substitute for that axis of regional power which disappeared with *somocismo* reveals the true nature of such a project. Even if, for cosmetic reasons, formal and ritualistic electoral activities are tolerated, the project's substance reveals itself as reactionary and militaristic.

That is why, ironically, the Sandinistas' inflexibility accords so well with most conservative projects not just for Nicaragua but for the entire region. It facilitates the creation of a military international which would put the region back onto a firmer and more stable base and, for some years more, restore traditional domination to the region. The reformist processes used to try to modify the Salvadoran situation would immediately succumb to pressure from ultra-right groups which, under cover of military solutions, would grasp the opportunity not just for revenge, but the chance to become the United States' oligarchic interlocutors for the whole Isthmus.

The utopian possibilities of a revolutionary international in Central America belong, in these circumstances, to the chapter of lost illusions, not just because of the international context but also because of the balance of social and political forces within each of the countries in question.

The only real way forward, modest and limited, but real (repetition is deliberate), is the reconstitution of a large democratic centre, on the basis of a programme of profound social change, economic development and regional integration resting on vigorous international public support, pluralist alliances like those which have wanted to see in Nicaragua's revolution a more coherent project which fits reality rather than Marxist-Leninist doctrine; and to reassure, by deeds, international public opinion, pluralist alliances *and* the United States that Central America will not become, in effect, a pawn of any global strategy threatening the balance of forces in the area.

Those who wish to help Nicaragua and the democratisation of the region can only do so by clearly opposing and not promoting that doctrinaire and dogmatic error which is leading inexorably to the final fragmentation of the region's democracy; and, independently of subjective ideological inclinations, by helping to direct the process towards the only goal which in present circumstances it is possible to achieve: a regional democracy which goes far beyond the traditional forms of power and social and economic organisation, but not nearly so far as the totalitarian structures expressed in the Marxist-Leninist concept of the dictatorship of the proletariat.

If this does not happen then the unrealised utopia would not in any case be consolidating any advance and would perhaps, at best, play only a symbolic role, like the Paris Commune. Its battles might amount to terrorism and rearguard battles. If not, what would remain? Putschism? Another Canton Commune, or another El Salvador, 1932? Another offer to turn the Nicaraguan leaders into propagandists of the revolution in Europe against American imperialism, as was suggested to Sandino in 1931?

That is why, in my opinion, one can only look, truly and not just as a temporary camouflage, for an advanced democratic solution, with effective political pluralism, real freedom of the press, concrete individual guarantees, profound social reforms. This would be the most profound revolution in Central America since Independence and, paradoxically, the only real revolution which could hope to create a new type of stable, positive and mutually beneficial relationship between this region and the USA. Possible alliances with Europe and the Contadora group, the helpful participation of international political groupings interested in a democratic outcome, and the notion of restraint and opportuneness in the demands of political leaderships would avoid the false question of all or nothing, and would put on the agenda the chance of something significant and historicallly decisive for the transformation of these countries. It is those profound reforms which are truly revolutionary from a national and democratic point of view; whereas revolution, in the dogmatic and Soviet sense of the term, is the end of even the possibility of transforming the societies of Central America for the remainder of this century.

Is there still time and, even more important, do the conditions yet exist to achieve this? I do not know. But my conclusion is that if this is not possible, then the chances for a maximalist position are even more remote.

Notes

1. On 4 November 1984 elections were held for President, Vice-President and constituent assembly, for the first time since the revolution. The Sandinistas obtained 67 per cent of the valid vote and there were about 25 per cent abstentions. For a full assessment which coincides with much of the analysis in this chapter, see Gabriel Zaïd, 'Nicaragua: El Enigma de las Elecciones', *Vuelta* (Mexico City), February 1985: 'It was the nine *Comandantes*, all by themselves, who sought out the troubles [*bronca*] they now face' (p. 18).

2. A local expression referring to the supposedly spontaneous Sandinista crowds who sometimes gather to harass opponents of the regime.

10 DEMOCRACY BY DESIGN: THE CHRISTIAN DEMOCRATIC PARTY IN EL SALVADOR

Terry Lynn Karl

Democracy is often a second-best option.* In general, democratic transitions have been the residual result of other desired scenarios – a by-product, as Dankwart Rustow once remarked, of different goals and intentions on the part of reactionaries and revolutionaries.[1] For anti-democratic actors, democracy is chosen only when no single other regime preference can prevail. A democratic compromise can emerge from and terminate a prolonged and inconclusive struggle that would otherwise bring significant losses to all political forces involved. Indeed, democracy's greatest attraction may well be this institutionalisation of compromise through the construction of a polity which is based upon uncertain outcomes yet offers definite rules for the subsequent negotiation of future change. Whether consciously designed or unintended, these 'second-best' political regimes are seldom the result of a grand strategy. Democracies arise in moments of political transition characterised by intense uncertainty, thus they are made 'on the instalment plan' as events unfold. They are the outcome of concrete steps and sequential decisions, unintended consequences and pure luck, which, when taken *in toto*, create the probability of a competitive or semi-competitive polity.

Yet democratisation rests on economic, social and political preconditions despite its somewhat incidental character.[2] However important sequential decision-making and political strategies may be, democracies arise from the demise of an authoritarian regime when specific factors beyond the control of political actors produce a structural opportunity which encourages a genuine compromise. These factors may include

---

*Author's note: The Tinker Foundation and the Committee on Latin American and Iberian Studies, Harvard University, generously provided support for research conducted in Mexico, Venezuela and El Salvador during the fall of 1983 and July 1984. The author visited El Salvador again in April 1985.

The incisive comments of the participants of the seminar 'Transitions to Democracy in Central America', held in San Jose, Costa Rica, 1-6 December 1984, the assistance of Phillip Oxhorn and Cynthia Sanborn, and the institutional support of the Department of Political Science, University of California, Berkeley, are gratefully acknowledged. A different version of this article, 'After La Palma: The Prospects for Democratization in El Salvador', appeared in *World Policy Journal*, Spring, 1985.

levels and rates of economic development, the degree of differentiation and organisation of social classes, and the extent and direction of external influence, etc. What is fundamental is that their combined effect produces a stalemate – often the first expression of a democratic possibility. Indeed, a meaningful structural opportunity for democratisation can be said to emerge in a political transition when a set of overarching vetoes, which may originate in both the domestic and international environment, rule out either a return to the old authoritarian regime or a revolutionary triumph. If these vetoes effectively prevent an outright military or political victory by any side, they can result in a stalemate which in turn may produce a democratic instauration by compromise.

Yet stalemate alone cannot produce democratisation. The main prerequisite for the creation of a durable democratic polity cannot be met until some type of broad social pact is forged in the context of this impasse. The extent of democratisation – the degree of participation, contestation, accountability and representation – will depend upon the parameters of this pact. This historic compromise must be designed by skilled leaders and a political party with a strategy for illuminating the path towards a future polity. The choice of democracy can appear to be the most beneficial or the least costly solution for contending forces unable to win clear-cut domination, but first this choice must be placed on the political agenda, coupled with a strategy for its achievement. If a party with a 'democratic project' is able to confront proponents of authoritarianism or revolution with the stark options of a viable compromise or slow mutual self-destruction, compromise begins to look attractive. This step ultimately depends on the ability of some political actors to produce acceptable interim agreements about the new rules of a political game as well as mutual guarantees that these rules will be respected by all parties concerned. This rule-making, which can take the form of explicated or informal political pacts, is crucial to the success of a political transition. In addition, it establishes the nature of a future democracy – from the range of left-right contestation to the extent to which it is characterised by elite or mass-based political power.[3]

The claim that stalemate, negotiations and bargaining agents are essential to a transition to some form of political democracy is relevant to the painful reality of El Salvador in the mid-1980s. By 1979, the rapid economic development of that country, the exhaustion of traditional authoritarian arrangements, the changes in class structures and political organisation and the deep involvement of the United States had combined to produce a regime transition of as yet uncertain political form. While it is unclear whether democratisation is a viable prospect in El

Salvador – a country which has been shaped by a powerful authoritarian history and which over the past five years has suffered at least 50,000 deaths and the displacement of 32 per cent of its population – the possibility for democracy is not closed. Indeed, to state the conclusion at the beginning, El Salvador in 1985 does have an opportunity for democratisation. As we shall see, this is the product of a stalemate which has been established between the government and the opposition FDR-FMLN as well as that which has emerged between the Reagan administration and the US Congress. Opportunity, however, does not mean that democratisation will occur – a forecast no political observer could make in the face of the tremendous uncertainties that exist in the region.

To some extent, the realisation of this opportunity depends on the political strategy and statecraft skills of the Christian Democratic Party (PDC). Within the context of stalemate, the PDC lies at the centre of current democratisation efforts – the place where domestic and international forces meet and where strategies and alliances are forged or discarded. In 1985, its actions are more decisive in the determination of El Salvador's future than ever before – a reality which, appearances notwithstanding, had not been the case until after the elections of 1984. As we shall see, the party's enhanced capacity to affect the direction of El Salvador's future is largely the product of changing circumstances beyond Christian Democratic control rather than the result of a self-conscious democratic strategy. Yet the Christian Democratic design for democracy has played an important role, particularly since 1984.

Ultimately, however, the PDC's contribution to the resolution of El Salvador's crisis depends upon the decisions of external actors, primarily the Reagan administration. Although the PDC has enhanced its own ability to exert domestic influence by making itself politically indispensable to the hemisphere's dominant political actor, it has not been responsible for the creation of a stalemate in El Salvador. This has occurred, somewhat inadvertently, through a combination of sequential political and military decisions in both El Salvador and the United States. Yet only the US government, particularly Congress, holds the power to maintain incentives which slowly can pressure the representatives of traditional authoritarian rule to play by democratic rules. If the US acts in a manner which supports negotiated compromise, then the choice of democracy will gradually appear to be more advantageous, or less disadvantageous, to groups which traditionally have rejected democracy in El Salvador. If it fails to do so, a ruinous civil war will continue unabated. That this decision is a foreign, not Salvadoran, policy choice is a poignant reminder of the depth of Central America's dependent status.

The Evolution of a Stalemate: 1979-84

The period from 1980 to 1983 marked a clear failure for democratisation in El Salvador, despite the trappings of party competition and externally-sponsored elections. In the wake of the abortive reformist officers' coup in October 1979, the decisive pressure of the Carter administration, rather than any basic transformation in the authoritarian regime, convinced the armed forces to accept the Christian Democratic Party in the ruling junta in 1980 and to lend at least rhetorical support to a land reform. Concessions from the armed forces regarding the holding of elections – an idea which they firmly opposed – were granted to the United States, not to their hated PDC allies.[4] Despite this slight bending under US pressure, the armed forces-PDC government ruled under a state of siege which suspended freedom of movement, speech and assembly. Army-led repression, which included the notorious death-squads, resulted in over 1,000 non-combatant deaths each month and the systematic slaughter of peasant and labour leaders. By the end of 1980, political activists and their followers who had built the popular organisations that later became the FDR-FMLN began to fight the army from the countryside.

US-sponsored elections, held in the midst of state terror in 1982, did little to improve prospects for democratisation. Since they were implemented to counteract strong internal and external pressure for a negotiated settlement to end an evolving civil war, they hindered progress by shifting the policy agenda from a focus on a political solution to a concentration on the trappings of formal electoral mechanisms. Elections excluded all forces to the left of the Christian Democrats and were characterised by fraud stemming from the efforts of all participating parties to inflate the turn-out. Although the electoral route was imposed by a US administration anxious to stem the tide of widespread criticism of its policies, the outcome was unexpected. The Christian Democrats were unable to win a decisive electoral majority. Instead, the ultra-right, represented by the ARENA Party, won the presidency for its candidate Roberto D'Aubuisson and gained control of the Assembly. Only US intervention in the selection of the country's president pressured the armed forces to veto D'Aubuisson, a man linked to death-squad activity, and replace him with Alvaro Magana – who had not even participated in the elections. Furious at this manoeuvre, the right blocked all efforts at land reform in the Assembly. Thus the 1982 elections, widely heralded as the expression of Salvadoran popular will, resulted in fraud, the end of reforms and the appointment of the president by the military and a foreign power.[5]

What changed the strategic context for all political actors in 1983 was the dawning realisation of the existence of a political and military stalemate. This stalemate could be delineated by several hard realities: on the one hand, the Reagan administration, pursuing a hardline strategy in Latin America, remained committed to the defeat of any revolution on its watch – a fact which ruled out a military victory on the part of the FDR-FMLN. At the same time the US Congress, the keeper of the purse strings which are the sole maintenance of the Salvadoran government and economy, refused to condone an alliance with the violent ultra-right represented by ARENA or a major escalation in El Salvador which might involve US troops. This ruled out the total defeat of the opposition as well as the full restoration of the old regime. On the other hand, by 1983 the FDR-FMLN had demonstrated that it was too strong, both politically and militarily, to be defeated by the Salvadoran military alone. Since it could deny an economic recovery or peace until its political demands were met, the FDR-FMLN retained the power to prohibit a viable centre-right alliance in El Salvador. In sum, El Salvador faced a series of international and domestic vetoes which effectively prevented the successful installation of an authoritarian or revolutionary regime.

By 1983, this system of vetoes began to translate into domestic turmoil in El Salvador and a brewing foreign policy crisis in the US. In El Salvador, the FDR-FMLN launched a highly-successful military operation in October 1982, culminating in an intense campaign to open the new year. The strength of this new offensive caught the army and the government by surprise. In January 1983 alone, it initiated 181 military actions, demonstrating a capability of attacking over large areas of the country, including the capital city of San Salvador, that belied the Mark Twainish reports of its early demise. In late 1983, it over-ran a major army base in Paraiso, drove hundreds of government troops from a crucial bridge at Cuscatlan and demonstrated the weakness of a US-sponsored 'National Plan' which was to be the crux of the army's strategy in the coming year.[6] Extensive US-backed counter-insurgency measures could not stem the tide of the FMLN offensive.

The success of the FDR-FMLN, coupled with the growing US pressure to hold down human rights violations of civilians, exacerbated growing divisions within the armed forces. Appalled by losses through deaths and desertions of up to 20 per cent of enlisted personnel and shortages of supplies due to the growing unwillingness of the US Congress to fund the war adequately, the army command was torn between a hardline and a reformist response. A faction, led by Defence Minister Garcia, began to support land reform in order to assure continued access to US aid – a position challenged by the January 1984 rebellion of Lt. Col. Sigifredo Ochoa. In a controversial compromise, both Garcia and Ochoa were eventually removed from their positions. Different factions of the army agreed to settle upon General Vides Casanova as the new commander, but the fragility of army unity could no longer be dismissed.

The governing political parties were also deeply divided over the prosecution of the war, the state of the economy and the extent to which reforms should be permitted. In early 1983, an alliance between ARENA and the National Reconciliation Party (PCN) – two rightist parties that had dominated the constituent assembly since the 1982 elections – collapsed in a shambles. The country became virtually ungovernable. After considerable turmoil, the Christian Democrats stepped in and used their skill in political pact-making with the PCN to forge a new, fragile, one-vote majority in the assembly based on the 'Pact of Apaneca'.[7] This pact established rules for power-sharing with the right, particularly at the municipal level.

Crisis erupted again at mid-year over the constituent assembly's adoption of the new constitution. ARENA and the PCN reunited to design a constitution which would block land reform through legal mechanisms, using death-squad threats as part of their new 'legislative' tactics. In return, the Christian Democrats tried to defend their programme of agrarian reform by resorting to the unusual tactic of mobilising peasants to march into San Salvador. In the tense period that followed, the Christian Democrats were forced to accept a constitution that provided new legal means to defeat much of their own land reform programme, narrowed the rules for political participation and gave disproportionate power to the right.

The Reagan administration also faced a bleak situation in 1983. Strong pressure for political negotiations instead of a military solution came from a variety of sources: the unexpected strength of the FMLN offensive, the deterioration of the Salvadoran military and government, the visit of the Pope to Central America, the formation of the Contadora group and the positions of European allies. In addition, Harris Polls from 1982 and 1983 showed that 79 to 85 per cent of US respondents were against sending US troops into El Salvador – figure which briefly dipped to 54 per cent after the invasion of Grenada. Most important, Congress began to demonstrate its displeasure with the administration as well as the Salvadoran government by blocking additional US funds to the Salvadoran military. The president, in his unusual address to a joint session of Congress in April, was unable to reverse the removal of Assistant Secretary of State for Latin America, Thomas O. Enders, and the formation of the Kissinger Commission. By November, Reagan was forced into the position of vetoing certification requirements for the protection of human rights – a political embarrassment of the first order.

As early as March 1983, the Reagan administration sought to resort to new elections in El Salvador to escape from its own policy dilemma. Elections might also alleviate the country's internal crisis – a tactic that had proved at least temporarily effective in 1982. This time the administration tried to ensure a Christian Democratic victory. Realising that the PDC offered the best public relations advantages to overcome an unpopular policy, the Reagan team poured over $10 million into the elections. It gave support funds to the PDC and to the Unión Popular Democrática (UPD), a confederation of unions allied with the AFL-CIO which backed the Christian Democratic Party, and later co-operated with the COPEI government of Venezuela and the Konrad Adenauer Foundation of West Germany to channel money through a Venezuelan-sponsored Christian Democratic public relations firm, IVEPO.[8]

The results were satisfactory for both the US and the PDC. In an election between D'Aubuisson and Duarte, marked by the abstention or failure to vote of 33 per cent of the eligible electorate, the Christian Democratic candidate won 53.6 per cent of the valid votes. Although the PDC still did not control the assembly, the party which had only nominally governed from 1980-2 and had remained on the political sidelines in 1983 was given another chance.

La Palma: The Road to a Democratic Compromise

The 1984 elections reshaped the political game in El Salvador to the advantage of the Christian Democratic Party. The PDC's victory gave its programme the domestic and international legitimacy it had lacked during the 1980-2 government. José Napoleón Duarte's first act as president was to bring in massive amounts of new foreign funding. The Reagan administration, delighted that it finally had an acceptable elected ally to present to Congress, brought the Salvadoran president to

Washington and arranged for him to address the Senate. His success was resounding. Duarte immediately brought in $61.75 million in supplemental military aid. Within three months of his inauguration, Congress had appropriated a total of $132 million in military aid and $120 million in economic aid, a sharp increase from the past. In addition, the amount set for fiscal year 1985 brought the total aid figure secured by the Duarte government to almost half a billion – a foreign aid amount third only to Israel and Egypt. The 1984 elections turned around the direction of Congress. Duarte then travelled to Europe where he received money and support from the leaders of West Germany, Portugal, Belgium and Britain.[9]

Using his new international backing as leverage, Duarte moved quickly to clarify the new conditions that would prevail under his government: access to the desperately needed foreign aid he could provide would depend upon curbing of the extreme right inside the armed forces and the political parties. Although there had been numerous pressures upon the military to put its own house in order in the past, Duarte's success in Washington brought home the message that El Salvador had to maintain a government acceptable to the US Congress in order to receive massive aid. Not surprisingly, given the sums of aid, the Salvadoran armed forces responded positively by partially restructuring the military command, dismantling the intelligence unit of the Treasury Police, sending death-squad leaders out of the country and replacing hardline leadership in the National Police and the Treasury Police with moderates and conservatives. ARENA also felt immediate pressure to lower its extremist profile. When threats surfaced of a coup to overthrow Duarte, the Reagan administration despatched General Vernon Walters – the traditional expert at dealing with recalcitrant militaries – to El Salvador to tell D'Aubuisson that a coup would not be tolerated. ARENA would have to play by recently-established party rules since the US would not tolerate actions which might jeopardise the diplomatic victory represented by the 1984 elections.

Thus Duarte's election marked an important shift in the balance of power between the Reagan administration, the Salvadoran armed forces and the Christian Democrats. In a sense, the least powerful member of this alliance – the PDC – had temporarily gained the upper hand. While this realignment did advance democratisation by propelling party politics into a more central role and restricting state violence, the actual changes introduced were still quite tentative. The war continued unabated. The private sector still blocked land reform in the constituent assembly and opposed the attempts of workers and peasants to organise.

Death-squad activities slowed but did not stop. There was no civilian control over the armed forces. The Duarte government knew that it was walking a fine line. As rumours of a leadership purge based on political sympathies spread throughout the armed forces, one high commander warned publicly, 'If it stops here, it is okay, but if it continues, it could be worrisome.'[10]

Yet the new president could not stop at this point if he wanted to succeed in future elections. Despite his initial actions, Duarte faced intense pressure from his party and electoral base. Worker and peasant organisations grew increasingly angry at his constant efforts to placate landowners at their expense. Impatient for change and trusting that repression would slacken under the new government, these new groups became active after the 1984 election. Strikes and labour disputes rose at an alarming rate and demanded solutions. At the same time trouble arose in the PDC's relations with the Unión Popular Democrática (UPD), an AID-linked umbrella organisation of labour federations and peasant unions. In the 1984 elections, the Christian Democrats had given promises of accelerated land reform in exchange for the UPD's support. But the PDC found itself unable to honour this commitment. Although Christian Democratic leaders explained that the peasant unions would have to build support for the party in order to win a majority in the 1985 assembly elections that could reintroduce the land reform programme, the Secretary-General of the nation's largest peasant union publicly threatened to withdraw support from the PDC if it did not deliver on its promises. Duarte recognised the gravity of the problem: 'If we can't have the land reform, what are we supposed to tell the peasants that are with us?'[11]

Other factors weakened the PDC's hold on its electoral base. The 1984 elections vividly communicated an important message: the party's constituency and the Salvadoran population in general favoured some form of political negotiations with the opposition to bring peace and economic recovery. Pre-election polls showed that 70 per cent of all Salvadorans considered the war and the economy to be the principal problems of the country. A striking 51.4 per cent favoured dialogue as the best way of resolving the war – a surprisingly high percentage since this coincided with the formal position of the FDR-FMLN. Only 10.3 per cent supported the military annihilation of the armed opposition (the position of ARENA), while another 10 per cent called for a military intervention by the US.[12] The reasons for these trends were readily apparent. The rapid deterioration of the economy since 1979 had dramatically affected the standard of living of most Salvadorans.

Between 1979-83, real minimum wages declined by 65 per cent and consumption levels fell nearly 50 per cent. Up to 80 per cent of the population was unemployed or under-employed.[13] At the same time, the war and uncontained human rights abuses took an enormous toll on the country, displacing over 1,600,000 persons in this country of only five million inhabitants. The popular base of the Christian Democratic Party clamoured for some visible and significant change.

Thus the 1984 electoral victory created a painful dilemma for the governing party. On the one hand, the PDC was restricted by its key allies – the United States and the Salvadoran military – who had been opposed to any form of negotiations with the FDR-FMLN. On the other hand, the party had been given a mandate to negotiate by the Salvadoran people. To the extent that voters were free to choose in the elections, they had expressed a clear preference for a programme of reforms, an end to the war, the termination of human rights abuses, an opening towards the FDR-FMLN and the defence of the right of association.[14] Throughout the campaign, Duarte had offered the promise of a social pact, a government that would reconcile and integrate all Salvadorans into an effective plan for peace. Now he had to deliver on his promise.

The continued pressure of the FDR-FMLN compounded all these difficulties. It engaged in a heavy sabotage campaign through June and July, repeatedly seized control of the nation's roads and launched a spectacular attack on the Cerron Grande dam, demonstrating a military capability that surprised US advisers. Despite a lull in the combat as the FMLN adjusted to an escalated air war – and despite frequent pronouncements in the US press about the new successes of the Salvadoran armed forces – the enormous influx of aid following Duarte's election initially did not appear to diminish the opposition's capacity to continue fighting. The FDR-FMLN made its position clear: there would be no peace or economic prosperity until the fundamental issues of the distribution of power and wealth were resolved. Referring to its mid-year offensive, the opposition said, 'The attack is to make the government aware that there is no military solution. It is urgent that they take our dialogue proposal seriously.'[15]

The Christian Democratic leadership was aware that the 'honeymoon' opened up by the presidential elections would soon expire: the constituent assembly elections scheduled for March 1985 would determine the fate of reform and of the PDC. If the party could not gain majority control of the legislature, it could not hope to implement a land reform. Its tenuous position was obvious. As PDC leader Eduardo Molina explained:

> There is no military solution to our conflict now, unless it is a military victory by the guerrillas . . . If we continue to attempt to resolve the conflict militarily, we will lose. Only a dialogue and eventual incorporation of democratic elements of the left into our ranks offer any exit for us now . . .[16]

President Duarte, pushed from all sides, saw only one way out. The guerrillas had an apparently limitless capacity to maintain the war while the Christian Democrats could only weaken if they did not show some results before the 1985 assembly elections. A coup from the right or a victory of the left perpetually threatened to bring down the Christian Democrats or to provoke a future intervention by US troops – a disaster from the point of view of nationalist members of the party. Yet continued backing from the United States was critical. Duarte understood that the two leading forces historically opposed to negotiations – the Salvadoran military and the Reagan administration – needed him in order to extract aid from a sceptical US Congress. After surprisingly little consultation with the United States, Duarte gambled on his own indispensability to the US and Salvadoran hardliners. In a dramatic speech to the United Nations, he invited the FDR-FMLN to begin a dialogue on 15 October 1984 – the anniversary of the start of El Salvador's political transition.

The decision to meet with the FDR-FMLN at La Palma and to hold a subsequent meeting at Ayagualo opened up new political space in El Salvador. This was reinforced by the Christian Democratic Party's electoral sweep over a combined slate of ARENA and the PCN in the March 1985 assembly elections. The PDC's position was further enhanced by a surprising move on the part of the military: on 3 April the entire high command of the Salvadoran armed forces – demonstrating an awareness that their fate was now linked to their former enemy, President Duarte – publicly repudiated PCN and ARENA attempts to annul the elections. Although a major new military escalation on the part of the US and the army belied these signs of political accommodation and threatened to close this emerging *apertura*, the combination of dialogue plus an assembly majority represented an important moment of increased autonomy for the PDC. Whether this could be turned into a process of genuine democratisation would depend in part on the statecraft abilities and strategies of the Christian Democratic Party.

The Christian Democratic Strategy to Democratise El Salvador

The key decisions of the Christian Democratic Party during El Salvador's political transition – the alliance with the military in 1980, the support for an electoral strategy prior to negotiations and the initiation of dialogue with the FDR-FMLN – have their roots in Christian Democratic ideology and practice as well as in specific partisan interests. In this sense, the tendency of observers to attribute these decisions solely to US government influence is overstated. Perhaps more than any other political force in El Salvador, the Christian Democratic Party has understood that its own long-term survival ultimately depends upon the successful construction of an alliance that can forge a compromise on the procedures for democratisation and the parameters of a future political regime. Its actions must be viewed in this light.

There can be little real debate over the PDC's credentials for this bargaining role. Since its inception, the party has played a pact-making game – first with the left in a formal alliance for the 1972 elections, then with the right after 1980. The PDC has been the most important political organisation to appear during the flurry of associational activity that took place in El Salvador over the past two or three decades. Formed in 1960 when International Christian Democracy was showing substantial gains throughout the continent – especially in Venezuela and Chile – the PDC rapidly demonstrated its ability to construct a durable organisation, build a mass base in largely urban areas and govern the city of San Salvador. Its success resulted in part from the popularity of party leader José Napoleón Duarte, a politician who had been able to build a loyal mass base while mayor of San Salvador. By March 1972, the PDC was able to produce a national electoral victory in coalition with two other parties (now in the FDR-FMLN) which was subsequently snatched away through electoral fraud by the armed forces.

Although party critics emphasise recent US influence over the PDC to explain its political behaviour, the party's current strategy for democracy owes more to its participation in the Christian Democratic international movement than to direct US pressure. Its guiding principles are based upon certain key Christian Democratic tenets: anti-communism; the importance of consensus-building; a conception of private property rights that includes agrarian reform; the preference for individual expression through the right to vote over forms of collective action; and the defence of the existing structures of law. This vision has a strong conservative bias stemming from Catholic precepts of natural law or ordained order and zealous opposition to the spread of atheistic thought represented by communism, yet the emphasis upon socio-economic change gives the party a reformist cast. The occasional ideological discord which results from these twin preoccupations of order and reform has often resulted in a confused political definition, strong internal factionalism, party divisions and rapidly shifting alliances with other parties.[17]

The PDC's strategy of democratisation has been influenced by the party's two decades of political practice. During its formative years, the PDC was forced to grapple with the question of allying with the military. At that time, it rejected any type of collaboration, preferring to continue to build its own separate political base. The party kept its policy of non-co-operation with the military, choosing to ally with parties of the centre-left until 1972 when the military denied the PDC its victory. Forced into exile in Venezuela, Duarte and other party leaders came to the conclusion that any future reform in El Salvador could only be achieved in alliance with the army, particularly the young officers. Thus the groundwork was laid for the highly controversial decision to join the military government in 1980 at the very moment when other civilian parties were moving into armed opposition in response to army-led repression. This decision, which prompted a fifth of party activists to leave in protest against participating 'in a regime which has unleashed the bloodiest repression ever experienced by the Salvadoran people', became the central component in PDC strategy.[18]

To a unique extent, the experiences of other Christian Democratic parties, particularly those of Chile and Venezuela, have also affected the Salvadoran party's strategy and perceptions of reality.[19] The Venezuelan experience in regime transformation in 1958 has had a particularly strong impact because Duarte was exiled to Caracas and developed close political relationships with the leaders of the Venezuelan Christian Democratic Party (COPEI). Venezuela provided an important example of the 'democratisation of the military' – the voluntary transfer of power to a civilian government. In 1958, in exchange for an amnesty for past human rights violations and political crimes as well as substantial economic benefits, the Venezuelan armed forces accepted a new self-definition as an 'apolitical, obedient and non-deliberative body' and accepted the authority of President Rómulo Betancourt. Although conditions in Venezuela were quite different – the military was so deeply divided that different services began to attack each other, much of the leftist opposition was unorganised and the guerrilla war broke out *after* the establishment of some form of political democracy – the Venezuelan example was powerful. It is not surprising that Duarte considered himself El Salvador's equivalent of Betancourt.[20]

There were additional lessons for El Salvador in the elite agreements that established the rules of the game in Venezuela's democracy. The Pact of Punto Fijo, signed prior to the holding of any elections, guaranteed that all parties would respect the result of the elections, whatever they may be, and established a political truce between parties previously in dispute, particularly the Christian Democrats and the Social Democrats, while excluding the Communist Party and other forces of the left. Although the pact did not commit the parties to explicit quotas of power-sharing, as did a similar pact in Colombia, it did recognise that the benefits of state power must be equitably distributed to guarantee the prolonged political truce necessary for the formation of a coalition government. Thus, regardless of who won the elections, each party was promised a share of the political and economic pie through access to state jobs and contracts, a partitioning of the ministries and a complicated spoils system that would assure the political survival of all signatories. The Salvadoran Pact of Apaneca, an agreement which actually borrowed from the language of Punto Fijo, represented a similar attempt to form a power-sharing alliance with the right.

The Venezuelan parties had also negotiated an economic pact with the private sector that established the broad outlines of a development model – an important means for limiting the uncertainty which generally affects investment decisions during the formative stages of a regime transformation while winning elite support. All political parties in Venezuela agreed to respect foreign and local private capital accumulation as well as to subsidise the private sector. While this agreement ruled out the possibility of expropriation, it did provide for a programme of land reform based on compensation paid for by Venezuela's petroleum wealth. In return for their support of basic property rights, the parties won the elite's acquiescence to the expansion of the state, the right of workers to organise and a policy of guaranteed benefits in health, social security and wage rates. The economic pact was closely tied to an informal *modus vivendi* with the United States. The US government refrained from intervening to support its previous ally, the dictator Pérez Jiménez, and eventually promised its full backing to the new regime in exchange for assurances that US holdings would not be expropriated and that Venezuela would maintain a pro-US foreign policy. PDC leaders hoped that a similar arrangement could be made in El Salvador. US aid, rather than petroleum revenues, could provide the financing required to underwrite these accords.

To a lesser extent, the experiences of Chile, where a democratic political system was overthrown by the coup of 1973, also influenced the Salvadoran Christian Democratic Party. Unlike their Venezuelan counterparts, the Chileans were more sceptical about the possibility of using simple persuasion on a military characterised by El Salvador's history and suggested that this task be left to the United States. Meanwhile, the PDC should concentrate on building a pragmatic 'centre'. Chilean Christian Democrats felt that their party had failed to continue the practice followed by its predecessor, the Radical Party, of occupying the political centre by forming alliances with both the left and the right. Indeed, the party had become sectarian, adopting a *partido único* majoritarian strategy in the mid-1960s that polarised politics, making it more difficult to formulate compromises. This factor, combined with party tactics emphasising mobilisation at the expense of clientelistic relationships, upset the normal rules of Chilean democracy by encouraging popular organisation and political competition in previously unincorporated rural areas. This contributed to the polarisation that eventually provoked the 1973 coup. 'We have to avoid that here', argued José Miguel Fritis, a Chilean PDC member working in El Salvador, 'by building a pragmatic centre-right coalition in this country.'[21] Once cemented, this alliance could later turn its attention to negotiations with the left.

The combination of Christian Democratic ideological predispositions and party experience in several countries produced clear, if inconsistent, guidelines for the democratisation of El Salvador. First and foremost, the Salvadoran party believed that it should attempt to 'turn enemies into partners'. This explains the decision in 1980 to govern with this traditional enemy, to give unqualified support to the Salvadoran armed forces despite the level of repression, and initially to renounce all active efforts to seek a political solution to the war.

Second, the party has been committed to occupying the centre of the political spectrum wherever it might be – through pragmatic policies, non-mobilising actions and historically alternating alliances with both the left and the right. Since post-1980 strategy has been aimed at assuaging the fears of the private sector and the political right, this has resulted in the gradual abandonment of its centrist position. In order to regain the moderate bargaining position which initially produced a popular base, the party has been under pressure from below to make some move towards the left.

Third, the PDC has attempted to maintain a reformist image with regard to the polity and economy. Thus it believed in the importance of pursuing a careful programme of agrarian and technocratic reforms combined with an electoral strategy. If successful, this could improve the efficiency of the market and the state while cementing a social base for a conservative political democracy. In practice, given the restrictions of its alliance with the military, the importance of and timetable for various reforms has shifted constantly according to the prevailing political winds.

Finally, like all other forces in El Salvador, the PDC believed it should seek international support for its own programme – an awkward task as the party twisted and turned through these other imperatives. As Christian Democratic fortunes dipped from 1980-4 and international criticism grew over its alliance with the military, its only firm external ally has remained its sister members of International Christian Democracy, particularly Venezuela's COPEI. Even the Reagan administration, opposed to a programme of state-led reform, occasionally shifted its allegiances to the parties of the right.[22]

The Prospects for Democratisation in El Salvador

There is no viable political democracy in El Salvador today despite the existence of semi-competitive elections of 1982, 1984 and 1985. At minimum, democracy depends on the achievement of a compromise protected by law – a fundamental agreement over a set of secure rules that determine who wins and who loses, that guarantee the game can be played again in the future and that set the broad parameters of a model for economic development. Clearly such an agreement has not been reached – and may never be reached – in this deeply divided country. Yet the 1985 political stalemate in the United States over policy towards Central America and the military stalemate that has prevailed in El Salvador since 1983 have created a different set of possible political outcomes and an opportunity for democratisation. Whether a durable *apertura* will result remains an open question.

There are certain hopeful signs. The understanding that total victory is unlikely by either side has already begun to change the perceptions of key domestic forces. The army, affected by the strains of continued combat and fearful of losing US congressional approval for badly-needed aid, has tentatively agreed to attend talks with the opposition. However, it has insisted that all discussions be limited to the parameters established by the 1983 Constitution. Some sectors of the military understand that the violent ultra-right in its ranks has become a hindrance, that some form of land reform must occur and that its own access to US military assistance may ultimately depend on negotiations.[23] Certain groups in the private sector have also lowered their level of opposition to negotiations and to President Duarte – a departure from their attitude in the past, when they feared the Christian Democrats as much as or more than the FDR-FMLN.

Stalemate has moderated hopes for victory on the other side as well. The FDR-FMLN renewed efforts to meet with the government following the 1985 assembly elections. In a rare public statement, FMLN commander Joaquin Villalobos, the reported hardliner opposed to dialogue, gave his endorsement to political negotiations. Villalobos called for immediate 'partial accords to humanise the war such as prisoner exchanges' and permanent mechanisms of communication between the government and the opposition. He proposed a ceasefire in exchange for the termination of US aid to the Salvadoran military. 'It would be a beginning . . . An end to aid would be a guarantee to us. A ceasefire would be a guarantee to them.'[24]

Most important, the Salvadoran people have proved to be a persistent force for peace. Both the government and the FDR-FMLN have found it necessary to produce signs of progress after their meetings in order to please their mass constituencies. Nationalism also encourages dialogue. Strong demands to keep out foreign influence – 'from the United States to the Mexicans and the Venezuelans' – can be found on both sides of the Salvadoran conflict.[25] Finally, the small size of the country and the high degree of associational activity also facilitate the process of forging an agreement.[26] The political importance of the national mood should not be under-estimated. The Salvadoran people have expressed their desire for peace in numerous ways and, if negotiations fail, they can be expected to withdraw their support from whichever side is responsible.

Yet the present barriers to democratisation are great. There is a wide gap between Christian Democratic and FDR-FMLN visions of democracy. The Christian Democrats, as we have seen, emphasise elite pact-making, generally with parties of the right, electoral mechanisms, clientelist relationships, the importance of individual political rights over the rights of workers and peasants to organise and a slow pace of reform. The competing vision of the FDR-FMLN, whose members span a political spectrum from dissident Christian Democrats to Marxists, is mass-based and stresses political organisation and mobilisation as tools to achieve rapid socio-economic reform. Within the FDR-FMLN itself, there are different notions of a political regime, with some guerrilla factions contending that a Leninist party is a viable model for the future a view not shared by the majority of the current leadership.

These distinct visions create substantively different interpretations of the current situation in El Salvador and of the steps necessary to achieve a basic compromise. On the one hand, Duarte's government maintains that profound changes have actually taken place between 1979 and 1985: that human rights violations are slowly being brought under control, that the anti-democratic character of the armed forces has changed, that the power of the landowners has been broken and that all political parties – including those of the opposition – can now participate freely in fair elections. Asserting that the repressive conditions which provoked the outbreak of civil war no longer exist, Duarte equates negotiations with a ceasefire. He offers a general amnesty to the FDR-FMLN if it will lay down its arms, a process of resettlement to those who wish to leave the country and the right to participate freely in future elections. These elections would be based on the rules established by the 1983 Constitution – a document drawn up in negotiations with ARENA and the PCN which excluded the left. The Christian Democrats, according to Duarte, are wedded to these parameters:

> My responsibility as president of the Republic is the Constitution and . . . I cannot go beyond the Constitution . . . Therefore, if this sector [the FDR-FMLN], which today does not believe in the Constitution, wanted to change the Constitution, the Constitution itself provides them with the instruments to do that. These instruments are to participate in the elections, elect deputies, carry their propositions to the assembly and win the adoption of their propositions.[27]

The FDR-FMLN offers a radically different interpretation and peace plan. While agreeing with Duarte that certain changes have occurred in El Salvador, it maintains that the military and the death-squads continue their systematic violations of human rights, that land reform has been blocked and that as long as the country's repressive forces remain intact, the safety of opposition leaders and supporters could not be guaranteed during an election. Rejecting a settlement based on the 1983 Constitution, the FDR-FMLN leaders offer a three-stage plan, to be implemented over an extended period. In the first phase, the government would present a concrete formula to guarantee security, end human rights violations, stop weapons imports and send US advisers out of the country. In exchange, the FDR-FMLN would agree to an arms freeze and to the termination of economic sabotage. During the second phase, there would be a formal ceasefire, with territorial concessions to both rebel and government forces. The final phase would include a broad national dialogue, the formation of a new government, a new constitution and the reorganisation of the armed forces. Only at this point would national elections be held.[28]

The greatest obstacle to democratisation, however, has been the post-La Palma military escalation by the United States. Even if the Duarte government and the FDR-FMLN could find common ground in their different political visions, this militarism undercuts efforts for a political solution. In 1984-5, the Reagan administration deepened and transformed the nature of its military activity through support for aerial bombardments of the countryside, daily reconnaissance flights over El Salvador, the introduction of AC-47 gunships and an expanded helicopter fleet, increased training of the army and the direct involvement of US personnel in combat-related activities. According to a congressional report, these activities revealed 'a step-by-step escalation of a strategy for military victory' – despite the existence of political negotiations.[29]

This rapid US military build-up threatened to replace political calculations with the logic of war, thereby undermining any progress on democratisation. By mid-1985, it had already begun to alter the perceptions and stances of key political forces in favour of a military solution. The army command – growing confident with the help of $1.7 billion of US aid – set narrow parameters on President Duarte's ability to negotiate, ruled out a formal ceasefire and refused to co-operate with the government in investigations of the murder of Salvadoran citizens. Death-squad activity, one key indicator of army sentiment, rose steadily after the La Palma talks.[30] The private sector began to hint at the possibilities of victory.[31] In response to this escalation, the FDR-FMLN began to alter its political and military strategy to prepare for prolonged war. 'We are a veto force. We cannot be liquidated. We can sabotage the infrastructure, . . . fight in smaller groups, and engage in activities in the cities . . . There can be no democratic solution that excludes us.'[32]

Political democracy, characterised by the principles of citizenship, contestation, representation, participation and accountability, is possible in El Salvador. The realities of a stalemated war have created powerful incentives to forge a compromise which might represent a 'second-best' option to prolonged mutual destruction. Successful democratisation, however, is far from certain. On the one hand, this stalemate must be maintained over time. Yet this cannot be assured until the Reagan administration is forced, through a combination of domestic and international pressure, to relinquish its strategy of military escalation in the region.

On the other hand, US policy decisions alone cannot design the final shape of a democracy. The core of any democratic transition lies in an historic social compromise. While the successful negotiation of this compromise may include electoral mechanisms, it is principally based on conscious trade-offs and concessions between many actors, including an external hegemonic power. The Christian Democratic Party is well situated to play this central bargaining role between domestic forces and with the United States. Although its history of forming shifting alliances with a range of forces has branded the PDC with a reputation for opportunism, it has also given President Duarte the diverse connections essential to the creation of a social pact as well as the distinct advantage of capturing the 'centre'. Whether Duarte is capable of forging this compromise depends upon his personal character, his leadership skills and his ultimate capacity to use the United States as a sturdy, if reluctant, shield in the pursuit of accommodation.

The essence of democratisation is compromise. In El Salvador, successful political negotiations imply that the Reagan administration, the oligarchy, the military and the PDC may have to accept a social pact that is significantly broader in scope, more participatory in means and more indigenous in content than one which they might design among themselves. The FDR-FMLN also may have to settle for considerably less than its vision of full mass 'participation in national solutions that historically have been at the hands of the establishment of the day'.[33] Until this mutually acceptable 'second-best' agreement is reached, democracy in El Salvador will have to wait.

Notes

1. Dankwart Rustow's seminal article, 'Transitions to Democracy', *Comparative Politics* (April 1970), pp. 337-66, regarded democracy as a 'second-best' scenario in this sense. This discussion of democracy (confined here to the political rather than the social or economic realm) has been influenced by participation in the 'Transitions to Democracy' seminars sponsored by the Wilson Center, Washington, D.C. See the four volumes of this series, edited by Guillermo O'Donnell, Philippe Schmitter and Laurence Whitehead, especially *Political Life After Authoritarian Rule: Tentative Conclusions about Uncertain Transitions* (Baltimore: Johns Hopkins University Press, 1985) and Adam Przeworski, 'Some Problems in the Study of the Transition to Democracy', in this series. Also see Giuseppe DiPalma, 'Party Government and Democratic Reproducibility: The Dilemma of New Democracies', presented at the workshop 'The Future of Party Government', European University Institute, Florence, Italy, June 1982.

2. For a summary of some of these conditions, see Kevin Middlebrook, 'Notes on Transitions from Authoritarian Rule in Latin America and Latin

Europe', Rapporteur's Report (Washington, D.C.: The Wilson Center, Working Papers, No. 82, 1980).

3. For a discussion of the importance of pacts in the transition to democracy, see Terry Karl, 'Petroleum and Political Pacts: The Transition to Democracy in Venezuela' in Guillermo O'Donnell, Philippe Schmitter and Laurence Whitehead (eds.), *Transitions From Authoritarian Rule: Latin America* (Baltimore: Johns Hopkins University Press, 1985). Also see note 1.

4. For descriptions of the post-1979 period, see Raymond Bonner, *Weakness and Deceit: U.S. Policy and El Salvador* (New York: Times Books, 1984); James Dunkerley, *The Long War: Dictatorship and Revolution in El Salvador* (London: Junction Books, 1982); and Kenneth Sharpe and Martin Diskin, 'Facing Facts in El Salvador: Reconciliation or War', *World Policy Journal* (Spring 1984), pp. 517-47. For an historical description of the party, see Stephen Webre, *José Napoleón Duarte and the Christian Democratic Party in Salvadoran Politics, 1960-1972* (Baton-Rouge: Louisiana State University Press, 1979).

5. By 1983, both ARENA and the PDC privately admitted fraud in the elections. See Edward Herman and Frank Brodhead (eds.), *Demonstration Elections: U.S. Staged Election in the Dominican Republic, Vietnam, and El Salvador* (Boston: South End Press, 1984) for a critique of these elections.

6. For details of this military offensive, see 'Cronica del Mes: Enero de 1983', *Estudios Centroamericanos* (February 1983), pp. 186-7. This journal is the most complete source of information available on El Salvador.

7. On 3 August, the PDC, ARENA, the PCN and a smaller party signed this agreement to set up a transitional government of 'National Unity' as well as a timetable for the constitution and the next elections. See Thomas R. Campos, 'El Pacto de Apaneca: Un Proyecto Politico para la Transicion', *ECA* (Sept.-Oct. 1982), Ano XXXVIII.

8. The firm, named IVEPO, a Venezuelan-sponsored institute staffed largely by Chilean Christian Democrats, denied receiving funds from the US. However, employees of IVEPO privately credited Konrad Adenaur, the Venezuelan government and the US for its money. Their campaign advice (provided free to the PDC) and their financing launched Duarte's campaign and kept the electoral process functioning. Jorge Rochac, the chief planner of the Elections Council, said: 'IVEPO just pays the bills. They haven't said no to anything I asked for. The beauty of it is, IVEPO can give help in ten minutes that would take ten years if I had to go through the government.' When asked where the money originated, he replied, 'Sometimes it is better not to know things in this country.' The US government also gave money to the PCN to help draw votes away from ARENA. *Boston Globe*, 4 May 1984; *Time Magazine*, 21 May 1984. Interview in IVEPO, San Salvador, October 1983. For a detailed look at campaign finances, see Ricardo Chacon, 'Las Campañas de los Partidos', *ECA*, pp. 229-52.

9. Before Duarte's first visit to Washington after winning the presidency, one senior official remarked delightedly: 'We will run him all over Capitol Hill, putting members of Congress in the palpable position of voting against democracy if they vote against aid to El Salvador.' *Boston Globe*, 6 May 1984. For a report on Duarte's international trip and subsequent aid statistics, see *Central American Bulletin* (July-August 1984) and *Latin America Weekly Report*, 27 July 1984.

10. *New York Times*, 25 May 1984; 31 May 1984; 14 June 1984; and 1 July 1984.

11. Interview with Napoleón Duarte, San Salvador, October 1983.

12. These polls, obviously limited in their reliability due to the atmosphere of intimidation in which they were conducted, are one of the few indicators of public opinion in El Salvador. The statistics favouring negotiations are particularly surprising since the expression of support for negotiations, an FDR-FMLN position,

was difficult in early 1984 without risking reprisals from the ultra-right. See Ignacio Martin-Baro and Victor Antonio Orellana, 'La Necesidad de Votar: Actitudes del Pueblo Salvadoreno ante el Proceso Electoral de 1984' in *Estudios Centroamericanos: Las Elecciones Presidenciales de 1984* (April-May 1984), pp. 255-6. This entire edition contains several excellent analyses of the 1984 elections.

13. See, Segundo Montes, 'Condicionamientos Socio-Politicos del Proceso Electoral', ibid. and NACLA, *Report on the Americas*, vol. 18, no. 2 (March-April 1984).

14. See the analysis of party programmes by Ricardo Chacon, 'Las Campañas de los Partidos' in *Estudios Centroamericanos*, pp. 229-52.

15. *Central America Bulletin*, Berkeley, California, June-July 1984.

16. *The Christian Science Monitor*, 8 and 30 March 1984.

17. For a discussion of Latin American Christian Democratic ideology, see in Michael P. Fogarty, *Christian Democracy in Western Europe: 1820-1973* (London: Routledge & Kegan Paul, 1957); Edward Williams, *Latin American Christian Democratic Parties* (Knoxville: University of Tennessee Press, 1967); and Mario Solórzano Martinez, 'El Papel de la Democracia Cristiana en la Actual Coyuntura Centroamericana' in Hugo Assman (ed.), *El Juego de los Reformismos frente a la Revolucion en Centroamerica* (San Jose, Costa Rica: Colleccion Centroamericana: DEI, 1981).

18. Important leaders like Hector Dada, Ruben Zamora (now leader of the FDR) and Roberto Lara Velado resigned from the party at this time.

19. This treatment of Christian Democratic democratisation strategy is drawn from interviews conducted by the author in El Salvador, Mexico and Venezuela. Discussions with Napoleón Duarte, Fidel Chavez Mena (PDC), Hector Dada (former leader of the PDC), José Miguel Fritis (IVEPO), Rafael Caldera and José Rodriguez Iturbe (CARE, Venezuela) were particularly useful.

20. As Duarte remarked. 'We believe that we can do what the Venezuelans did . . . We are following the Venezuelan example and I am Rómulo Betancourt.' Interview with Napoleón Duarte, San Salvador, October 1983.

21. Interview with José Miguel Fritis, Chilean Christian Democratic working in IVEPO, San Salvador, October 1983. For an analysis of the destruction of the political centre in Chile, see Arturo Valenzuela, *The Breakdown of Democratic Regimes: Chile* (Baltimore: Johns Hopkins University Press, 1978).

22. The Reagan administration briefly flirted with offering support to the ultra-right in 1981 and later lent backing to the PCN, particularly during the 1985 assembly elections. For a discussion of Venezuelan support for El Salvador, see Terry Karl, 'Regional Powers and Central American Peace: Mexico, Venezuela, and the Contadora Initiative' in Moss Blachman, William LeoGrande and Kenneth Sharpe (eds.), *Confronting Revolution: Security Through Diplomacy in Central America* (New York: Pantheon Publishers, forthcoming in 1985).

23. The views of the FMLN Commander Fernan Cienfuegos, expressed in an interview by Chris Hedges, are instructive here. He divides the military into ultra-rightists, whose power is diminishing, apolitical technicians trained in the US, and nationalists, who form the support basis for a political settlement. *Christian Science Monitor*, 18 October 1984.

24. Interview with Joaquin Villalobos, Morazan, El Salvador, April 1985.

25. This was a common theme in interviews with party members ranging from ARENA to the FDR-FMLN and also with Salvadoran entrepreneurs in April 1985.

26. The small size of the country and its elite, a plus in forging democracies, has led to poignant moments during the La Palma talks. The FDR-FMLN military commander, Fernan Cienfuegos, reportedly asked the Salvadoran Defence Minister, General Eugenio Vides Casanova, who was part of the government

delegation, to send regards to Mr Cienfuegos' family since the general was a friend of his parents. In other unexpected encounters, representatives of the two sides often embraced, sent messages to each other's families, and traded social gossip. *New York Times*, 19 November 1984.

27. Transcript of President Napoleón Duarte's press conference, held 16 October 1984 in San Salvador following the La Palma meeting.

28. See FMLN-FDR Political-Diplomatic Commission, 'La Palma: A Hope For Peace', November 1984.

29. See 'U.S. Aid to El Salvador: An Evaluation of the Past, a Proposal for the Future', *A Report to the Arms Control and Foreign Policy Caucus*, from the offices of Rep. Jim Leach (R-Iowa), Rep. George Miller (D-California) and Sen. Mark Hatfield (R-Oregon) US Congress, February 1985. Immediately following La Palma, the US introduced new airships into El Salvador and permitted military advisers to accompany Salvadoran officers into combat. See *Washington Post*, 19 October 1984.

30. The number of death threats, including those aimed at the president and leading Christian Democrats, and human rights violations rose in the wake of meetings between the government and the FDR-FMLN. In addition, the rightist assembly blocked all efforts to investigate disappearances and murders. According to Americas Watch, deaths attributable to death-squad activity rose from 8 in December 1984 to 22 in February 1985.

31. As a representative from ANEP explained: 'We have two years of US aid and three years until we have to deal with another election in our country or yours.' Interview, San Salvador, April 1985.

32. Interview with Joaquin Villalobos, Morazan, El Salvador, April 1985.

33. *New York Times*, 17 October 1984.

11 THE PROSPECTS FOR A POLITICAL SETTLEMENT: MOST OPTIONS HAVE BEEN FORECLOSED

Laurence Whitehead

Introduction

This chapter begins from the judgement that a political settlement of the conflict in Central America would require the fulfilment of a series of conditions that at the time of writing (mid-1985) seem quite unlikely to be met. If there is no political settlement, many will argue that it was in any case never really possible. The history of the region, its geo-political setting and its inherited socio-economic structure all look highly unfavourable. The dominant ideology of the main revolutionary forces can also be presented as an insuperable obstacle to peaceful compromise, although that leaves open the question whether their intransigence was chosen or forced upon them. However, the argument presented here is that it was not inevitable, five years ago, or one year ago, or even after President Reagan's re-election, that there could be no peaceful settlement. Over that period there has been a succession of decisions, misjudgements and non-decisions that has cumulatively foreclosed most of the options for peace, and narrowed the alternatives to the point where few possibilities remain for any kind of *salida politica*. This chapter is an attempt to justify that mode of interpretation – which gives priority to the realm of political calculation, rather than to socio-structural necessity. In such an exercise there is bound to be at least some implicit attribution of blame, but that is not my main concern. In order to minimise that aspect of the argument I shall try briefly to sketch what I believe to be the reasons and justifications that would be invoked by the key political actors at each critical conjuncture.

Clearly the task of writing an accurate history lies well in the future, but meanwhile we urgently need realistic and reasonably well-informed judgements based on the information currently available. An interpretation couched largely in terms of a series of critical conjunctures raises the question whether, given an alternative sequence of choices at key conjunctures, the result would have been a stable and peaceful settlement, or merely some rather different manifestation of the basic underlying conflict. An assumption made here is that none of the contending forces in Central America – probably not even the USA – is powerful enough to impose an outcome entirely satisfactory to itself. (How far this incapacity represents a genuine lack of power, or alternatively a lack of realism about what is attainable, will vary from case to case.) Consequently, the contending forces must either reach a stable compromise, or pay the price of an indefinite and inconclusive prolongation of the conflict. The possibility of a political settlement has always depended – and still depends – upon general recognition of this logic. So long as any of the major forces in contention can persuade themselves – however unrealistically – that an outright victory is attainable (or that the other side still believes an outright victory to be within its reach) there will be no stable peace. A minimum level of at least tacit co-operation is required to stabilise a peaceful outcome. That minimum requires a willingness to distinguish between negotiable and non-negotiable demands, and to take some risks in trusting to the good faith of adversaries. At several critical conjunctures where such a climate of opinion might have been fostered, the path of polarisation was chosen instead. Such choices are cumulative and have progressively eliminated most possibilities for a lasting peace.

Like the term 'democracy', references to a 'political settlement' can carry differing connotations depending upon the standpoint and interests of the observer. For Washington policy-makers, only an outcome which gives paramountcy to US security concerns (including the most hypothetical of these) would count. It sometimes seems as if *any* outcome which met that condition, and did not involve the direct use of US troops, would be deemed to qualify. From a Sandinista viewpoint there can be no 'political solution' that leaves an imminent threat of counter-revolution in place; the more radical view would be that there can be no lasting political settlement based on propping up a bankrupt social order in the rest of Central America, either. As will become apparent, this chapter, although not espousing any specific package of proposals for a political settlement, reserves the term for those outcomes in which all the main contending forces substantially reduce their demands upon each other, establishing a *modus vivendi* in which each can surive without posing, or being charged with posing, an imminent threat to the vital interests of the rest. Such an outcome does not require convergence of viewpoints about all the issues in contention, but only a reasonable degree of confidence on both sides that remaining agreements will not be pressed to the point of military action. In this sense Britain and Eire reached a 'political settlement' by the 1930s, as did even the US and Cuba after 1962.

In the next section of this chapter I shall briefly review the stance of the various political actors most involved in the conflict, trying to identify the crucial moments at which they defined their priorities and foreclosed their options. I shall attempt to suggest why each crucial decision may have been taken, and to indicate the main consequences (often unintended or unanticipated) that followed. Next I will discuss what I mean by the term 'political settlement' in the Central American context, and assess both Washington's approach and the Contadora approach. Although my conclusions are fairly pessimistic, it would be contrary to the standpoint of this chapter to view a failure of current peace efforts as predetermined in advance. Therefore the final section considers what scope may still remain for a negotiated solution, taking into account the presumption that 'some issues can't be fudged', but also recognising the facts of growing war-weariness and 'disenchantment' throughout the Isthmus. Some comparisons with analogous situations elsewhere tend to confirm the case for pessimism, but also indicate that in certain 'critical conjunctures' apparently unrealistic solutions can acquire an irresistible momentum.

A Brief Survey of the Contending Forces, and How They Became 'Locked In'

Simplifying drasticially, I shall classify the contending forces as 'left' 'right' and 'centre', including both external and local actors under each heading. (Tom Anderson rightly refers to a 'series of overlapping conflicts' rather than a single region-wide divide, but the degree of overlap is so great that it is hard to see how the separate conflicts could be disentangled or resolved in isolation from each other.) The focus on 'actors' means that I shall only discuss the strategies of organised political forces (above all, leadership strategies and perceptions). It will not be possible to consider the broader social context within which these political forces operate. Much is omitted by this approach, but there is also some gain in clarity. At times of open civil war it is the interlocking strategies of the well-organised minorities that drive the rest.

The Left

Starting on the left, I shall run through the supposed 'domino' connections from Moscow through Havana and Managua to the FMLN. In my view, however, each of these is substantially autonomous, each has quite distinct interests in the conflict, and each has contrasting perceptions of its dynamics. Furthermore, none of these centres of decision-making on the left can select a strategy towards the regional conflict that disregards the broader international setting. On the contrary, I would argue that international developments *outside* Central America (indeed totally unrelated to the circumstances of the Isthmus) can have and have had the most powerful influence in shaping the strategy of the Central American revolutionaries and in foreclosing some of their options.

First, the USSR. Moscow's protégés had suffered three foreign policy 'defeats' in Central America before the Nicaraguan Revolution: the communist-led peasant uprising in El Salvador was crushed in 1932, the Costa Rican CP was faced down in the 1948 civil war, and the Guatemalan party was crushed following the CIA operation of 1954. Even in these three cases, it remains doubtful whether Moscow took all that large or direct a part in supervising the activities of these local parties, or whether these defeats were considered particularly surprising or damaging. It seems most likely that Soviet strategists quickly drew the lesson that the Central American Isthmus was too strategically sensitive, too strongly under US control and too lacking in any 'rearguard', to offer promise of advantage in the global geo-political struggle. Despite the Cuban Revolution (and ignoring Cuban advice about the prospects for the Sandinistas), Moscow apparently continued to disregard revolutionary prospects on the Isthmus until after the fall of Somoza. By February 1981, of course, the State Department was publicly proclaiming in the famous 'White Paper' that 'Cuba, the Soviet Union, and other Communist states . . . are carrying out . . . *a well-co-ordinated* [my emphasis] covert effort' to impose a communist regime in El Salvador. On the other hand, Alexander Haig has himself acknowledged that Havana and Moscow were far from well co-ordinated at this time.[1] Since 1981 there have been further signs of divergence between Moscow and Havana on how to respond to the regional crisis. Over the Grenada invasion, in particular, whereas Castro forcefully condemned the murder of Bishop, the USSR equivocated, and indeed there may have been some degree of Soviet complicity with the Coards.[2] After the CIA attacked Nicaragua's oil refineries the USSR replaced Mexico and Venezuela as the leading source of crude oil imports to the Sandinista revolution. Military assistance from the eastern bloc may also have been greatly increased over the past year or so.

Of course the conditions attached to such aid are a matter for speculation, and we have no direct evidence of how far the Russians are willing to go, or of whether there are differences of opinion within the Soviet bloc over aiding Nicaragua (and conceivably the left in El Salvador). Nevertheless my reading of the record is that Moscow has always been wary of over-involvement in Central America, unwilling to take another exposed position (the alliance with Cuba has been demanding enough), and by no means confident that the isthmian revolutionaries can withstand the inevitable American backlash. Undoubtedly Moscow will be obliged to lend some degree of support to revolutionary movements that act in accordance with Soviet ideology, and of course they will seize opportunities to make life difficult for their rivals in Washington, where this can be done at low cost or with little risk. What is far more doubtful is their willingness to enter into the sort of long-term open-ended commitments that are probably necessary if pro-Soviet regimes are to be consolidated anywhere on the mainland. If this broad assessment remains correct, Soviet support for the Central American left will be motivated mainly by calculations about the state of their global competition with the USA. To be precise, I would assume that the deteriorating Soviet position in such places as Afghanistan and Poland, and the post-1979 intensification of the Cold War, contribute more to explaining the Soviet posture in Central America than any specifically regional analysis.

From this perspective, the critical steps defining and limiting Moscow's freedom of manoeuvre in Central America were (i) the 1960 decision to shelter/incorporate the Cuban Revolution (voluntary and costly but fairly successful); (ii) the 1975 decision to act through Cuba in Angola (voluntary, costly and quite unsuccessful); (iii) the 1979 decision to invade Afghanistan (probably involuntary, very costly and of indeterminate success). Central America was always unfavourable terrain for Soviet activism, and these three decisions each provided strong arguments for those Soviet policy-makers opposed to overcommitment on the Isthmus. From Moscow's point of view, even if the Central American revolution is massively defeated, a *limited* degree of support would be obligatory. It would, moreover, be worthwhile provided that in consequence the USA became deeply entangled and discredited.

The view from Havana must be radically different. The Cubans' highest priority must be to avoid a massive defeat in Central America, for that would plunge them back into isolation, it would dangerously demoralise domestic public opinion, and it might even tempt the US into a direct assault on the Cuban Revolution itself. Whereas in Angola and Ethiopia they could despatch their own forces to block the defeat of overseas allies, this would be a reckless and counter-productive step for them to take anywhere in the Caribbean Basin. Moreover, Cuban forces are presently so over-stretched in Angola that the military reserves are lacking for additional overseas adventures, even if the prospects were more favourable. Viewed from Havana, recent Soviet leadership is unlikely to have inspired great confidence. Apart from the obvious deficiences of the ruling groups, Soviet foreign policy must deal with such urgent difficulties closer to home that, from Castro's standpoint, the problems of the Caribbean probably receive insufficient priority.[3] The problems of the Soviet economy also leave Cuba quite exposed. In particular, the acute dilemmas arising from the joint Cuban-Soviet presence in Angola must put the relationship under considerable strain. Equally, the Cubans must view their wayward allies in Managua with misgivings, especially after the shock of witnessing the sudden auto-destruction of the Grenadan Revolution. Havana will no doubt give all the advice, support and indeed, direction it can to its Central American allies, in order to minimise the risk of total defeat, and to improve the chance of extracting some lasting advantage from the conflict. However, I consider it most unlikely that the Cubans seriously envisage the creation of what President Reagan has described as a string of 'Cuba model' states in Central America in the foreseeable future. The risks attached to the pursuit of this unlikely goal must seem far too great (far greater than the risks as perceived from Moscow). I believe this is a judgement they must have made at least two years ago (i.e. before the Grenada invasion), if not much earlier. This would help to explain Cuban verbal support for the Contadora process, and perhaps also such 'unexpected' developments as Managua's willingness to sign the draft peace treaty of October 1984 (which would require *inter alia* the withdrawal of any Cuban forces in Nicaragua). But Cuban perceptions and interests are not identical with those of all the Central American revolutionaries, nor is Havana always able to control the policies of its regional allies, even when mistakes by those allies could threaten Cuba's own prestige and security.

What led Havana to its current constrained and vulnerable position? First and foremost, of course, was the 1960 decision to undertake a wholehearted 'reversal of alliances' – not only to defy the USA, but fully to embrace the USSR. Castro's endorsement of the Soviet invasion of Czechoslovakia (in 1968) was another watershed, although it probably just brought to international attention a strategy that had been determined some time earlier. In practice it was not until the early 1970s that the full consequences of this decision worked themselves out, but in my opinion there was only one fundamental choice. The rest followed more or less naturally, if not inevitably. The underlying issue, which is also of obvious relevance to the contemporary Central American left, is whether some modified version of the Cuban Revolution could have survived in the absence of such a full-blooded pro-Soviet realignment. If not (and I am reasonably persuaded that Castro was right to conclude that he would end up like Arbenz unless he achieved a massive pre-emptive mobilisation and realignment) then the next critical 'moment of choice' came in 1975, when the Cuban revolutionaries for the first time exploited their privileged links with the USSR to achieve (by military action) a foreign policy success that undoubtedly reflected their own ideological priorities, but that would have been entirely unattainable without Soviet logistics and Soviet finance.

The Angolan operation proved a great short-term triumph, yet the long-term consequences cannot have been fully anticipated by its authors. The unanticipated consequences constrain Havana's room for manoeuvre in the Central American crisis, and perhaps also reduce the chances for a peaceful settlement there. Apart from the direct military and economic costs (which have become more long-lasting and more onerous than the Cubans can ever have anticipated), the element of surprise used then now helps to justify a US posture of over-insurance; and the scale of the military operation now invites a grandiose counter-strategy in Central America. Moreover, the intimate nature of Cuban-Soviet co-operation in Africa can be cited to cast doubt on Cuba's capacity or inclination to act as a regional power (rather than a mere 'Soviet proxy') in the Caribbean.

Cuba's third critical decision was to back the Sandinista revolution (despite Soviet scepticism) and subsequently to generalise the Sandinista formula from Nicaragua to El Salvador and Guatemala. In this case the internal degeneration of the Somoza dynasty was, I would argue, a process largely beyond Cuba's capacity to accelerate or prevent. It accorded so well with Havana's worldview, with Cuba's domestic experience, and with the island's urgent strategic need for at least one reliable Latin American ally, that a posture of support for the Sandinista front was almost mandated by the circumstances, rather than actively chosen. Even in 1979, when the Carter administration presented an image of the US at its least threatening, the Cuban leadership already seemed aware of the dangerous nature of the game they were playing. Thus, in May 1979 Castro sought Mexican assurances that would provide a broad international front to protect the prospective revolutionary regime in Nicaragua, and would make it possible to reduce/mask the intensity of Cuban support for the Sandinistas. Since 1979 Havana's advice to Managua has by all accounts emphasised the need to avoid the early mistakes of the Cuban Revolution, to maintain as broad a basis of international support as possible, and to pay great attention to US public opinion as a brake on the predictable hostility of Washington. Thus it seems that the Cubans have been rather consistently more prudent and defensive than either the Soviets (who have little to lose) or the Sandinistas (who, in the first flush of their revolution, have tended to place too much confidence in the rightness of their cause, and to over-estimate their strength).

Nicaragua's *comandantes* have recently been taught some harsh lessons in realism but, partly because of their own choices and mistakes in an early phase of the revolution, they now have little scope to benefit from what they are learning. The Israeli operation to oust the PLO from Beirut, and the US invasion of Grenada, were both viewed with foreboding in Managua because they underlined how isolated a revolutionary movement may be at its moment of supreme need. Compared to either the PLO or the NJM, the Sandinistas have been far more skilful in protecting themselves, both in their management of international relations and with regard to internal questions. However, on both fronts their position has clearly weakened for reasons that are not entirely external. Although in general their international diplomacy has been quite impressive, they made some critical choices with regard to the USA that have subsequently come to haunt them. They overplayed their hand with President Carter, misjudged the likelihood and implications of a Reagan victory in 1980, and based too much of their defensive strategy on the expectation of another 'Bay of Pigs'. In the event they have had to contend with a much slower and more systematic war of attrition: this slow strangulation has indeed worn them down. However it is not, in my opinion, their foreign policy judgements and choices that have most harmed them. On the international front they were always at a grave disadvantage, despite which they have done quite well. On the home front, by contrast, they started with huge advantages and with a considerable leeway for choice. As Rodolfo Cerdas argues in his chapter, I would judge that they unnecessarily alienated the support of many potential allies, out of a misplaced belief that they could thus keep the revolution 'pure', and also to consolidate an effective monopoly of power. The question here is not whether such a strong and pure revolutionary regime might by some criteria be *desirable*, but whether this scheme was ever *realistic*. It is understandable why the

Sandinistas should fear the long-term consequences of sharing power with their bourgeois, Social Democratic and clerical allies in the struggle against Somoza. All of these groups were potential rivals who might strike a deal with the US against the revolutionaries. But I suspect it was a serious over-estimate of the gains attainable through military and bureaucratic means that induced the *comandantes* to try to 'go it alone' internally. Under the combined effects of mounting external pressure, economic scarcity and dislocation, and the loss of political momentum internally, the Nicaraguan revolutionaries now face demands for concessions that could once have seemed magnanimous, but that would at present seem an indication of weakness. With their options narrowing all the time, and with their defensive strategy only serving to postpone, but not lastingly to alleviate, the pressures against them, the problems of maintaining internal cohesion are likely to intensify. Most of them probably feel (and this would be correct) that their revolution has gone too far for them to change course now. Unfortunately there may be some resemblances with the later stages of the Allende government, in which the scope for realistic accommodation was eliminated and a 'Masada complex' developed.

The Salvadoran guerrillas probably never had any scope for realistic accommodation with the armed forces and state bureaucracy of their country. In their case a 'Masada complex' would be fully justified from the outset, and indeed validated by a history dating back at least to 1932. Naturally they have drawn encouragement from the Cuban Revolution (although some key leaders have been quite anti-Cuban and/or anti-Soviet in their ideological orientations) and have used Managua as a base area and operations centre. However it seems most unlikely that these international backers can exercise sufficient control to impose a strategy on the Salvadoran left against the wishes of the FMLN's own leadership; and for objective reasons the Salvadoran revolutionaries have substantially different interests, and different perceptions, from their external sponsors. Their primordial interest must be to purge or remould the Salvadoran armed forces at least enough to offer the left some chance of physical survival and organised existence after formal hostilities cease. Although that might appear an unduly limited objective, in fact, in Salvadoran conditions, it has extremely far-reaching implications, and may only be attainable (if at all) after very costly and protracted confrontations. Neither the Cubans nor the Sandinistas have the same interest in pressing the Salvadoran conflict so far. For the leaders of the FMLN and for their social bases this minimum aim is a question of sheer survival (few of them can achieve a bearable future in exile); whereas for the leaders of Cuba and Nicaragua (and even more so for their respective peoples), the price of an indefinite and inconclusive struggle in El Salvador has increasingly come to seem out of proportion to any possible gain. The ill-chosen rhetoric of the 'final offensive', and subsequent triumphalist language from Radio Venceremos was probably prompted, at least in part, by the urgent need to cover up this underlying divergence of interest between revolutionaries of different nationalities. Of course, all the radical left forces in Central America are coalitions, made up of a variety of elements, each with a distinctive history and ideology. It is only with the greatest of difficulty, and under severe duress, that the more militarist and sectarian components of these coalitions can be persuaded to co-operate with rival factions; especially since questions of revolutionary strategy are also questions of physical survival for each organised sub-group. Counter-insurgency strategists are always on the look-out for ways to exploit these internal tensions, and in some cases (notably the Salvadoran FMLN) there is no shortage of new material for them to work on.[4] In any case, much of the Salvadoran left may be thinking more in Central America-wide terms than their Cuban or Nicaraguan associates. 'Socialism in one country' is a reality for Cuba, and an apparently feasible aim for Nicaragua, but much harder to envisage in El Salvador, because of the country's social structure and its geographical setting. Any conceivable revolution in El Salvador probably does require the 'dominos' to fall (especially in Guatemala). This is not the case in Nicaragua. In short, the predicament of the Salvadoran left has long been far more desperate than that of the Sandinistas.[5]

The same applies *a fortiori* to the Guatemalan left. There have been no political options open to them in their tragic and largely isolated struggles. For that reason I shall pass directly to the forces of the right, from the ascendant right in Guatemala, to their counterparts in El Salvador and Nicaragua, to the backers in the USA.

The Right

It was at least a generation ago, if not more, when the repressive right in Guatemala went too far ever to turn back. In the 1940s Arévalo feared that the reflexes of 'reactionary despotism' were already so deeply entrenched that he might as well attempt the most quixotic counter-measures. Washington disregarded all such danger, and sanctioned a counter-revolution that unleashed all the most extreme impulses towards repression and intolerance. It was a grave choice made by the USA in 1954, not one that can subsequently be forgotten or undone. But we should also give due weight to the equally grave and irreversible choices then made by the Guatemalan right. Arguably there have been substantial periods since 1954 when conservative interests were so well entrenched and secure, and popular and revolutionary movements were so thoroughly cowed and dismembered, that the right had the opportunity to offer reforms from a position of strength. However this may be, no strategy of conciliation has ever been seriously promoted, as the chapter by Martínez Solórzano indicates. Since 1954 the repressive right has enjoyed a remarkable ascendancy, based on the principle that if you intimidate or suppress all moderate and centrist forces, the opposition will have no choice but to join the revolutionaries. Then, by posing a stark choice between the status quo and violent revolution, the repressive right can gather round itself many groups who otherwise dislike or fear its methods. (Among others the Americans will be obliged to accept the right.) The methods long used in Guatemala are indeed detestable, but from the standpoint of their promoters they have also proved strikingly effective. Although to some extent this repressive formula may be varied from time to time (as after the 1982 coup, and perhaps again after the 1985 election), it is far from clear how the essentials of this structure can be changed from within. Nor does it seem likely, for the foreseeable future, to be changed from without.

El Salvador also has a repressive right, as deeply entrenched as in Guatemala, and as relentless in its conduct. But the conservative classes of El Salvador have not always relied so consistently and exclusively on this formula to preserve their interests. On the contrary, they have from time to time endorsed a variety of strategies, including some quite inventive forms of institution-building and conciliation. Perhaps because they have never faced a challenge on the scale presented by Arévalo/Arbenz, and also because they were never reduced to sheltering behind the CIA as Guatemala's conservatives have been, the Salvadoran right long enjoyed considerable room for manoeuvre. The decision to deny Duarte/Ungo their electoral success in 1972 was not predetermined, but once taken it pushed El Salvador down the Guatemalan road. The coup of October 1979 is the object of many conflicting interpretations, but even if its main thrust was to pre-empt the waves of radicalism spreading out from Nicaragua, the point is that in Salvadoran conditions pre-emptive reformism contained some genuine potential. This was squandered *either* because the Salvadoran left was too euphoric, *or* because the repressive right was so skilful in provoking a polarisation (or, most likely, through some interaction of the two), but *not* because all the preconditions for reformism had been systematically eradicated before the attempt began. Herein lay the crucial difference between Guatemala and El Salvador, one that even now offers more hope of a negotiated settlement in the latter country than in the former.

Nevertheless that hope is relatively slender, largely because of the choices made in 1980 made on the centre and right, especially inside the armed forces and the business community, and in Washington, which chose to tolerate, if not actively to sanction, a campaign of provocation and intimidation launched by the far right. In other circumstances at least *some* of these sectors might have put up a more effective resistance to this 'Guatemalanisation' of El Salvador, as Archbishop Romero appealed to President Carter to do. But in 1980, with the shock waves still spreading out from Nicaragua's revolution, and with US power mocked in Iran, a wide spectrum of conservative forces tacitly accepted the 'death-squads' as lesser evils. That choice doomed El Salvador to a protracted civil war.

The Nicaraguan right has once again a different history, a different relationship with the USA, and made its critical choices at a different time. Somoza and his National Guard were, of course, the embodiment of the 'repressive right' until 1979, when they were destroyed. The 'new right' in Nicaragua owes its origin quite directly to meetings of the US National Security Council held in 1981. To be specific, it originated in November 1981 when President Reagan authorised the CIA to launch its 'covert' war against the Sandinistas. Without that decision in Washington it seems doubtful whether the counter-revolutionaries would ever have amounted to a serious force. A re-elected Jimmy Carter would not, I am convinced, have made the same decision as President Reagan. In a sense, therefore, it was the American electorate (whose minds were on many other questions rather than Nicaragua) who opted for the reconstitution of a violent right capable of seriously challenging the Sandinista revolution. (Here I am referring mainly to the 'Contras' – for centrist opposition see below.) There would, in any event, have been *some* opposition to the Sandinistas – including armed opposition; but it does seem that the Contras are considerably more dependent on Washington than the violent right in Guatemala, or even El Salvador, or indeed any of the left-wing forces are on Havana. Consequently I assume that any 'critical choices' concerning the Nicaraguan right were made not by the Contras as such but by their paymasters in Florida and Washington.

Therefore this discussion of the Central American right concludes with a brief consideration of their various external backers, i.e. the Cuban exile community, the Argentine military, the Begin administration in Israel and so on. This diversification of support has to some extent cushioned them from attempts by the majority in Congress to limit and qualify American support. Nevertheless the US government has been the back-bone of support to the Nicaraguan Contras. It has also exerted considerable influence over the right in Honduras, but enjoys only limited influence with the Salvadoran right and has rather little control in Guatemala. Of course the term 'US government' is imprecise. To understand Washington's Central American policies it is vital to distinguish between the rival bureaucratic agencies within the executive, and to recognise the complexity of the relationship between the executive, the legislature, the media and even public opinon at large.[6] According to official statements Washington is supporting the democratic centre against extremes of both left and right in Central America, but it is hard to make sense of these declarations in view of the arbitrary and self-interested way in which Washington policy-makers apply the labels 'democracy', 'centre' and 'right'. Official usage bears only the loosest of relationships to isthmian realities.[7]

The explanation for this practice is, of course, that prior to 1979 the US regularly acquiesced in, and benefited from, the dominance of unashamedly repressive and reactionary regimes on the Isthmus. By its acts of commission (e.g. Guatemala in 1954) and omission (e.g. the Salvadoran electoral fraud of 1972) it acquired a substantial complicity in situations that could in no way be defended or even explained to domestic public opinion. Rightly or wrongly, US policy-makers judged that their strategic or other interests were so well served by this situation that they must simply accept the status quo and hope that its characteristics never became an issue of public controversy at home. The result of this long-standing policy was that the Nicaraguan Revolution placed Washington in an extremely awkward predicament. It drew national and international attention to the iniquitous character of some of America's local alliances, and it demonstrated the fragility of official hopes for the creation of a respectable centre that could block the revolutionary left and take over from Somoza without damaging US security interests. (My own interpretation is that it was not any major security interest that was at stake, rather it was US prestige and domestic harmony on foreign policy matters,[8] but that judgement is not essential to the interpretation presented here.)

In its final year, the beleaguered Carter administration hesitantly chose to confront these difficulties, as they arose in El Salvador, by extending its classification of the 'centre' to cover almost all the real forces on the right and by extending its classification of the 'extreme left' to embrace many of the forces and interests without whose participation there could never be an authentic democratic centre. After January 1981 the Reagan administration extended the same procedure to Nicaragua (and eventually to the whole of Central America) and abandoned Carter's *arrière-pensées*. All this was necessary to relegitimise US policy before the domestic electorate. It also had the consequence (which we might very charitably characterise as an unintended consequence) of rehabilitating the repressive right; of restoring its confidence in the availability of international support (notwithstanding US official rhetoric to the contrary); and of tying US prestige – and perhaps even US security interests – very tightly to the fortunes of Central American reaction.[9] In particular, US prestige has become closely tied to the battle fortunes of the Salvadoran army and of the Nicaraguan counter-revolutionaries. What requires brief consideration here is the strictly reactionary component of the counter-revolution, and in particular the choices, perceptions and misjudgements of those in Washington whose emphasis on a military solution may have tilted the balance – whether knowingly or not – towards the restoration of reactionary despotism in much of the Isthmus (and especially in Nicaragua).

We must consider two rival Washington agencies, each quite distrustful of the other, and each with a set of bureaucratic objectives extending well beyond Central America. Obviously there must be coordination between the CIA and the Pentagon, but the relationship is far from smooth. Until 1985 responsibility for the so-called 'covert war' against Nicaragua was located in the CIA, which has been trying to restore its position in the foreign-policy process after the grave setbacks it experienced during the 1970s. Until the spring of 1985 it was claimed that this 'covert war' was only intended to press the Sandinistas into a satisfactory compromise.[10] In reality it always implied the overthrow of the Sandinistas and their replacement by a government of Contras willing to use maximum force to make the counter-revolution irreversible. This is what the CIA had achieved in Guatemala and Iran in the 1950s, and what they aimed for in Cuba in 1961. To overthrow the Sandinistas by force would inevitably lead to the establishment of an extremely repressive and 'reactionary' regime. Anything less would be inappropriate or even counter-productive. It is because many in the US Congress recognised the logic set out above and flinched from the implications of an outright drive to overthrow the Sandinistas that funds for the 'covert war' were so strongly opposed. It would be foolhardy to predict at this stage how the CIA's Nicaraguan policy will eventually turn out. What is already clear is that by betting so heavily on the revival of *somozismo* the CIA has pre-empted Washington's alternatives for containing the Sandinista revolution, and has narrowed to near vanishing point the scope for peaceful accommodation between the US and the existing Nicaraguan government.

In El Salvador and Honduras, by contrast, prime responsibility for US policy rests with the Pentagon, since it is through the established military that American influence flows. My belief is that the Pentagon has the strongest of bureaucratic reasons to avert any situation that could require the despatch of US troops. Once American ground forces became directly involved, the local military would expect the new arrivals to do their share, or more, of the fighting. The cost in terms of US lives, morale and domestic consensus would be very high. El Salvador does not present favourable conditions for American troop operations, and the only kind of landing that would make any sense would be an overwhelmingly large intervention paving the way for an indefinite stay. (According to some semi-informed estimates, 100,000 men might be required.) If the order was given, the Pentagon would of course comply, but in the meantime the US military have every incentive to promote strong and effective local armies so that no such order will ever be required. Viewed from this standpoint the Salvadoran 'death-squads' are a doubtful asset. Political conciliation and social reform could have some appeal to American military planners, and a 'purged' more technically efficient Salvadoran military might seem preferable to the blunt old instrument of what Baloyra has called the 'reactionary despotism'. Since 1984 the balance of war seems to have swung in favour of the Salvadoran military. The Pentagon's contribution to this has been through extensive training and re-equipment and perhaps some pressure for internal reform, combined with a very lavish application of air-power.

Contrasts between the CIA and the Pentagon may have been quite significant. If so, the Pentagon's more nuanced position may leave Washington some scope to disengage itself partially from the repressive right in El Salvador and Honduras. This would leave the US government with a somewhat greater margin for manoeuvre than in Nicaragua, but not a very large margin. However, it is hardly necessary to rehearse once more the very close and dependent relationship between the Salvadoran and Honduran military and the US military, nor to repeat well-known evidence about the extent of the entire Salvadoran high command's complicity with the death-squads. Moreover, the Pentagon's capacity to reform or restructure the Salvadoran high command must be constrained by the exigencies of the war. Washington still needs the full co-operation of the Salvadoran armed forces as an institution if it is to avert a situation calling for the landing of US troops. Consequently any progress in shifting the Salvadoran high command from 'extreme right' towards the 'democratic centre' could only be very slow, incomplete and uncertain. There is every incentive for Salvadoran officers to pose for the foreign press as moderates and respecters of human rights (as even President Romero explained quite explicitly to his fellow officers shortly before the 'reformist' coup of October 1979). But there are very few incentives to alter actual military behaviour in accordance with this rhetoric. On the contrary, the public prominence and continuing impunity of Major d'Aubuisson illustrates only too clearly how strongly the internal incentives still flow in the opposite direction. It is not obvious that the Pentagon could fundamentally change the repressive and reactionary character of its Salvadoran protégés even if (unlikely hypothesis) it had the clear determination to do so. Thus Washington's past choices – particularly the decision to rely so heavily on a military response to the FMLN-FDR challenge – have foreclosed most of the potential options in El Salvador almost to the same extent as in Nicaragua.

The Centre

Whereas the categories of 'left' and 'right' may be relatively well defined, the 'centre' is always an elusive and in many ways unsatisfactory concept. This is above all the case when generalising about five different countries in a region undergoing intense political polarisation. One way of posing the underlying conflict on the Isthmus is to ask what kind of organised political centre can hope to survive in such a setting, and on what terms. The organisations discussed in this section are extremely heterogeneous. They can be defined negatively as all those political actors who belong neither to the left nor the right as described above, but this still leaves a great range of rival interests and competing ideologies. More positively, they all have an interest in preventing further polarisation and internationalisation of the conflict, and they all potentially contribute in diverse and competing ways to the search for a political settlement. On the other hand, they each have other interests to serve, as well as the wish to prevent polarisation, and they differ profoundly amongst themselves over what would constitute a desirable or practical political solution. Consequently they have found it impossible to establish a unified and coherent 'centrist block' that would underpin a well-defined settlement. I shall consider first the forces within the USA that fall into this category; then Duarte and the Christian Democratic International; then the Socialist International and its protégés in Costa Rica, Nicaragua and El Salvador; and finally, the Contadora nations.

Beginning in the USA we find a complex situation. In rhetorical terms, nearly all US organisations claim to favour the 'centre' and a political settlement. I have already outlined the reasons why these claims should not be taken at face value, and have claimed that the US executive, in particular, has in reality worked in at least tacit alliance with the repressive right. However even within the executive branch there has always been considerable ambiguity on this question. A 'two-track' policy would seem the obvious strategy. A display of ruthless determination should demoralise and intimidate the revolutionaries; whilst a simultaneous programme of concessions and reforms might create a pro-American centre, detach some waverers from the leftist alliance, and reassure US public opinion that the Central American policy was morally justified. The difficulty with this approach has been that it would require the right messages to be received only by the right audiences. It would therefore require a clarity of purpose and a capacity for co-ordinating the various agencies of government probably beyond the powers even of a Henry Kissinger. Between 1980 and 1984 the authors of America's Central American policies mostly lacked the sophistication, and certainly lacked the centralised control, to make much use of the 'two-track' approach. After the Salvadoran elections of May 1984 however, the State Department assumed a more leading role, and scored at least some points for the use of more subtle tactics. It seems likely that this was merely an expedient shift timed to dampen down tension until the President was safely re-elected. Since the beginning of 1985 the administration has shifted tactics once again. It no longer seems so concerned to present a conciliatory image either to its domestic critics or to its foreign allies.

It is Congress that has exerted strong pressure for compromise with the left and disengagement from the far right, and within Congress this has been more true of the Democrat-controlled House than of the Republican-led Senate. This is not to say that the division has been entirely on party lines, nor that Congress has successfully formulated a coherent Central American policy to challenge the Reagan administration's strategy. On the contrary, Congress has only the bluntest of instruments at its disposal for influencing the executive's foreign policies and such instruments have frequently been used only in a negative or unconstructive manner. The precedents that loom so large in congressional reasoning on this issue (the Gulf of Tonkin resolution, the Watergate scandal, the Angolan débâcle) are all rather poor guides to the management of the Central American crisis. Congress may veto certain items of expenditure, and may urge alternative priorities on the administration, but this will only produce the desired results where the executive is willing to listen to criticism and therefore to formulate new policies that accurately interpret the intentions of the legislators. There has been no such convergence of views on Central America at any time since 1979. Since President Reagan's re-election, however, there does seem to have been a shift in the congressional balance that has given the administration a freer hand. The major explanation for this shift is not, in my opinion, that the Sandinista 'threat' has become more real. It is simply that uncommitted congressmen have come to the conclusion that the Reagan administration will not be deflected from its course by any but the most drastic of congressional restraints (e.g. impeachment). Realising that 'the votes are not there' for whole-hearted obstruction, and accepting the *fait accompli* of confrontation brought about by President Reagan in his first term, wavering liberals seem to have lost their will to resist.

A major development that has encouraged the administration and suprised some of its critics has been the course of events in El Salvador since the election of Duarte as Salvador's President in May 1984 (an election achieved with substantial US funding and after much arm-twisting to block ARENA). Duarte's record in El Salvador from 1980 to May 1984 was a source of considerable embarrassment to his international backers. Sister parties in Venezuela, Western Europe and elsewhere must be hugely relieved that after so many vicissitudes Duarte not only won the presidency, but in the March 1985 congressional elections he also appeared to regain the political initiative, securing an opportunity to justify his claim to be a peace-maker and a progressive democrat. They have every reason enthusiastically to support Duarte's current position in the hope that he can become sufficiently strong and successful to outmanoeuvre the right, to domesticate the military, and to steer the left into a compromise that would leave the Christian Democrats strategically well placed and ideologically vindicated.

The decisive issue, then, is whether Duarte's past acts of ommision and commission, and his current system of alliances, leave him with sufficient credibility and room for manoeuvre to achieve a centrist settlement of the Salvadoran civil war. As Terry Karl's chapter indicates, he made two strategic choices that define the scope and limitations of his present position. There was the decision to preserve his alliance with the Salvadoran military, however unsavory or indeed threatening their behaviour might be in the short run, on the view that eventually – with sufficient international and domestic pressure – they could be reformed. The second strategic choice was to define the insurrectionary left as the essential enemy, and to insist that this enemy could only be defeated – as defeated it must be – by a determined application of force, combined with reform. For several years it seemed as if this stance would lead him into complicity with the crimes committed by the right, without ever establishing the political efficiency of his reforms. To the popular sectors he risked appearing as just a particularly two-faced spokesman for the *ancien régime* while the conservative classes might well view him as a dubious ally trying unnecessarily to upset the status quo. To construct an effective 'centre' in El Salvador he needed to escape from this disjuncture, which has for so long threatened to destroy him. At the time of writing this still seemed a relatively open issue, although the peace overtures of La Palma seemed unlikely to prosper, and the Archbishop of El Salvador seemed inclined to blame both the guerrillas and the US (which has stepped up its military aid) in fairly equal proportions.

If international Christian Democracy has recently gained at least a modicum of encouragement from the latest turn of events in El Salvador, the reverse is true for the Socialist International and developments in Nicaragua. Continuing revelations concerning the CIA's unscrupulous tactics against the Sandinistas more or less oblige the SI to support the Nicaraguan Revolution. But SI unease has grown as the Sandinistas became more isolated, both regionally and within their own country. Attempts to persuade Arturo Cruz to stay in the November 1984 election failed, and at least some international supporters attribute this partially to Sandinista intransigence. Edén Pastora also retains *some* credibility within the SI, and of course he argues that there is no alternative to continued armed struggle, even in association with the FDN. Finally the democratically elected government of Costa Rica, under a party which is a long-standing member of the SI, has come close to arguing that the Sandinista revolution poses such a threat to its unarmed neighbour that an OAS peace-keeping force may be required. In my opinion there is an even more basic reason why the SI finds itself in such difficulties in Central America. Its importance was always as an *interlocuteur valable*, in good standing with both sides, rather than as an independent actor in its own right. Given Nicaragua's weakness, the SI could readily retain some measure of influence with the left, but its problem was always to achieve some degree of co-operation from the US. As the Reagan administration has gradually shifted the terms of the debate within the US, has worn down the Sandinista regime, and has now won itself an additional term of office, the SI's stock of political capital has been progressively reduced.

The presently contrasting fortunes of international Christian Democracy and the SI should not distract attention from the underlying similarities of their position. Just as the CD had to bear with Duarte during the four years when his room for manoeuvre seemed exhausted, so the SI will seek to assist and influence the Sandinistas in the hope that their centrist tendencies may also regain the political initiative in Nicaragua. The SI's strategy therefore depends on the prospects of like-minded elements within Nicaragua, El Salvador and Costa Rica. But these elements are widely dispersed, divided among themselves, and often even lack organisational autonomy. For example, broadly like-minded Nicaraguans can be found within the government, within the legal opposition, and even among the counter-revolutionaries fighting in the south. Obviously with this degree of dispersion the SI's protégés lack cohesion and tend to fall under the control of other better-structured groupings. For my purposes the most important sector is the so-called Social Democratic current within the leadership of the FSLN. It is unnecessary to repeat here the catalogue of concessions made by this sector in order to stay within the Frente and to preserve the revolution. As US hostility has mounted, they have been obliged to close ranks with the radicals – after all, no incentives are being offered to reward moderation. Their position has been broadly comparable to that of Duarte in relation to the Salvadoran high command, with the important qualification that they have no clearly identifiable figurehead, and no separate organisation with a distinctive ideology.

It is a characteristic of even the most structured political forces of the 'centre' that their room for manoeuvre is sharply constrained by their dependence on more intransigent allies. Only the church still seems relatively capable of maintaining its distance from the polarised alternatives, while retaining at least a certain degree of (in some sense apolitical) leverage. There can be no peaceful settlement based *only* on such invertebrate forces. The conventional wisdom that a peaceful settlement requires the commitment of hardliners from both sides is correct.

Finally, some comments on Contadora belong here. This has been a remarkable episode in international diplomacy, backed only by the promise of subsidised oil, and the threat that if negotiations failed the result would be worse for all concerned (including the four Contadora nations themselves, where the spill-over from a Central American war could prove highly disruptive to relatively open societies). The initiative began in January 1983, as the scale of US support for the Nicaraguan Contras became apparent. It always seemed to me an exercise in buying time, while hoping for a change of emphasis in US policy. The key issue has been whether Contadora's promises of reassurance would ever inspire enough confidence in Washington to induce the US to shift towards regional *detente*. The denouement came in September 1984 when Nicaragua accepted all Contadora's terms, whereupon Washington found fault with the verification procedure. That would seem to confirm the limitations of this approach as a means of securing substantial changes in US policy.[11] However Contadora *has* helped to buy time, and *did* slightly improve the climate for negotiation. The question once Reagan was securely re-elected became whether that extra time and improved general climate would provide the basis for a political settlement. The next section concerns that issue.

What Constitutes a 'Political Settlement'?

The term is so imprecise that almost all contending forces can envisage some kind of 'political setlement' that would meet with their approval. This section attempts to identify the probable ingredients of any *realistic* political settlement – i.e. one that would elicit consent from a sufficiently wide range of political forces to have a good prospect of durability. This can be contrasted with alternative forms of settling the conflict that do not merit the label 'political'. In practice, however, the distinction between 'political' and 'imposed' settlements is unlikely to be very clear-cut. My position is that there will have to be some real losers if any durable settlement is to be achieved ('some issues can't be fudged'), and that there will have to be some forceful imposition of the settlement on those losers who do not accept the outcome. A related point is that if none of the contending forces has the strength to impose a chosen pattern of settlement (as I believe to be the case) then the only kind of political solution that can realistically be encouraged will be sub-optimal – or indeed downright disappointing/worrying – from the standpoint of all concerned. The choice will be between a 'lesser evil' and the very great evil of an indefinitely protracted and inconclusive conflict.

This 'disenchanted' view of the kind of political settlement that may be attainable derives not just from the analysis presented above of the particularities of the Central American case, but also from a comparative survey of the forms of settlement achieved in comparable situations elsewhere. Current negotiations between South Africa, Mozambique and Angola provide one illustration of what I have in mind. The British settlement with an independent Eire, shorn of the Protestant north, offers another rather discouraging example. The US accommodation with the Mexican Revolution, also during the 1920s, constitutes a third demonstration that political settlements can be demanding and disillusioning. In all these three instances the dominant power made fewer concessions than the 'underdogs' considered either just or adequate. The dominant power was willing to buy peace with its weaker neighbours provided the price was not excessive. Such concessions still left the weaker partners in a poor condition, not even fully secure despite the great sacrifices that had been made. But for the weaker partners, the alternative was a continuing conflict that threatened their very existence. For the dominant power the alternative was also unpalatable (otherwise no concessions would have been offered) but by no means a matter of survival. This is the essential point that must underline any political settlement in Central America. At various points before 1985 it seemed as if the USA might be induced to make some accommodation with the Central American left, but only if the other side made entirely disproportionate concessions. However, President Reagan's re-election has reduced the pressure from Congress and the US media. Unlike Congress, the administration no longer has to worry about being re-elected. This leaves only two motives for the US to concede anything: (i) to eliminate any contingency that might require the landing of US troops; (ii) to buy off hostility that would otherwise fester and create long-term enmity, given that the Central American left can only be suppressed, not expelled or dissolved. Therefore in principle the US has a long-term interest in avoiding the creation of more Guatemalas and Chiles. But this is only an *interest*, not an overwhelming necessity and not, apparently, a source of much concern to the present administration.

On this 'disenchanted' view, all sides would need to make concessions, to attain a result that would seem far from satisfactory. It seems unlikely that Washington will be prepared to make any concessions for now, but the question of *what kind* of concessions could in principle constitute a realistic basis for a settlement still seems worth considering. A stable political settlement cannot be achieved merely on the basis of undiscriminating concessions. What are the inescapable sticking points in the Central American conflict? Let me briefly consider US security interests, territorial integrity, cessation of hostilities, economic reconstruction and internal political structures.

There can be no political settlement unless some irreducible US security concerns are respected.[12] A political settlement that excludes Soviet influence from Central America is a possibility, but there can be no such settlement that excludes Cuba (as a regional power). Cuban influence can perhaps be entirely excluded from Central America by force, but not by political negotiation. The US would therefore have to acknowledge that the Cuban Revolution is not *merely* an instrument of Soviet imperialism, but has some basic interests of its own that were not to be disregarded. Likewise the Mexican Revolution has some autonomous legitimate interests in the Isthmus, not reducible to US interests, that would have to be respected.

There can be no political settlement if the national sovereignty and territorial integrity of the various states is still being seriously violated. This is the essential insight of the Contadora approach, namely that any state being subjected to large-scale external aggression inevitably comes to represent a threat to the security of its neighbours. Thus a political settlement must contain genuine negotiations to achieve bilateral accommodations between each pair of antagonistic states. It is not so clear to me that any settlement must necessarily involve the withdrawal from *all* countries of *all* foreign troops. To make the withdrawal of US forces from Honduras an essential precondition for a settlement seems to me unrealistic. (US troops have yet to withdraw from Guantanamo Bay in Cuba, after all.) The minimum requirement is that each state feels secure in its relation to the others. In Nicaragua's case, if the counter-revolutionary war was suspended this security might be attainable even if all Cuban and Soviet bloc forces were withdrawn.

Turning to internal matters, there can be no political settlement without a negotiated cessation of hostilities in the Nicaraguan and Salvadoran civil wars. This is not to say (as Malcolm Deas' account of the Colombian amnesty example makes clear) that all hostilities must actually cease. But the major leaders on both sides must achieve a minimum degree of understanding that offers the insurgents the possibility of returning to normal life without persecution, or alternatively that gives them somewhere else to go where they can be safe. The Greek Civil War ended when the communist forces crossed into Yugoslavia, Bulgaria and Albania. The Cuban Revolution achieved its consolidation when the opposition migrated *en masse* to Florida. The Nicaraguan conflict might be ended by an agreement to relocate the counter-revolutionaries outside their homeland. The Salvadoran civil war is harder to resolve in this manner, for the insurgents have nowhere else to go, and the Salvadoran state lacks credibility as a guarantor of their security if they ever disarmed.

There can be no durable political settlement without some reconstruction of the war-devastated economies. Assuming that there is no prospect of the Soviet bloc paying for the reconstruction of the Nicaraguan economy, this means that aid must be obtained either from the USA, or from Western Europe, or from the wealthier countries of Latin America. Aid from these sources will only be available to mixed economies, and not to those that are entirely socialised. Therefore, as even the programmes of the guerrilla forces generally acknowledge, the more doctrinaire variants of socialist economic transformation are incompatible with a political settlement. A large public sector and an elaborate programme of welfare provisions and redistributive policies may be practical politics, but a Cuban-style economic policy is not.

Finally, as far as internal political life is concerned, I do not see that any particular formula of government is necessarily ruled out by the requirements of a political settlement. It may be desirable, or even necessary, to observe the formalities of periodic elections, but this has been the case for many years in Mexico and indeed in Guatamala without greatly affecting real political life. Committees for the Defence of the Revolution could be compatible with a political settlement, although in the absence of a fully socialised economy they would possess less total control than their Cuban counterparts. On the other side, a corrupt judiciary and a lawless police force might also be retained, within the framework of a political settlement, provided their conduct could be reconciled with minimum requirements for the return to normal life of ex-insurgents. (The fate of ex-Cristeros in Mexico after the war ended in 1929 provides an example.)

These, then, are what I would consider to be the minimum requirements for what might loosely be labelled a 'political settlement' of the conflicts in Central America. It will be apparent why I have described mine as a 'disenchanted' view of what such a settlement might entail. The only virtue of this approach is its attempt at realism. What remains for consideration in this chapter is whether even this very minimalist definition of a 'political settlement' has any prospect of materialising. The last section takes up this theme.

How Much Prospect for a 'Political Settlement'?

It would seem that the prospects for a political settlement (as I have defined it) must be rather poor. More likely would seem an American drive for what I would call an 'imposed' settlement (probably involving the attempted destruction of the Sandinista revolution). Most likely of all, either through continued stalemate or the failure of such an American drive, would be no settlement at all. I earlier emphasised the gulf still separating the perceptions and interests of the main power contenders, and how heavily past history weighs on them all, constraining their potential for mutual accommodation and reassurance. Even if Moscow, or Havana, wished to call off the Salvadoran left it is far from clear that these power centres would have the means to do so. Even if Washington decided to accept the peace offerings of the Sandinista regime the Contras and their regional allies and Florida friends might well be able to sabotage such a change of policy. Even if Duarte established some minimum degree of rapport with the left over the need for peace and reconciliation, his alliance with the (probably unreformable) army high command might well not stand the strain. If one follows my earlier analysis all of the above are distinctly optimistic hypotheses, but a political settlement would require not just *one* isolated change of heart. It would need a whole series of major shifts in perception and conduct all round, and these shifts would have to be well co-ordinated. Moreover, these changes of heart would have to take place not in the cause of some highly attractive overall settlement, rather on behalf of a solution that would be in varying degrees disappointing or even threatening to all. The major political forces in conflict have been motivated by highly optimistic visions of what may be achieved once their side manages to prevail. Can expectations be so drastically scaled down that they will relinquish their visions of complete victory and accommodate themselves to a most discouraging new realism? Clearly, there is no shortage of reasons for doubting the viability of any negotiated political compromise, more still the durability.

Nevertheless the kind of settlement outlined earlier, when discussing what constitutes a 'political settlement', should not be written off, even yet, as a complete impossibility. The emphasis of this chapter has been on political choice rather than socio-structural necessity as the appropriate explanatory level for this type of analysis. This means that under appropriate conditions key political actors may engage in abrupt shifts in strategy and even in objectives. Examples from elsewhere (e.g.

the South African, Irish and Mexican examples cited above) seem to confirm the relevance of this approach. To conclude then, let us consider whether the present Central American conflict contains appropriate conditions for an all-round re-evaluation of methods and priorities, paving the way to a political settlement.

One such condition might be war-weariness. This certainly exists in El Salvador (not only on the left), and perhaps to an increasing extent in Nicaragua as well. On the other hand the Guatemalans never seem to tire of their unending struggle. In any case, war-weariness can produce a variety of results, not all of them favourable to constructive compromise. On the contrary it might, for example, encourage the forces of the 'right', with their abundance of equipment and money, to hold out for total victory. One aspect of war-weariness can be to produce a preference for ending the conflict at any price, no matter how great the brutality, provided there is a clear verdict. The Salvadoran guerrillas and the Nicaraguan Contras have both attacked soft 'economic' targets in an attempt to intensify and generalise war-weariness. In both cases this has had the incidental effect of alienating public sympathy for the insurgents, and thus reducing their chances of winning support after a political settlement. Although there is no *mechanical* relationship between war-weariness and the disposition to accept a political settlement, it does nevertheless provide a climate within which appropriate political leadership may achieve unexpectedly favourable results. It was this intangible factor that gave Duarte's initiative in El Salvador its initial momentum (subsequently dissipated).

'Disillusion' is a related, but distinct, product of interminable conflict that could also favour a political settlement. On the left we have traced a series of major disappointments that must have shattered many of the illusions of 1979. The scale of external support for a Central American revolution has proved quite limited; the breadth and depth of internal support has also been revealed as less than overwhelming; and the objective difficulties confronting any attempt at revolutionary social transformation have also been shown to be formidable. All this is a severe contrast to the euphoria accompanying the initial Sandinista victory, and it may contribute to a new willingness to settle for modest advances, rather than to risk everything on a relentless escalation. I have argued that Cuban advice almost certainly reinforces the new sobriety of some sections of the Central American left. The forces of the 'centre' have also experienced a series of disillusionments. Both the Sandinista revolution and the 'reformist' coup in El Salvador inspired some initial hopes that with goodwill the stark confrontations of the past could be dispensed with. But subsequent events have revealed how deep-seated the underlying conflicts remain, how little room for tolerance exists, and how limited is the capacity of external actors to support or build up a 'democratic centre' in highly polarised societies. In the light of these experiences, those centrist forces that have not been driven to throw in their lot entirely with one warring group or the other may be eager to promote any form of compromise that increases the weight of reasoned argument, and reduces reliance on blind force.

Some encouragement can be drawn, therefore, from the likely effects of 'disillusionment' on the expectations and perceptions of the 'left' and 'centre'. However, the most crucial requirement for a political settlement is that this effect should also operate with comparable force on the attitudes of those groups I have labelled as the 'right'. Does the recent progress of the Christian Democratic Party in Guatemala indicate some change of heart on the part of essential components of that country's right? Time will tell, but the grounds for optimism are quite slender, as Martínez Solórzano's chapter makes clear. Did President Duarte's success in securing military assent to his discussion with the guerrillas reflect a genuine recomposition of the balance of forces within the Salvadoran state apparatus? There are, perhaps, rather more grounds for believing this about El Salvador than Guatemala, but it still requires a great leap of faith. Have the Nicaraguan counter-revolutionaries drawn any sobering lessons from their failure to make more military headway against the Sandinistas, or from the high turn-out in the November 1984 elections, or from the evident distaste of liberals in the US Congress for many of their methods? Present indications suggest not. The FDN is in any case so dependent upon external support and direction that the outlook of these foreign backers will be decisive. In April 1985 the Reagan administration told Congress its aim was to increase the numerical strength of the Contras from 20,000 to perhaps as much as 35,000.[13]

My final conclusion, therefore, is that thc prospect for a political settlement still depends, above all, as it has for so long, on the outlook of the US government. Are Washington policy-makers so disillusioned by the experience of the past five years of conflict that they are willing to make significant concessions? Apparently not. America has committed its prestige to the prevention of revolution in Central America, and has given many hostages to fortune in the process. To retreat now would be far more costly than at some earlier stage, and moreover Washington believes its policy is working. While the US administration feels itself in a position of great strength, there is little likelihood of any concessions on the other hand. Equally well, Washington finds it very difficult to show flexibility when on the defensive. Here then lies the most important reason why the prospects for a political settlement in Central America remain so elusive.

Notes

1. In the early months of the Reagan administration 'Castro had more reason to be nervous than he knew. In my conversations with Dobrynin I continued to press the question of Cuban adventurism in the Americas and in Africa as well. Dobrynin's response convinced me that Cuban activities in the Western hemisphere was a matter between the United States and Cuba . . . Castro had fallen between two superpowers.' *Caveat* Alexander Haig, (London: Weidenfeld & Nicolson, 1984), p. 131.

2. 'Leninism in Grenada' by Jiri Valenta and Virginia Valenta, *Problems of Communism*, October 1984, is a valuable study based on the captured documents, although in my opinion it under-estimates the autonomy of the local actors.

3. In an effort to offset this, the first Comecon summit was held in Cuba at the end of October 1984 and promised more support for Nicaragua.

4. See e.g. Gabriel Zaïd, 'Enemy Colleagues: A Reading of the Salvador Tragedy', *Dissent* (New York), Winter 1982, an interpretation the relevance of which has been confirmed by subsequent internecine killings.

5. They may have made one crucial error of judgement (abandoning the 'reformist' junta before its possibilities were entirely exhausted at the beginning of 1980), although I half believe they had no choice even then. For the rest I would not claim that they unnecessarily foreclosed their options, since I doubt whether they had any.

6. I have expanded on this point in my article 'Explaining Washington's Central American Policies' in the *Journal of Latin American Studies*, November 1983. An updated version (to July 1984) appears in *Politica Internazionale* (Rome), October 1984. A recent example is provided by the congressional decision to bar funds for the Nicaraguan counter-revolutionaries, an apparently clear-cut vote taken in April 1985, but then effectively rescinded in June. In the meantime, since any 'agency or entity of the US involved in intelligence' was legally debarred from helping the FDN, the CIA suspended that programme. However the National Security Council promptly took over the task, with a military officer in the White House directly supplying military advice to the Contras. The administration denies that this step violates any law.

7. I develop this point with particular reference to the term 'democracy' in 'International Aspects of Democratization in Central America' (paper presented to the APSA Convention in Washington DC, September 1984).

8. The Sandinista revolution was harmful to US prestige for a variety of reasons that are worth separating out, since different causes point to different remedies. It was harmful because Washington failed to anticipate events (corrective action should have begun as early as, say, 1972); because as the crisis unfolded the US seemed paralysed by it (various of America's allies showed greater alertness and capacity to respond); because once the history of US involvement with Somoza came under scrutiny it became apparent that America's critics occupied the moral high ground; and because – as the very name 'Sandinista'

implied – the revolution gave encouragement to all those very miscellaneous forces round the world who had some time or other been defeated or suppressed with the help of American power. As if these were not sufficient reasons to create internal dissension with the USA, the Somoza regime could count on the vociferous support of a substantial and well-financed block of congressmen, whilst the Sandinistas also proved quite adept at attracting a following from the Vietnam War protest generation, radical Christian groups and the human rights lobby.

9. I regard this as a *choice* made in Washington rather than an inevitability. The 1980 'Dissent Paper' gives fairly clear evidence that at least one alternative strategy existed, and was taken quite seriously in some policy-making circles.

10. Initially the US objective was supposedly to interdict the supply of arms to El Salvador. Subsequently American demands escalated. See Roy Gutman, 'Nicaragua: America's Diplomatic Charade', *Foreign Policy*, no. 56 (Fall 1984).

11. Washington's complaint touches on a basic weakness in the position of the Contadora powers. Conflicts as extreme as those in Central America cannot be settled entirely on the basis of mere promises of good behaviour from all the contending forces. Some losers will cheat, unless they can be prevented. To me it never seemed likely that the Contadora nations would actually send troops to police their own settlement, so verification must require a degree of mutual trust, which is precisely what is missing. However, despite all the setbacks, Contadora refuses to die, as the creation of a Costa Rica-Nicaragua border commission under Contradora auspices seems to confirm.

12. What should count as such irreducible security concerns? Any prudent government will identify a certain range of hostile actions that pose such a real and present danger they must be prevented at all costs. However, Washington's anti-Sandinista rhetoric does not seem to discriminate with any care between really serious security threats, and much more minor irritations. At the time of writing it is being stated that the introduction of advanced MiG-21 planes into Nicaragua would be viewed with the 'utmost concern', and would constitute grounds for a surgical military strike. On 8 July 1985 President Reagan listed Cuba and Nicaragua among five so-called 'terrorist states' accused of training, financing or controlling anti-American terrorists. 'We are not going to tolerate these attacks from outlaw states run by the strangest collection of misfits, looney tunes and squalid criminals since the advent of the Third Reich.' This sounds more like threat (or bluster) than a cool appraisal of serious security issues.

13. On 17 April 1985 the *New York Times* summarised a 22-page 'top secret' document (dated 3 April) from the White House to congressional committees reviewing its request for a $14 million appropriation to resume funding for Contras. This claimed that an enlarged Contra force would 'prevent the consolidation' of the Sandinista regime, and thus help achieve 'a negotiated solution', in which Nicaragua reduces its armed forces, sends home Cuban and Soviet military advisers, halts aid to Salvadoran guerrillas, accepts free elections and a free press, etc. The Sandinistas observed, correctly, that this is in practice a demand demand for unconditional surrender rather than a negotiated settlement. Never-the less, Congress eventually endorsed it.

LIST OF PARTICIPANTS

Antonio ABREU
Dominican Republic

Thomas P. ANDERSON
Eastern Connecticut State U.

Horst AUGUST
Naumann Foundation
Costa Rica

Burckhard BLANKE
Naumann Foundation
W. Germany

Jorge CACERES
CSUCA, Costa Rica

Rodolfo CERDAS CRUZ
CIAPA, Costa Rica

Margaret CRAHAN
Occidental College,
California

Malcolm DEAS
St Antony's College,
Oxford, England

Giuseppe DI PALMA
UC Berkeley

Esperanza DURAN
Chatham House, London

Rosario ESPINAL
Washington University

Fernando FLORES PINEL
Universidad Centroamericana
El Salvador

Wolf GRABENDORFF
Director, IRELA
Madrid

Alfonso HOYOS BOTERO
Bogotà, Colombia

Francisco HUERTA MONTALVO
Quito, Ecuador

José Miguel INSULZA
CIDE, Mexico

Terry KARL
UC Berkeley

Robert KAUFMAN
Rutgers University, New Jersey

Manina LASSEN-GRZECH
Naumann Foundation, W. Germany

Luis MAIRA AGUIRRE
Chile

Mechthild MINKNER
Hamburg, W. Germany

Ernesto PAZ AGUILAR
Honduras

Sonia PICADO SOTELA
San Jose

Victor REYES MORRIS
Colombia

Caesar D. SERESERES
UC Irvine

Mario SOLORZANO MARTINEZ
Costa Rica

Constantino URCUYO
CIAPA, Costa Rica

Jiri VALENTA
Naval Post Graduate School
Monterey, California

Virginia VALENTA
Naval Post Graduate School
Monterey, California

John WEEKS
American University
Washington D.C.

Theodor WEMERUS
Head of the Regional Project
Naumann Foundation
Quito, Ecuador

Laurence A. WHITEHEAD
Nuffield College,
Oxford, England

Jorge WITTE
Naumann Foundation
Honduras

INDEX